Abou

Douglas Gageby was born in
Belfast Royal Academy and t
the *Irish Press*. From there he ....p round the *Evening Press*, where he stayed until moving to *The Irish Times* to act as joint managing director. He edited *The Irish Times* from 1963 until 1974, was recalled to there in 1977 and retired as editor in 1986.

He is the author of *The Last Secretary General*, TownHouse, 1999.

Publishers' Note

Tucked away on the Letters To The Editor page in *The Irish Times*, the column devoted to the natural world, *In Time's Eye*, ran daily from the mid-1980s until early 2001. The pieces, collected in this volume of the same name, have been culled from selected years between 1985 and 2000 and are reproduced here as originally published.

The material has been arranged season by season, starting with spring. However, to give the book further coherence, there are thematic categories within the seasonal sections. These have been loosely designated as foliage, fur, feather and fin, plus some pieces on the environment and other matters that fall outside these categories. These groups of thematic pieces, randomly arranged within each season, give a sense of the authors' preoccupations and the changes observed over the years.

Most of the pieces in the selection have been written by Y, now revealed as Douglas Gageby, the distinguished editor of *The Irish Times*, but also included are 23 pieces by H, the pen-name of the political writer, John Healy.

H, as Douglas Gageby acknowledges in his introduction, was a co-originator of *In Time's Eye* and contributed to the column until his death in 1991.

IN TIME'S EYE

Y

THE IRISH TIMES

TOWN
HOUSE
DUBLIN

First published in 2001 by

TownHouse and CountryHouse Ltd
Trinity House
Charleston Road
Ranelagh
Dublin 6
Ireland

1 3 5 7 9 10 8 6 4 2

A CIP catalogue record for this book is available from the British Library.

ISBN: 1 86059 148 5

The publisher would like to express its appreciation to and acknowledge the
assistance of *The Irish Times*, the author, Sally Berman, Maria Gageby and their
families, and Áine Crowley.

Cover illustration: *Untitled,* 1986, by Gerald Davis (Private collection, Dublin)
Woodcuts: Liane Payne
Cover design: Terry Foley
Typeset: Red Barn Publishing, Skibbereen
Printed by WS Bookwell, Finland

Contents

Introduction

It all began when the late John Healy and myself were fishing on the lovely River Borora. Hares were common in those days, but we had the remarkable sight of a string of them, seven or eight, running across the horizon of a steeply rising field just across from us.

"We should note that," said John. We did, and continued to write in the same vein.

Cities and Thrones and Powers,
Stand in Time's eye,
Almost as long as flowers,
Which daily die:

"Cities and Thrones and Powers" by Rudyard Kipling

SPRING

Spring

WHEN WE WERE VERY YOUNG   10 March 2000

These were wonderful days when we were eight or ten years old. One great thrill was frogspawn. We collected it in jam jars, kept it in basins or baths in the garden at home, and also had it in school where in nature study class, we watched the little dot at the centre of the egg lengthen and grow and eventually break out as a tadpole, finally losing its tail and becoming a tiny frog. What happened next? Either the teacher or a couple of the pupils bore the small glass tank away and decanted the whole into a suitable pond. There was a waterworks nearby. Away from school, some of us in the district were fascinated by an old mill-pond which held newts as well as frogs. Lovely, in memory, highly coloured, and a text-book tells us that the males "develop striking breeding dress". Exactly. Nowadays you don't collect frogspawn without a licence. Why? Are we short of frogs? Well, part of the answer anyway is that moving frogspawn from place to place might bring weeds with it which could contaminate, if that is the word, other waters. Anyway, to complicate things, you must have a licence. After some conversation with a friendly voice in Dúchas, this corner received a licence form to fill up. Teachers, by the way, have no trouble in getting permission, so that classroom instruction can continue as it should. By the way, a dog walker tells us that on the Dublin mountains there is, in one busy area, a huge supply of the commodity. Fertile frogs up there.

Bread-and-cheese was another feature remembered from spring, that is, of course, the just-sprouting leaves of the hawthorn. Have they any nutritional or health value? For children used to chew them as they walked home from school. Now, of course, roadside hedges would carry too much contamination from petrol fumes. In England, Richard Mabey relates in *Flora Britannica*, a massive and entertaining as well as informative tome, how in Leicestershire "a spring dinner" was made by covering a suet crust with young hawthorn leaf buds and thin strips of bacon, and rolling and steaming it as a roly-poly. The elder is well in leaf now in our parts, and soon we'll be into recipes for the flowers. But, of course, today so many children are ferried to and from school by bus or by parental car that hedges are in no danger of being stripped.

And are cleevers or goosegrass forgotten? That sticky plant which adhered to clothes and hair and was so often used in boy versus girl warfare. Childish courtship. And wasn't March for kite-flying? And wasn't it time for spinning-tops?   Y

DOUBTS ABOUT SPRING   25 March 1995

It has been spring for two days in these eastern parts. Spring is not necessarily followed by automatic progress to summer. It may lapse into winter. Every year we remind ourselves of William Cowper: "Our severest Winter, commonly called the Spring." But for two days it has been magnificent. A farming friend even admits that the land is drying off quickly. Things are bursting out. Big, mushy leaves emerging from the horse chestnut tree. Hawthorn showing glimpses of the buds that will soon be bread-and-cheese for children. Or maybe that's all gone. Among the herbs, a few skinny borage plants, which didn't develop last year, amazingly put out brilliant blue flowers. Where no rabbits have been seen for nearly a year, a friend reports on his lawn a vest-pocket-sized precursor of what may be a big brood – just near a flower border. And for two days, sniffles and wheezes seemed to abate. Creaks and pains, said some, were eased to vanishing point. Self-delusion? Couéism? In a suburban garden, after a couple of months when the badgers came only fitfully to the nightly feed of peanuts and scraps of bread, no less than three were seen, bold as brass among the daffodils. And haven't local authorities or road authorities really treated us to daffodils on a Wordsworthian scale? So much so, that it's hardly worth while now hooting at people gathering armfuls of them, as was seen on the Clonee end of the entry to the M50. Christina Rossetti, in her day, was wise to be cautious: "Sing, robin, sing;

I still am sore in doubt concerning Spring."

But never mind. The river is down a foot and a half.

That brown, murky, thunderous mass of water may now be fit for the fly-fisher and his first trout for tea.   Y

THIS TIME IS IT REAL? 4 April 1998

 We have been fooled before, but last Monday really was something. In these eastern parts, anyway. Across the river, the cattle had just been let out of the sheds. They were visibly unstiffening, slightly dazed in the sunshine, maybe. Moving slowly. The human beings were saying, not for the first time, "Is it really here at last?" The river was low and clear. A kingfisher flashed by – then another.

The signs of winter were still around, of course; half-haystacks of dead reeds and twigs and grass hung from the alders, now nearly ten feet above the present level of the water. Twenty yards into the trees, similar debris lay around like seaweed on a shore. But the buds were moving. The dogwood in the drive, brilliant yellow and red stems, were showing leaf. Now to be cut back at once by about four feet. And still they will come on again. For autumn they are unbeatable in the colour competition. Scarlet oaks and even liquidambar have nothing on these large leaves with their shades of yellow into apricot into blazing red and then down to purple and a dusky death.

Everywhere under the trees, the oaks especially, you now notice a deep, damp carpet of the leaves. Sweep it up? No. And grass is bleached in lumps and flat stretches. Nearly white. And the reeds, the phragmites. You'd like to see them grow more and more. As they used to do before the river was drained. And birds have never attacked the nuts and grains in the feeders more eagerly. Building up their strength for mating and laying and the parental drudge of having to work from morning to night to feed young squalling hungry mouths.

As far as the rabbits are concerned, we are not clear of the winter yet, for they keep on digging holes in among the ash, and even on the lawn, to get at soft roots. Isn't it enough for them to have half consumed a clump of new broom within days of its planting? Moral: take nothing for granted.

But the warmth and the sun! Get the last of the tree-pruning done. And felling. Better to plant too many and then take out some than plant too few and then have to supplement with undersized specimens.

In spite of all this, in spite of the warm glow, you order more central heating oil. And a cheerful call from Geneva, that night, announced four inches of snow on the ground and still coming down.   Y

REAL FREE RANGE   29 April 2000

"This Easter," he said, "I didn't hear of any children colouring eggs and rolling them down hills. Come to think of it, I haven't heard of the practice for a long time. As children, we didn't question it, we just did it and the colouring was an important part. The deep yellow you got from boiling them in a pot with handfuls of whin flowers. The source of the blue I don't remember, but it came from something in the kitchen. Hens were big in our lives then, even in towns. At our first house in the suburbs my mother got into business (as she hoped) with about 150 hens and cocks. Or was there just one cock? Anyway, after a few years, she gave it up. So many friends who came visiting just had to have a dozen eggs and perhaps a newly killed bird to go away with. It was a chore for the children to feed, and often to find the damned things, for they at times 'layed out', i.e. in shrubby corners or nettle beds rather than in the henhouse proper. They had, after all, an acre to roam over. That enterprise of my mother's soon collapsed. But on holiday in County Antrim we stayed with a former sea captain who added to his pension by keeping hens in some number, and in a little market gardening. There, children sometimes being perverse, it was not a chore to go searching for hens laying out, but fun. There were four fields running down to Larne Lough – the shore field, the middle field, the fetchfer and the upper field. Every one of them had, at times, to be scoured for errant fowl. (Fetchfer is a word that no Scots–Irish dictionary has yet interpreted. It was the steepest.)

"But all that is a world away. A recent article in an English magazine shows that even the breeds of fowl are different now. While we were familiar with Black Minorcas, Rhode Island Reds, White Wyandottes, this article in *Country Life* on a man who shows eggs in exhibitions and is apparently the number one, gives the names of the breeds as Marams (grey-barred) which give deep-brown eggs, Araucanas which produce blue eggs, Welsummers which again lay brown eggs and Leghorns whose eggs are described as being as snow-white as their feathers. The article concentrates on a Cumbrian farmer George Taylor whose passion seems to be not eating the eggs but admiring them on plates of sawdust for showing. His exhibits are perfectly formed and elegantly coloured, brown, green and white in the examples photographed. All are free range, i.e. they do range freely in the open. But this is perfectionism. He says it may take two weeks' laying from a good hen to produce three matching eggs for exhibition. There could be 30 dozen eggs on the table when he begins sorting for his show entries."

Mrs Beeton says that eggs are better when new-laid than a day or two afterwards. Don't you wish you had room in the garden for a few hens?   Y

WEXFORD'S MOUND OF LIGHT   1 May 1999

 This is a new-old form of commemoration – Tulach a'tSolais at Oulart Hill in Wexford. A commemorative mound, as at Newgrange, we know; but at Oulart the mound is bisected, and this is to show the division between the old world and the world after it was changed by the enlightened ideas of the French and American revolutions. The Irish title means Mound of Light and an article in the *Wexford Association Yearbook* and in a comprehensive information sheet issued by Brian Cleary, who is chairman of the organising committee, reveals the thought and hard work that has gone into what is a unique memorial. The split which bisects the mound, leads through a central chamber which houses two massive oak sculptures. These "very large sculptures" curve towards the light. They were saplings in 1798 and Brian Cleary writes that they represent the

people of Oulart and similar communities everywhere reaching upwards.

The chamber, it is pointed out, will receive maximum light on Midsummer Day, June 21st, which incidentally is the date of the battle of Vinegar Hill. The dividing line, of course, is on an east–west axis. And the inner chamber is paved granite on the floor, while the walls are concrete painted white, so the light is enhanced. Tulach a'tSolais itself is an important step on the way to the concept of "Oulart, the '98 Village". When complete, the monument will be handed over to the Oulart Hill Co-op and they will be responsible for it. Every person in the parish, writes Brian Cleary, should realise that this hill is in their care, that it ranks among the great outdoor monuments of Ireland, that every effort be made to keep Oulart Hill clean and tidy, and that no developments should be built there.

Already there is a trickle of visitors to see this, the work of Scott Tallon Walker, architects; Michael Warren, sculptor; Ove Arup Ireland, consultant engineers and, of course, the Oulart Hill Co-operative Society. The concept of a mound as a memorial, particularly with its corridor through, and its light signifying enlightenment, is certainly worthy of Wexford and all it stands for.   Y

LADYBIRDS   7 May 1988

Are the ladybirds a sign of a fine summer? This spring has seen a very good presence of ladybirds in back gardens and in cold greenhouses. This insect is associated with warm weather and in a dry warm summer they seem to thrive. In one of the fantastic summers of the last decade the ladybirds swarmed over everything, including people sunbathing in back gardens and public parks. If the heavy incidence of the tiny insect is any guide, we appear to be in for a jolly fine summer.   H

GROW, TREE, GROW 19 March 1986

So many schoolchildren spent so much time and effort planting during last week – Tree Week – and all the weeks before it; and not many of them got a mention in the papers. But it was worth while, and trees grow quicker than children may impatiently think. On St Patrick's Day, twins looked at a row of oaks that had been seedlings, just up above ground level, two inches high, the week they were born in September 1977. The oaks are now between 12 and 15 feet high.

That was fast for oaks. But the really impatient can plant willows. A few cuttings put down last February were recently clipped when they reached six feet, clipped so that the young trees would branch out and thicken. Then the bits cut off were replanted. This time next year they will be six feet high and will be clipped and the clippings planted, and so it goes on.   Y

EASY TREES 9 March 1998

And the last word on trees – for a while, as the special week ends. It comes from the current newsletter issued by Crann, those pioneering folk. There is one way of growing trees on the farm that doesn't involve any planting, doesn't take up any extra space, and with a little careful arrangement could provide some valuable timber in the future, says this article. And that, we are told, is in the hedgerow. And the article claims, there are more broadleaf trees growing in Ireland's hedges than in its woods! A surprising thought. But a walk around your hedgerow, the article goes on – and of course it is aimed at the farmer – will show you dozens of young saplings growing under the protection of the hedge.

It's a simple job, apparently, to mark suitable ones, and you are advised to tie a strip of fertiliser bag on these to make sure they're not decapitated during routine hedge-trimming. Then the list of advantages of leaving growing saplings is given. First, the trees are already well established and suited to the site. Then, most saplings will be of native species and thus better for wildlife. Further, self-set saplings make more stable trees than transplants. And, on top of all this, there is no fencing involved and it's cheaper.

Of course not all trees are suitable as hedgerow trees. For example, beech, sycamore and chestnut cast a dense shade. The article suggests as more acceptable ash, oak, cherry, rowan, holly, willow, birch, crab apple and hazel. The suggestion is made that it is a good idea to let the odd blackthorn or hawthorn grow on, for they provide pollen for bees. And are a source of food for the birds. Neil Foulkes and John Matthews, of Crann Leitrim, Hyde Street, Mohill, County Leitrim, can supply further information on their Hedgerow Project.

And by the way, hawthorns left to grow into trees, as happens in open fields for protection and shade for the animals, give, when felled, a first-class wood for your fire. They burn long, they burn well. And you can safely put a log into the dying fire late at night and be sure that a small blow of the bellows will bring it into life again, even after seven or eight hours. Much more in this newsletter. Every week is Tree Week for Crann. Good luck to them.   Y

REPLANTING   14 April 1998

Replanting is only one way of restoring woodlands, though the most effective. As in Britain, for example, following the disastrous storm of last October. (An air traveller to Heathrow from a southern direction, on that morning, in a plane which had to circle for quite a time before the gusts diminished, said that looking down on the south eastern counties was like looking down on a child's board game on which all the pieces had been scattered in every direction.) As well as replanting, there is coppicing. Thus, a neighbour who lost a few small ash through cattle damage, points out that in each case, where he sawed the tree off at ground level, he now has five or six more healthy boles rising. Pollarding can be done on trees that were cut off six or eight feet from the ground. Again, new life sprouts and you have the possibility of cutting in continuous cycles, making of the tree an everlasting source of energy.

Anyway, that is a thought from the handout accompanying a little book published by Lennard House in Luton, in association with the British Woodland Trust, which is trying to raise half a million pounds. The book, *Trees: A Small Appreciation*, is pocket size, just over 40 pages, costs £4.95 (stg), has some lovely paintings of trees, faced by literary quotes on the same subject and is introduced and recommended by Gloria Hunniford. She now lives in Sevenoaks. Nice booklet, sent to *The Irish Times*, but charity begins at home, and we have Crann and other schemes to deal with first.   Y

TREES FOR TOWN BEES   12 May 1998

The last thing you might think of in planting a tree or shrub in the urban situation, might be: "Will this be good for the bees?" Other people's bees, in most cases. For, yes, many bee-lovers keep hives within city boundaries, even in the metropolis of London. A writer in the English periodical *The Dendrologist* lists those trees and shrubs that are among the best yielders of nectar and pollen. In April and May all the rosaceae give generously. They cover a lot: hawthorn, rowan or mountain ash, pear, quince and medlar; also plums including sloes; then peach, almond and cherry. Whitebeam, too, now being more widely planted, including on housing estates. You know it, gooseberry-fool colour leaves, white underneath.

By the way, the writer, Virginia Purchon, who herself lives and beekeeps in London, says that cherry trees which have double flowers are no good for this purpose. Oddly enough, a tree that is much looked down on, the sycamore, which propagates like a weed (and don't children love the propellor-like seeds which come whirling down in autumn), is an excellent source of spring nectar. All maples are good bee trees. Also, she says, horse-chestnuts, white and red. "I live in the part of north London where both kinds of chestnut grow within the bees' flight radius of two miles, and I can tell when the trees are in flower by the baskets of red pollen being brought into the hive."

Earlier on, the bees have to make do with hazel and goat willow – that tree or bush with the fat sausage-like catkins. Alder is said to be good, too. But the main source of honey to beekeepers in London is the lime trees, planted long ago. Many will recall sitting under a big lime in June or July and being intrigued by the constant hum of the bees; almost a boom, in fact. And planting urban trees of the right sort, the writer points out, is good not only for bees but for other pollinating insects. Then you get berries for birds; they disperse the seeds in their droppings, says the article, and on we go.

The writer seriously advises going for native trees or those closely related or long-established like sycamore or horse chestnut. Exotic or Mediterranean species may grow well, but their nectar production is much more dependent on hot weather. Honey for what? Milkless tea; honey in coffee. Honey by the teaspoonful. Two at night helps you sleep, say some.   Y

QUICKS COME SLOW   7 March 1996

 One of the hardest and slowest ways of making money must be in cultivating hawthorn quicks, or plants, from the haw – a fruit that humans don't eat, and that birds tend to leave while there are juicier things around, like blackberries. To grow these hawthorn quicks, according to one written source, you store the haws in sand in a box, covering layer after layer with the sand. About November, according to this formula, you then rub off the pulp from the seed – no easy task. You then sow one inch deep in a seed-bed and, the following October, transplant the bigger seedlings to where they are to grow. The rest can be moved the next year. That's from the *Field Book of Country Queries*, published over forty years ago.

It sounds very much of a short-cut according to a landscaper friend who recently provided hundreds of quicks, grown in the following way. The haws are piled into a clamp, like potatoes, in ridge formation, straw above and beneath and the whole covered with earth. Not the following spring but the one after that, you take them up and plant out on flat beds, covering lightly with soil. You keep the beds weed-free and then in autumn you line out the biggest and best. But it will probably be another year before your plants are ready for the market, and they will be even more saleable the following year.

A few hundred bought recently by a friend may have been even three years in the seed-bed, for they were very well rooted, sturdy and two-and-a-half to three feet high. Of all the safe fences, there is surely none to beat the thorn, well-looked after and not allowed to grow too leggy.

Of course, the hawthorn may be left to grow into a tree, and handsome it can be, while its wood is dense and heavy. Excellent fuel after a year or two. It is said in *The Tree Book* by Edward Milner that haws have been used to make jellies, wines, liqueurs and ketchups. Never come across these, though the flowers could well be, like elders, used in wine-making.

N.B. Quick in this sense has nothing to do with speed, obviously. It is quick – meaning alive. "Medicine is able to quicken a rock", Shakespeare.   Y

BORING OLD IVY?   23 March 1999

Don't be too hard on ivy. It's all a matter of context – i.e. just where it is. For years, a great thick, luxuriant, bulbous growth at the top of a tall hawthorn tree was tolerated for two reasons: one, that a woodpigeon nested there; two, that the mass of greenery seemed to protect the front of the house from the worst of the north wind. But the woodpigeon seemed to have abandoned the site last nesting time, and the growth had become so heavy that it was feared a strong wind gust might bring it down – and thus on top of the car or five cars regularly parked in front of it. The man who was to do the job was just a bit reluctant, until it was pointed out to him that at the next gale his car might be in the line of the falling tree and ivy. "Ah, well, if that's what you want." So, off with the top.

A defender of ivy is an English arborist, Andrew Pinchin, who wrote recently in *Horticulture Week* magazine during December. Ivy, for him, has charm, and in the right place does little harm. Its rightful place is in the midst of woodland, and it may be a nuisance in manicured parkland or suburban front gardens. But it is not a parasite, as is mistletoe, which roots itself directly into the host plant. For the ivy's feeding roots are firmly in the ground. And the little hair-like roots do not suck life-giving sap from the tree it climbs. Mind you, there may be competition at the roots for moisture. Ivy's natural habitat being woodland, it can survive when light levels are low, writes Mr Pinchin. Ivy stems, too, can grow to ten centimetres in diameter, and with a weight of growth on top (as in the example at the beginning of this piece) may add to the possibility of the tree's windthrow. And ivy can cover flaws and cavities in trees. But ivy, argue its defenders, gives shelter to invertebrates, to some birds and maybe bats. Its flowers are sought by bees and the berries by birds.

If you must cut it, take a good section out of the stem (a mere cut might join up again) and later, as it withers, you can remove the whole. And, writes our friend, suppose ivy did kill a tree in a wood, think how the dead wood would become a small universe for the insects, etc. And, in a wood, dead trees may stand for a long time. Now, of course, along roadways it's a different story. But don't forget the virtues. It is handsome.   Y

POOR RELATION TREES   1 April 1985

 If you've a bit of messy, wet ground you want to cover up, the usual formula is to put down sallies. For a change, mix them with alders. They have to be the hardiest of trees and are among the fastest growing, though they don't normally reach great height. But their toughness, especially in wet conditions is formidable. As the water in the river has gone down in past weeks, the lower portion of the banks are seen for the first time in months. And there, in one bend of the river are scores of tiny alder trees, some no more than six inches, some over a foot, but with one thing in common – all have been entirely submerged on and off for months at a time.

We all know about trees which do well with their feet in water: these have actually led a subaqueous life almost from the sprouting. Not beautiful trees, but in early spring their purple buds and dangling catkins are fine; later, too, their miniature cones.   Y

14

BUSH FOR EVERYONE   8 April 2000

The buds of the lilac flowers are already showing their colour, promising elegance and beauty in a few weeks. Near them another bush, or small tree, is also pushing up flower-buds, not colourful as the lilac, but useful. This is the elder, a rather ungainly plant but one with a diverse contribution to make in spite of its often tawdry appearance. (It does now and then make a stately tree, but that is the exception, for it is often the bush of the scrapheap, the untidy corner of the yard.) Its reputation is, in some cases, sinister, with connotations of witchcraft. Charles Nelson in his majestic *Trees of Ireland* tells us that the wood is cursed. You must never put elder wood on a fire because, if you burn it, you will see the Devil in the flame. Don't make boats or babies' cradles out of it. In the latter case the fairies could easily steal the baby and leave a changeling in its place. These statements come under the heading of folklore, let it be said.

On the other hand, the elder can be useful and beneficial. From the schoolboy hollowing out the soft pith from a short length of twig to get a fine pea-shooter, to the cook in her kitchen, to the winemaker. It could be said that it is so useful, we take it for granted. The leaves in a room are said to keep out flies. Sometimes sprigs of it were put under the headbands of horses in the field for the same reason. The Henry Doubleday Research Station found the leaves could be used as a remedy against blackspot on roses and gooseberry and rose mildew. (Up to a pound of leaves in a quart of water, simmered, strained, cooled and then sprayed on.) Also said to kill aphids. Elderflowers make a fine drink. There is a better use, some think. Dipped in batter and fried with your bacon or whatever, they add a lot to a routine meal. Flowers, of course, are kept on their stems, thus easy to handle. The berries, later, make a fine wine. And you can also have a chutney with blackberries and elderberries, according to Nelson.

We ought to be grateful for the abundance of these berries. Birds go for them voraciously, and that's why you find the bushes everywhere, sprung from the seeds in their droppings. Richard Mabey in *Flora Britannica* gives many examples of its uses. It was planted near dairies to keep flies away and also sited beside outside privies. Elderflower water, he tells us, has still a reputation as a skin-cleanser and he asserts that it is recognised as an eye lotion – presumably commercially produced. But it is principally for food, and he finds "the flower eaten straight off the bush is refreshing as ice-cream soda, but they are not to everyone's taste".   Y

PRIMROSE PROMISE   4 April 1987

The yellow city forsythia may mark the spring for the urban dweller, but for the country person the sight of the first primroses on the sunny south-side of sod ditches is always a heart-warming sight. The snowdrop and crocus (or domestic daffodil) may mark the new year and the first of spring but they do not have the promise, as the primrose has, that the worst of winter is gone.

The first primroses venture from a soft mossy ditch and then, like a measle rash, the ditch is alive with the delicate yellow blossoms. You can feel the sun warm on your back just by looking at them!   H

YELLOW   15 April 1986

Is there any significance in the fact that so many early-year flowers are yellow? To show them up better against the green? A signal to bees or birds, in a code that we don't yet understand? Anyway, there are the lesser celandine, the coltsfoot, the dandelion, the primrose, the whins; and, in gardens, the daffodils. All yellow. Later in the year, when the herbs bloom, the colour is mainly blue. Ask a beekeeper. They are knowledgeable people.   Y

YELLOW SPRING   16 April 1996

It seems to be the yellowest spring in memory. For a start, two people come down from Belfast, exuding delight at – according to them – the miles and miles of daffodils along the road into Dublin. And, sure enough, if you are on the road to the west from Dublin

you'll see them, too, in profusion. And even when you go off the M50 on to the dual carriageway towards Dunshaughlin and Navan. There may be miles and miles of them elsewhere. And in gardens, on this east side, anyway, after a late start, they are flourishing.

Even if you don't feel it in your bones, the plants do, and the seeds. For example, in a cardboard box in a greenhouse, a few score acorns waiting to be potted are breaking out of their skins. And some of the exotic kermes (or chermes) oaks, *Quercus coccifera*, picked up on the roadside in France last year, are poking up tiny holly-like leaves. In ten years they will probably be about two to three feet high. Before the shoot appears, the root has gone down into the compost of the pot, so it would be as well to keep a little water in the saucer.

And, of course, the usual spring drama or tragedy with the garden birds. Blackbirds built on a join of two outside pipes, just beside a neighbour's back door. It looked safe-ish, and anyway, there was a barking, leaping dog loose for much of the day in the garden. Two days ago there was much piping and throaty sounds from the birds. The nest had been raided by a local cat. Only one scaldie remained, fairly well-fledged and big. It was put back into the nest. The parents returned, and a huge protective screen of chicken wire was extended to prevent the cat getting up again.

It didn't keep a magpie from descending the next morning and making off with the last of the brood. You can go over all the arguments again. It's the magpie's nourishment. You can't argue with Nature. But a local, overfed, pampered cat? They are all implanted deeply with the hunting instinct. One specialises in laying mice at its mistress's bedside. Or shrews. Or birds in season. And a normally-behaved dog goes wild when it comes across ground-nesting birds' eggs. Pheasant, duck, slurp, slurp. And we humans eat . . . ? Let's not get into that. The blackbird was nearly like a bereavement in the family.

Bright point of the day. A relative rings up his wife from Granada to announce that he is sitting out in the shade, as the temperature is 24 Celsius. Damn.   Y

OAKS HAVE PERSONALITY   19 April 2000

It wouldn't be classed among the top trees in Ireland, the oldest, the highest, for, although it is of some age, it has had a hard time: that storm in the early 1960s (was it 1961?) took the whole top away. Fortunately, and to the surprise of the owners, branches grew straight upwards and thick and regular, as if it had been pollarded, which would have been ridiculous at its age. And good heavy and long branches, over a foot thick, have in the past half-century been cut off, firstly to let vans and cars reach the house, secondly to allow a couple of girls to ride ponies around the large paddock, as it was then. (It's now two lawns.) You see, it is a pedunculate oak, throwing generous arms out sideways, and as they do, here and there, they turn upwards at right angles, then after some growth continue along parallel to the ground. A tree with personality. Its chief contribution to arboriculture has been in its profusion of acorns every few years. Maybe the original farmer here appreciated them for his pigs.

Nowadays there are always clients for a few acorns. This aspect first struck the owners when the lawn was not a lawn, but a paddock. One summer a cluster of plants was pointed out growing around the shadow of the tree. Out they go and find about a hundred miniature oak seedlings coming up through the moss and unmowed grass. They were carefully dug up with a trowel, put into pots and transferred to a place outside the city which was calling for trees. They flourished. In fact, too much so. The planter in the other place forgot that these were arm-throwing pedunculate oaks and put them too close. In the end, he may find that out of a hundred or so, his few acres can only tolerate, in order to give the trees their rightful space, about eight or ten. Anyway, when the parent oak was just in fields, well outside suburban Dublin, it was marked on a map of the 1820s. Or, to be pessimistic, a tree was marked there, in the very spot of this one. Who was the writer quoted here recently, who admitted that one could only really ever be certain, expertise bedamned, about the age of a tree when it was cut down and the rings counted?

18

Take it that this tree, battered, now circled by houses but with still plenty of space, may be the tree marked on that map of the 1820s and now, nearly 200 years on, stands, cut back, beheaded by a storm 40 years ago, but still thriving and the admiration of its owners. Just now the yellow male blossoms are appearing all over. The female, green and discreet. We have to wait a little for the leafing, while last year's acorns are slowly beginning to put out their shoots.   Y

THE BLACKTHORN   17 April 1998

 What a wonderful show now of all those flowering trees, perhaps most noticeable in mass in suburbia. Pinks and whites and blossom laid on blossom. One of the finest of the whites is the cherry-plum, called by Herbert Edlin in *The Tree Key*, the Asiatic cherry-plum. It is one of the beauties of suburbia that produces lovely fruit. Last year was the greatest. Edlin tells us that the orchard plum, *Prunus domestica*, came about as a hybrid of that same cherry-plum and the European blackthorn *Prunus spinoea*.

And surely the blackthorn, not in gardens but throughout the country, in hedges, in odd spots in field corners, in land despised for almost anything else, is the real king. There are parts of Clare, in memory, which are made even more glorious by seas of the white blossom. You meet it now in hedges, in odd spots along a river where a bird, perhaps, had dropped the stone of a sloe. Or maybe a child has spat it out after tasting its bitter astringent flesh.

The fruit is generally rejected, though not by jam-makers or jelly-makers. It adds piquancy to apple jelly in particular, and, its peak is perhaps in the liqueur, sloe gin. Only quince competes with it in this class. In recent days, in this eastern part, the white blossom is to the fore. Will we be lucky enough to get, this year as we did last year, and as was so pridefully announced, for the first time in decades, sloes (slight exaggeration, but only slight) as big as damsons?

For practical purposes, it makes what is, to man and

beast, an impenetrable hedge. Keeping in and keeping out. The thorns are long and painful and potentially poisonous. And yet, and yet!

The blackthorn stick of the more popular kind, the stick sold in tourist shops, is often a cod, a deception. It is ostentatiously painted black. In fact, the bark of the blackthorn varies in colour. A specimen, cut long ago from a hedge in County Limerick, just by the roadside, is as near as dammit to brown. And it was a blackthorn. The spines are the proof.

Some people go to great lengths to bend curved handles to the blackthorn. Better a natural nob from the root, it is not meant to be a polite walking-stick. (Do the District Inspectors of the RUC still carry them? Or, indeed, are there still District Inspectors?) They used to be slim, dressy sticks.

But just now, the emphasis is on the emerging white blossom. And, even in a neglected corner of a field, the small pokey branches and the light blossom are among the finest sights of spring. The lone thorn in the middle of the field, carefully ploughed around? That's an other day's work.   Y

BIT OF A FETISH?   20 April 1999

"Not for the first time," he said, "I thought I'd make myself a good blackthorn stick. Not that I haven't a few decent walking-sticks, not to mention thumbsticks, the best being from holly and one from a very old wild rose, a huge bush, which was later wiped out in one of those scarifying operations known as land drainage. Anyway, there were a fair number of blackthorns around, planted as quicks long ago in some cases, and, in the hedges not a few that had been there before me. It didn't seem any problem – that is, until you went around looking for a straight branch of suitable length and breadth. If you were the sort of patient person who can apply heat to a stick while it is held in a pair of joiner's vices, or even go through the process of suspending it from a beam in a warm room (or a room where heat can be applied directly, say by a fan) – and one writer says countrymen solved this by hanging it in the warmish cow byre – then fine.

But if you want an instant stick of correct length and straightness, you have a problem. For in, say, a hundred bushes you will find many straight branches and off-shoots, but some will not be long enough and if they are long enough they are not straight enough.

"Couldn't you let it have a slight bend in it? You'd better. For you won't find the ideal without a lot of patience. You need a knob as handle, which is best done by taking one straight from the root; otherwise hacking your stick from an offshoot of a biggish branch and sandpapering and cutting the thickness to fit the hand." So our friend had to do with a stick of appropriate length and thickness, but not dead straight. And the first thing he says about a blackthorn stick is that it is not black – unless so painted in the tourist shops. It is a sort of grey-green, no, a grey-brown. And the colours will vary, perhaps according to which side of the bush got most sun or some quality in the soil.

It has one distinguishing mark – the number of bumps which stood for the original thorns, now cut and smoothed to acceptable level. Back to the lack of straightness. Our friend recalled that there had been cattlemen in his family. The not-quite-straight element shows that the stick is a professional tool, good and rough enough (he's sorry he didn't leave a few more bumps in it) for prodding beasts. So, stick OK.   Y

SPRING GROWTH   20 April 1988

 Some people who were over here last week from Paris and other western capitals, remarked that growth of trees and shrubs around Dublin was well ahead of that in their own places. This is often enough the case, but the big difference is that we usually have a stop/go spring. In Paris and other parts, the burst, when it does come, leaves us standing and there is no going back. But this time, it appears, we are to have spring all at once, with warmish rain following all that sunshine. And at this time someone is bound to trot out the old saw about the oak and the ash. If the oak opens before the ash, we are assured in rhyme, then we are in for a splash. But if the

ash comes before the oak, then it's a serious matter – we are in for a soak, or a real wet summer.

But what if the oak in one county is out before the ash, but not in the next county or even parish? It's all a bit dotty. But then these rhymes may go back to days when people were not mobile. They knew what was going on in their own parish or townland and not much beyond. Evidence in all the rest of the country, whether England or Ireland or Scotland, might be the opposite. They weren't to know. But at least it all rhymed. (And in one corner of the woods, it's definitely the oak before the ash this year.)   Y

HOUSMAN'S CHOICE   29 April 1988

"Loveliest of trees, the cherry now
Is hung with bloom along the bough."

So wrote A E Housman. And the cherries of all varieties are splendid for a while. After that, nothing to write home about in many cases. Though that can be a matter of taste. Some people plant for spring beauty, i.e. blossom. Others plant for autumn colouring, as in red oaks or liquidambar. A rich show of fruit in autumn tempts those who put down mountain ash, or rowan. And the berries last a long time, for the birds find them bitter, as do humans. Decorative crab apples are an addition to any garden, but too much of a temptation to young boys.

You can also choose your garden trees largely for their bark, as in the several varieties of birch. And some of these have, in addition, spectacular autumnal foliage. In fact, if you are short of space, a trio of birch gives you, after a few years, admirable bark, good leaf colour in autumn and, at all times, trees of grace and vigour; trees which, moreover, can be contained as to spread.   Y

TREES FOR LIVING IN   22 March 1995

 Children love a house in a tree. Sometimes they look as if they are custom-bought, but the majority are descended from discarded packing-cases and bits of left-over linoleum. Or its today equivalent. But what of a tree which, inside its hollow trunk, could

contain a room "in which a floor, an entrance door and benches were fitted, so that 20 persons could dine in it with ease". Such was the case with the Bowthorpe oak in Lincolnshire, the oldest living oak known, according to Alan Mitchell, a well-known established expert. Older, he says, than any tree other than the big church-yard yews.

An account written in 1805 states that in 1768 it had "been in the same state of decay since the memory of the older inhabitants and their ancestors". The lower part, before it became gentrified in 1768, was formerly used as a feeding place for calves, the upper part as a pigeon house. Where the man put in a door has now become narrowed and it is back to use for livestock. Today's measurements are: 3.97m (13ft) in diameter and 11.9m (39ft 7ins) in circumference at 1.5m (5ft) above ground. Mitchell estimates that the tree is well over 1,000 years old. Pictures show that, while it has a good show of leaves, the trunk is bockety enough, fissured in at least two places and bearing a great number of burrs or nobbles.

Some of the finest specimens are in the eastern glens of Scotland, writes Mitchell, around Angus and Perthshire. He gives other examples of huge trunks in England itself, and then mentions an interesting tree in Ireland – at Tullynally Castle, County Westmeath, home of the Pakenhams. It is a tree of 38m (124ft) high, by 4.5m (15ft), presumably in girth, has a clear, nearly cylin-drical trunk for 11m (36ft), and only a branch or two for the next 10m (15ft), "a remarkable sight out in the field". All this from *The Garden*, for November 1994, journal of the Royal Horticultural Society. Note for diary – to go at long last to Clare to see the famous Brian Boru Oak.   Y

LOVELIEST FAIRY TALE   31 April 1989

One of the loveliest fairy tales of them all, and a true fairy tale – well, it ought to be true and it has truth in it – has just been published as a small booklet. It is Jean Giono's *The Man Who Planted Trees*. An animated film of it has been seen on RTÉ. Now an old friend makes an Easter present of this booklet which has fine woodcuts by Michael McCurdy. It should be a text not only for primary children but for PhDs too. The story of Elzéard Bouffier who, as a shepherd, roamed a bleak Alpine region of France, sowing everywhere acorns and later other tree seeds, and who thus caused an arid desert to flourish and to nurture a whole new population, has gone around the world, been translated into a dozen languages. Towards the end Giono writes:

"When I reflect that one man, armed only with his own physical and moral resources, was able to cause this land of Canaan to spring from the wasteland, I am convinced that, in spite of everything, humanity is admirable. But when I compute the unfailing greatness of spirit and the tenacity of benevolence that it must have taken to achieve this result, I am taken with an immense respect for that old and unlearned peasant who was able to complete a work worthy of God."   Y

BEYOND THE TREE MAN   29 April 1999

 Many, many people were thrilled by the exploits of one Elzéard Bouffier, a shepherd in the mountainy country of Provence in France, whose life task was in wandering the bare spaces of those high areas, planting acorns and other seeds, but chiefly acorns, and whose work was crowned by the flourishing of a society which had been more or less moribund. Depleted villages came to life, streams flowed as a result of the local climate changes brought about by the woods which grew and, after a life of such good works, the old shepherd died content in the hospice of Banon. Jean Giono told the story in *The Man Who Planted Trees*. And it reads utterly convincingly. But when editors sent investigators to the area for more detail, Giono had to admit that it was, of course, a fable. It is a lovely fable and may, anyway, have stimulated many a forestry project. Jean Giono (1895–1970) was one of France's leading writers, according to André Malraux. Henry Miller said of him: "Giono gives us the world we live in, a world of dream, passion and reality." There is plenty of passion and reality in another Giono book published in English in London

this year by Harvill Press, a neat, dignified paperback with woodcut illustrations. It is *Second Harvest*, a translation of Giono's 1930 *Regain* which might also be translated as "Renewal". For the basic theme again is of a village – inhabited by only five people, later only one man, the hero or main figure Panturle – which comes to life again. Life is not merely hard, it is basic, cruel, savage almost. Panturle lives on animals he traps and some potatoes. "Water and potatoes were at one and the same time, soup, stew and bread for him." Eventually, when he finds a woman to live with him, his great achievement is to raise wheat and so have bread. One of his fellow-villagers, who soon vanishes, "hunted in her own way. She went for sparrows. She boiled some old oats, some rue leaves and thorn-apples and then strewed the mixture in front of her door. The sparrows ate them and died on the spot. Before cooking she removed the gizzards, cut them open with old scissors and emptied the grain into a paper to use again." Panturle helped out by giving her pieces of hare, thrushes and sometimes whole small rabbits.

There are also lovely lyrical touches: "the wild purr of the juniper bushes" and the stream is almost a character on its own. A bit rough and bloody at times for children, perhaps. But life was hard in rural France, as we read in books by sociologists and historians. Now back to trees. Don't forget An Gúm's edition *An Fear a Chuireadh Crainn.* Y

OLD IRISH CUSTOM   20 April 1985

It seems to be an old Irish custom to plant trees in a perfect circle. If you go around the country with your eyes open, you will find that there are enormous numbers of the same. You will notice, too, that the majority are about a hundred years old or more. Antrim is one county where there seem to be a lot. These are not of aristocratic or landlord derivation, for many of the places are modest enough as to housing.

Could the habit have come from copying the trees which so often decorate the circumference of old raths or crannógs? In these cases, of course, there are trees within the circle, too. For the more obviously planted circles are clear of other growth and are so often of beech, even in upland Antrim where the winds tame them mightily. They stand a bit back from the house and are not to be confused with the shelterbelts. Next time you are going to plant a clump or a row of trees, change your mind and make a circle. Y

POISON IN THE GARDEN 17 May 1985

 Annual warning. Gardens are cascading with the lovely golden rain of laburnum blossom. There is hardly a handsomer sight. (Golden isn't actually the right shade, but that's what the Germans call it: golden rain.) It's handsomer, many say, than its frequent companion lilac. But later in the year it becomes deadly when the seed pods are falling. They look so like smaller versions of peas or beans that children may be tempted – and have been – to play at making dinners with them. If eaten, the result can be fatal. If you have young children about you'd be better to replace it with a lilac. Y

DOGS' DINNER 3 April 1989

It's understandable that the resident dog has his favourite patch of couch grass and makes for it at every opportunity. (He takes a daily dose.) But it is remarkable that a dog, whose owners are paying a visit of a few days, makes for the same area all on its own. It is said that the dogs use this grass for emetic purposes, and it does happen that they sick it up now and then. But in taking it daily – they must find it a general purpose tonic or pick-me-up.

Humans also use the grass but in the form of a decoction of the roots or rhizomes, and, according to a popular herbal, it is still well regarded in France. Who reads "Trilby" now? According to one book, Little Billee in the same is dosed with it. As a tisane or infusion it is described as being demulcent and sudorific, i.e. soothing and sweat-making. Humans reading this would be advised not to experiment on their own. If it is usable, herbalists will have it in a safe form. Tastes of liquorice, says one source. Y

LAST YEAR'S BOUNTY   9 April 1985

The untidy gardener wins again. Last year's herbs are still going strong in many cases because the herb bed was never properly tidied up and some of them lurked on in the shade of hopelessly overgrown fennel and sage. Thus, the piercing blue flower of the borage is upon us – this is of course also partly due to being in a particularly shaded enclosure – and the chervil is still thick and abundant. What a mighty power is in fennel; there is already enough frondy, brilliant green foliage to stock a flowershop with backing for their blooms. But it's not yet warm enough to sow seeds out.   Y

HERBS TO HELP   10 April 1989

Newspapers and magazines in the western world seem obsessed with diets and nourishment and sickness. The stuff of life, you may say. But, looking at a German magazine, you'd wonder if these people aren't the most hypochondriacal of all. It's a popular, glossy publication with BMWs and bimbos and booze, but with an unbelievable forty-four advertisements, some of them full-page colour, with remedies for every sort of ailment, and mostly of herbal origin. In some cases, conditions to be treated affect the stomach, or joints and muscles, or the circulation. But forty-four – and not one of them a small ad.

There are many people in Ireland who believe strongly in herbal remedies, but this has not led to massive advertising in newspapers and magazines. In Germany it seems to be big business. Some say that Germany has always led in this field. Also it may be argued that Germany has a very highly-developed orthodox medical system and this is just the overspill of a wealthy society. They are big on garlic, by the way. And even the advertisement for mineral water gives, on the French model, the information that it is good for catarrh of the stomach, heartburn and other things, not just pleasant to drink. The advertisements, of course, cover such ordinary remedies as aspirin: but that comes from the willow tree.   Y

PIMMS NUMBER ONE ETC.   18 April 1995

"It's not just spring that is coming," he said. "Today I saw the first sign of summer: a man in Grafton Street, Dublin, wearing a panama hat." He must have been a stranger, you'd think. But Irishmen also wear them. And boaters at regattas and such events. And white flannel trousers – or some material of the kind. And sip Pimms Number One.

Pimms might be described as a yuppy drink, though it was around decades before that term was invented. It has long been the summer drink of rowing regatta folk and garden party and croquet people. You find it, in summer, around Henley and places like that – and Islandbridge, Dublin, when the long boats are out. Or used to. The distinctive thing about Pimms Number One, which, old timers assert, started out as the Somerset Maugham favourite, a gin sling, was not just the drink, but the greenery. You had to have, brimming over the tankard, a whole herbarium. Some favour mint as the main theme, but the real, the authentic, the only one for the best tipplers, is borage. That hairy-leaved, clumsy plant which, in fact, tastes good in spite of its hairiness – tastes of cucumber – but whose crowning glory is the bluest of blue flowers. As blue, indeed, as the famed gentian of the Burren and elsewhere.

And the point of this dissertation is that summer is really coming when two garden shops have packets of seed of every herb in the catalogue, but their borage packets have all been sold. More will come in, they swear, but the herb will hardly be up and blooming in time for the regatta, or the croquet, or whatever. The real gardeners grow herbs from seed. The rest of us get ours in little pots at about £1 and then repot them. Fortunately borage is good at reseeding itself. A few plants promise well, having sturdily lived through the winter. They are lovely, not with Pimms, but with the flowers (edible) sprinkled over a green salad.   Y

HERBAL   6 May 1988

You have to admire the well-kept herb bed. One, say, made in the shape of a cartwheel, with bricks for spokes and the space in between devoted to the different varieties. Now, herbs may not do all those things for you that some health enthusiasts claim, but they smell well and give flavour to any dish you use them in. There is an added advantage for the lazy gardener – that's most of us – in that herbs in general are better grown in poorish soil. You don't have to bother measuring out fertilisers.

This excuse has been given here before and bears repeating: instead of the old practice of growing from seed, the tendency now is to buy herbs in pots for about 75p. One gardener deplored this in a garden centre. "Nonsense," said the owner briskly, "it's horses for courses. You have far more important things to do than to watch seeds sprouting. Let someone else do that for you. Was it six pots of parsley you said?"   Y

"AS SNOW TO ESKIMOS"   14 May 1999

 Thomas Hardy had a great eye for the world around him. Just now, when you may be cursing every morning at the layers of brown bud-casings of the beech tree which cover the bonnet of your car, you may not see the charm of these lines from his famous poem "Afterwards": "When the Present has latched its postern behind my tremulous stay,/And the May month flaps its glad green leaves like wings,/Delicate-filmed as new-spun silk, will the neighbours say/He was a man who used to notice such things?" For, indeed, the new leaves of the beech are delicate as silk and so are the leaves of the oak at the opening; especially, perhaps, the red American oaks. Later they all thicken up. Last Sunday, on a drive of about 100 miles through Kildare and Laois, a member of the company kept remarking on the green of the grass, also on the quantity of yellow, principally from the acres of whins – furze if you like – on the Curragh plain. But there was also brilliant yellow along a stretch of road. No time to stop to take a closer look – but then the question was answered: a bit

farther along was a field of oil-seed rape. And in the towns, here and there, laburnum in full flower. Not to mention dandelions, though they seem mostly to have gone to seed now.

But grass, that's a really serious matter to us all in this island. Has there ever been a year when it has grown faster? Enviable for animal-raising farmers, hell for the ordinary householder, with his lawn to mow. Lush is the picturesque word for it. Gross, some would have it. David Cabot, in his recent book, writes: "The most striking feature consistently noted about Ireland by visitors is the greenness, due to the extensive carpeting of permanent grassland pastures which, in the absence of low winter temperatures, keep on growing, thus staying green for a longer period than in any other European country. Growth can continue to December and restarts in March. Grass to the Irish is like snow to the Eskimo (Innuit?); it is all-pervasive and has played a pivotal role in the social, cultural and economic development of the country for nearly 6,000 years since the arrival of the first Neolithic farmers."

A friend, whose job involves grass-cutting on a big scale, as well as tree-culture and so on, says grass in his area in the Midlands, grows in December, too. He cuts it up to Christmas. Grass is less seen in small front gardens in Dublin these days. Put it into gravel (usually pink) and you are saved mowing. Pity?   Y

GOOD MANY BLOSSOMS   16 May 1988

Will 1988 be a good year for fruit? The May blossoms on the apple trees promise a heavy crop. We need to avoid frost now for the rest of the month and we can do without heavy winds. When blossoms make it to June there is every reason to hope they'll be out of the danger zone, but snow and frost in an Irish June, not to mention freak hailstone showers, are too well documented to allow the apple farmer to relax until the crop has set. The common chestnut trees have splendid candelabras or blossoms, not all of which will translate into chestnuts come September, but again the promise of a heavy crop is there.   H

BAREFOOT DAYS   17 May 1988

 The sustained run of summer weather we're having must have mothers repeating the time-honoured saying "ne'er cast a clout till May is out". In the past years weather like the last week would have the young fry importuning parents to be allowed to cast off the leather shoes to run barefoot to school. Going barefoot to school in high summer in the old days had nothing to do with hard times or lack of money: it was the preferred state of all fleet-footed youngsters.

Free of leather sandals or shoes you could, you felt, "run like the wind". But no matter how warm the days or how soft the tar on the road, sober parents always obeyed the dictum about not casting a clout. The word "clout" always sounded odd to the youngsters who interpreted the word as a slap. Clout is an old English word for cloth.   H

WEEDS   10 May 2000

A Dublin suburban reader has his problems. When he moved to his present house, he decided to re-landscape his sloping garden, thus making some use of three years of art training in Ireland and France. On his wife's best tea-tray he made a scale model in plasticine of what he wanted to do. The final plan included a small hillock, and to make this he got 16 tonnes of soil from a County Wicklow farm delivered to his front gate. The pleasant smells of "real Ireland", as he put it, added to the fun as all hands set to with borrowed wheelbarrows to move the earth around the house to what is now known as "Mound Everest". Neighbours and visitors were suitably impressed. "Ours was no formal garden with neat flower beds and dainty shrubs, but a 60-yard-long series of rises and falls on four levels."

But then the problem arose. With the rich soil, determined weeds smuggled themselves in. Not your modest things that you see even in the best gardens, but brutes like ragwort, thistle and docks "that are mentioned in notices outside rural Garda stations with warnings of penalties for neglectful landowners who harbour them".

Supposing a wandering Garda should look over the wall, he thought. On advice from a farmer he kept a slash-hook so that he could be seen attacking them. But the weeds spread from the hillock, not only on to his own lawn but also to the neighbours' finely cultivated patches. So, he thinks he has a problem. Does he sell the house and flee the district or mix up some evil brew – for these are formidable opponents? Well, the notices may still be up outside Garda stations, but the sergeant is unlikely to call at any neighbouring house that shows a burdock or two. They have more to keep them busy these days. Apparently the message is still carried, however, by notices in the press.

In all this, is there no mention of the most persistent of weeds – goosegrass, cleevers or cleavers, or robin-run-the-hedge, that sticky "abundant scrambling annual" that Richard Mabey tells us can grow ten feet in a season. You can find it even beside city or suburban footpaths. But yes, geese and hens eat it. In Staffordshire an old dame used to make beer out of it. The most persistent of all weeds, but easily pulled.   Y

BLACKBIRD SPRING   8 February 1998

Spring means different things to different people. It's not just a matter of date. You can't count the masses of snowdrops and crocuses. They are really end-of-winter apparitions. Some people claim to be able to detect spring in the easing of their joints. But mostly it's recognised in the life around us. Christina Rossetti wrote:
"There is no time like Spring
When life's alive in everything."
Yes, alive in a good and a bad sense. A friend who works in landscaping claims that spring has arrived when he takes out the sprayer and the bottle of Nettleban, and goes after the nettles and cleavers in one piece of land he supervises. No blood-cleansing nettle potion for him. Other country people mark the spring by the first appearance of blackthorn blossom. But surely nothing conveys spring more than the almost unceasing activity of the blackbirds. In one yard and nearby shrubbery, they are

restlessly visiting prospective sites. So far they have not ever returned to any previous nest of their own or their clan's making, though at least two are in fine condition. And there is not so much time to lose. A friend says they will often be sitting on eggs by the end of this month.

The blackbird is most tenacious. This is a story from an old *Field* (the English one) of 1899: "We were cutting down a holly this afternoon, and on its falling to the ground, a blackbird flew from beneath. On looking among the branches, we found its nest, with three eggs in it, turned upside down. The bird must have sat on them all the time that the digging was going on round the roots, and would not leave its nest even when it felt the tree falling . . . we did not know the nest was there, or else the tree would have been left until all the birds were fledged."

The old Gaelic poets were right when they so often made the blackbird the hero of their lyrics.   Y

BIRDS ARE BRAINY   1 March 1999

Bird-brain is not a sensible appellation for human beings to use. For, after all, birds could navigate unerringly before we could. We are told this firmly by the eminent scientist Hubert Reeves in his book *Oiseaux, Merveilleux Oiseaux*. And now, in a longish article on blue tits, coal tits and others of the species, Corine Lacrampe tells us some remarkable facts about their habits. For example, the coal tit (*Parus ater*), which in France, anyway, lives to a great extent in coniferous forests, often at some height, has its own style of laying away food for the winter. "You have to admire", the writer states, "the cleverness with which she stows away her provisions. Firmly holding the larvae or grubs of insects in her claws, she takes out the head and intestines with a few pecks of her beak. In this way the bodies will be preserved for a few weeks without deteriorating. To stock greenfly, of which she is very fond, the coal tit rolls them into pellets containing about thirty. And she takes care, this far-seeing tit, to put them in several different caches. If one is raided, she has others. The introduction of a monoculture of spruce on hillsides and on plains has extended her domain. And the coal tit, the smallest of the tits are those which are the earliest to lay in spring. Thus they can hope to have two or three broods in a year."

The coal tit, for the last few years in certain parts of the east of Ireland have been hugely numerous. Sometimes around the feeders they are like swarms of midges. Well, slight exaggeration, but this can be put down to the fecundity of the European birds, for the arrival of flocks here are noticeable. All due, the writer thinks, to over-population in north-eastern Europe and subsequent migration to the south west. The blue tit (*Parus caeruleus*), we are told, is most sensitive to winter hardship. If conditions are bad the blue tit will die of cold and exhaustion if it cannot find food for half of the short day.

On nests, the author tells us how this bird loves to use former residences of woodpeckers. In Irish conditions, any refuge will do. There is a picture here of a nest in an upturned saddle. In a fortnight the young reach their adult weight. An observer, Paul Isermann, saw 12,500 feeding flights by the parents in that period. Much more about all tits in the February edition of *Le Français*.   Y

TALKING TO BIRDS   28 March 1985

 You have heard of singular people who believe in talking to plants. So it's not so outlandish to talk to birds. In this case it's a blackbird that has nested in the greenhouse. You might think that everyone should go around on tip-toe and keep quiet as possible? Wrong. The thing to do, says the expert, is to keep up a continuous low talking, singing or humming when near the nest. This reassures the bird. For if you steal around trying to maintain silence, any sudden sound you do make will be a break in continuity and will startle the expectant mother. Clear the throat well before the approach.   Y

EGG-STEALERS   15 March 1999

It's the time of year when, walking along a hedgerow, or indeed anywhere in your own garden, you may come across a jewel in the grass – a fragment of a wild bird's egg. Bird-nesting has long been declared illegal and socially unacceptable and that fine essayist Robert Lynd gives over two of his meditations to this: "The Morals of Bird's Nesting" and then "The Morals of Bird's Nesting: Second Version". In the first, he tells us how he nearly took up that nefarious hobby. He found a hedge-sparrow's nest and "borrowed" one to give as a present to a lady who was ill. He pricked it at each end, blew out the contents in proper fashion, and laid it on the table beside her bed. "It looked prettier than any diamond that was ever stolen from an Indian temple. It was much admired."

Next day he set out – in a heat wave – on further exploration. He found a robin's nest and took one of the four eggs. He did not blow it. A good thing. For on this occasion, the hospital nurse, the children's nurse, the housemaid and the cook and even the patient set up a hue and cry: "He's robbed a robin's nest." He swore he would return the egg safely and as it had been in his hand all the time, was certain that the "poor little robin inside" would survive. So off again in the heat wave, up a hill to the nest and he delivers it safely. Five days later, or so, he visits the nest to find the full complement of four young robins alive and hungry. He had felt, he said, under the strictures of the nurse, the housemaid, etc., as if he were the man who shot the albatross.

In retailing all this he got deflected from his subject – the morality of it all. And he puts it straight: "I may say at once that I am a sworn enemy of bird's nesting." And, "I doubt if the possession of the loveliest egg in the world is worth the song of a single hedge-sparrow." And he acknowledges that some of the finest of the "old-fashioned" naturalists such as Richard Jefferies shot kingfishers "and as good men as he have robbed birds' nests". But if you must collect, he advises, why not follow the example of a child he knows who collects the broken shells that fall out of the nests when the young are hatched?

He had seen this collection, laid in cotton wool "and I assure you it was one of the most attractive collections I have ever set eyes on". That's Robert Lynd. But without some egg collection where would the world's natural history museums be? TV is fine, but . . . Anyway that is all gone and the egg-stealer is an outlaw. Rightly so.   Y

35

SWALLOW TIME 25 March 2000

 It's nearly April, and so, nearly swallow time. That is, normal swallow time, with the bulk arriving in May, but with all this global warming upsetting our calculations, who is to say that they won't make it in the last days of March? We get a powerful invasion of them – 250,000 pairs breed throughout Ireland, Cabot reckons in his *Irish Birds*, with swifts at about 200,000 pairs and house martins a mere 100,000 pairs. Swallows are the ones with the lovely long tail streamers. The bird the poets celebrate: "Swallow, my sister, O sister swallow." The gathering of the birds on telephone wires when ready to migrate back to Africa is a feature that even the most unobservant of humans recognises. Ever hear how long it takes them to get to their goal? Well, in the current English *Field*, Willy Newlands tells us that the young swallows migrate by making hops of 125 to 180 miles every five days or so, speeding up as they get farther south. They take a full four months to get down to South Africa. "The adults travel faster and can cover 6,200 miles in forty days."

And part of the question as to where the swallows go in winter can be "into West African cooking pots". For a patch of tall grass, says the *Field* article, on a hillside at Ebok-Boje in southern Nigeria is one important stopover for migrating swallows. At peak season, a million birds are estimated to roost overnight – and more than 200,000 are eaten by local bird-catchers. It's not all as it was for the swallows who come to Ireland, Cabot reminds us. Farming methods have changed, and there is not the same flying insect life about the modern yards as there used to be: bluebottles, hoverflies, horseflies, etc. Also farm buildings have changed and are not so accessible. Even some of our rivers, polluted or at least less pristine, do not offer the same fly life as in the past. The sight of a swallow diving down, weaving around a bend or two and then soaring up into the sky, again and again, was one of the thrills of summer.

House martins are thought to be declining. One house, near a river, which has deep eaves has not for two years seen the nests of this bird which were of long standing. Finally a footnote from Cork in the *Field*, dated 1958: a letter reads, "I noticed a swallow flying up and down over a pool on the river Lee on February 10th. I watched it for long periods and am in no doubt as to its identity." (Two other observers identified it.) And the writer asks if this is not extremely early for a swallow to be seen? The editor answered that swallows will occasionally remain here through the winter.   Y

BIRDS CAN NAVIGATE? PREPOSTEROUS   24 April 1998

This is the first time for those famous firsts: the first swallow and the first cuckoo. The first swallows to be seen by this pair of eyes came on Sunday 21 April on the Moynalty river, though a friend announced one on the previous Thursday in Navan. No doubt someone will come in with earlier reports.

The Moynalty lot were working over a river in heavy flood. It was raining lightly, muggy sort of weather, and the birds were skimming the surface sort of picking up flies. But the flies were not visible to the naked eye. First there seemed to be two, soon it was possible to count seven. "The vitality of them," said one of the observers on the bank, "compare the strength and ease of those power-dives with the fussing and fluttering of the birds at the feeding devices." And the eye found it hard to follow the bird skimming into a circle which brought it back to the water again and again. Seven of them, it seemed, though it was so hard to follow amid all the gyrations.

If this was their first landfall, the expert said, they may move on in a day or so. And on Monday they certainly weren't on the same stretch. That, of course, was the day after the night of the wind. Anyway, they're well represented. At the meeting of the Boyne and Blackwater on the main road through Navan on Monday the air seemed thick with them. Of course, we all laugh now at old Gilbert White with his theories of hibernation.

Richard Mabey in his book on White writes: "Migration was one of the most vexed questions in eighteenth-century science and philosophy, and many thinkers found it impossible – or just over-humiliating – to believe that blind instinct could achieve feats of navigation that superior human intelligence was just mastering. No wonder many old superstitions about swallows hibernating, in ponds or caves, were revived as eighteenth-century 'modern myths': dumb sleep was so much less unsettling as an instinctual gift."

And Mabey makes a nice point. It was not just a scientific problem for White. "He was intrigued and delighted by the annual return (or re-awakening) of his favourite parish birds, the swallows, swifts and martins; and increasingly their loyalty to the village seemed to echo his own not entirely rational attachment to Selbourne." Now you, too, be grateful to your own swallows: village or townland or city. Cuckoos another time.

(*Gilbert White* by Richard Mabey, Century Hutchinson, 1986.)   Y

CORNCRAKE WITH GRAVY   3 March 1988

 Keats wrote his "Ode to a Nightingale"; Shelley "To a Skylark", the blackbird figures in early Irish poetry. But to judge by the interest which is awakened every time the corncrake comes into the news, this has to be one of the most evocative of birds. Older people say that the summers were better when they were young and the evenings loud with that odd, clacking cry. The youthful feel they have missed something and are curious, for hardly any of them have had the experience.

The corncrake has declined disastrously in numbers. Some of this may be due to silage cutting and modern farm machinery in general. A main cause may reside in Africa, where the corncrake spends the winter. There could be other causes for, yes, Mrs Beeton has a recipe for landrail or corncrake. You need four for a serving, she says. And she tells you how to bring the head under the wing, the thighs close to the body and skewer the lot . . . and so on . . . and serve on fried breadcrumbs with a tureen of brown gravy. "When liked, bread sauce may also be sent to the table with them." Anglers know the rail fly, a wet sedge, using the soft cinnamon wing feather of the corncrake or landrail. Other feathers from the same bird, too.   Y

CREX CREX AND A MOUSE   8 May 1999

Sean Mac Connell's Midlands Report of last Thursday, pin-pointing Banagher Bridge as the centre for those who wish to hear the corncrake, made one wonder what Gilbert White of Selbourne had to say on the bird. No mention of corncrake in the index of an 1891 edition of his famous book. Look under landrail and there it is. "A man brought a landrail or dakerhen, a bird so rare in this district that we seldom see more than one or two in a season and those only in autumn. This is deemed a bird of passage by all the writers; yet from its formation seems to be poorly qualified for migration; for its wings are short, and placed so forward, and out of the centre of gravity, that it lies in a very heavy and embarrassed manner, with its legs hanging down and can hardly be sprung a second time, as it runs very fast and seems to depend more on the swiftness of its feet than on its flying."

But naturalists in those days and even later were always concerned with the inner workings. White goes on: "When we came to draw it, we found the entrails so soft and tender in appearance they might have been dressed like the ropes of a woodcock. The craw or crop was small and lank, containing a mucus; the gizzard thick and strong, and filled with small shell snails, some whole, and many ground to pieces through the attrition which is occasioned by the muscular force and motion of the intestine." As there was no gravel among the food, he supposed the shells might perform that function. He bemoans the fact that landrails used to abound. "I remember, in the low, wet bean-fields of Christian Malford in North Wilts, and in the meadows near Paradise Gardens in Oxford, where I have often heard them cry crex crex.

"The bird mentioned above weighed seven-and-a-half ounces, was fat and tender and in flavour like the flesh of a woodcock. The liver was very large and delicate." Eating birds in the interest of science or whatever was, until some time in this century, the norm for a curious naturalist. Under this piece by White, in very small print is a footnote, by Marwick, to whom many of the letters are addressed. It states that the landrail or corncrake is a regular migrant notwithstanding the shortness of its wing. "The food is somewhat varied; we once took a mouse from the stomach of a landrail."   Y

KESTREL IN THE CONSERVATORY   3 April 1998

After reading this, you might consider being less free with the pejorative "bird-brain". A couple of days ago, two young people who live on the outskirts of Dublin became aware of a commotion in their conservatory. It is big and high. And, as everyone knows, when a bird makes its way into such a place, the wisest thing to do is to do nothing. Small birds can injure themselves by dashing against the glass if you try to help them out. Just sit and wait. They will eventually find a way out. This was somewhat different. It wasn't the usual small bird. It was a kestrel. Not our biggest predator, but at 32–35 centimetres, according to Cabot, no mean size, especially indoors.

So the young people kept their cool. Next thing they see a remarkable sight. The kestrel is hanging upside down – by the heels, so to speak – against the glass, with his feet on one of the beams or struts, right up against the window. Below him is a louvred or sloping glass, as in so many greenhouses or conservatories. So our bold kestrel lets go, slides down, the belly to the glass, Niall confirmed, flaps his wing before he can hit the ground and is off.

The kestrel is known for many traits and stratagems, but this has to be one of the most intelligent birds even among them. "He was hanging upside down," said Niamh more than once. Maybe he'll be back – or she, if it was the less-colourful female. A learned book, *British Birds of Prey* by Leslie Brown, begins the chapter on the kestrel by declaring it is the most familiar bird of prey in Britain, even familiar to people who travel up and down motorways at speed, for "kestrels hunt voles in the long grass on the embankments and sides of cuttings . . . and are often seen hovering with the traffic roaring past a few yards away. "They are most conspicuous hovering over fields. Later on, the word 'hovering' is qualified somewhat. The bird spreads its tail and "winnows the air with its wings". When it sees its prey it glides down and, when a few feet over the quarry, "raises the wings vertically above its back and plunges, feet foremost into the grass to grasp the prey".

Interesting economy of effort: they don't build nests. A cliff ledge; the ledge of a building; viaducts, or even the abandoned nest of another bird. Cabot estimates we have about 10,000 pairs in Ireland. (Brown's book was published by Collins in 1976.)   Y

PHANTOM FIGURE   12 April 1998

Did you see *Animal Hospital* with Rolf Harris on BBC1 the other night, when one of the creatures dealt with was a barn owl, a young one, found near death from dehydration and starvation? Not much hope for its recovery was given by the vet, but it did survive and thrive, even. This, it seems was a tame owl that had escaped, for, hard as it is to believe, the *Field*, a knowledgeable journal, had an article a year or so ago telling us that while barn owls in the wild in Britain have dropped to not much more than 3,000 in number, there are no fewer than 25,000 in captivity. The article quotes a former Director of the Royal Zoological Society of Scotland as recommending a pet-lover to get a pair of barn owls.

The *Field*'s view is that the best way to preserve the species is to support wild pairs. Some lovers of these birds have started by acquiring a pair of hand-reared, tame birds and, by giving them suitable quarters – in a barn or attic, say – in the country, of course, and by feeding them with the right food at the right time, encouraging them to breed in the hope that their young may take off on their own to help check the general decline. The *Field* writer quotes a farmer, who must breed a lot of chickens, as feeding dead chicks to the owls. Others, in similar circumstances, can buy dead chicks, and also may use liver when short. Food must be regular.

A comprehensive book on owls of many varieties, their habits, history and superstitions about them, was published by David and Charles in 1970. The authors are John Sparks and Tony Soper. It also includes instructions about nest-boxes and general care of barn owls in particular. A man who has spent a lifetime moving around the country, often at night, usually angling, sometimes just rambling or working at his trees, still can count only rare encounters with this bird, but numbers them as among the most fascinating of all: the huge wings, white from below, the pale moon-face, the silence of its movements. Probably the source of many a ghost story. Once he came face to face on a cliff-top with this white face, and the bird just looked for a few seconds and with no haste dropped out of sight. James Fairley in his *An Irish Beast Book* writes that: "The owl's enormous lenses result in the eyes being fixed almost immovably in their sockets, but this is compensated for by the extraordinary mobility and rapid reflex action of the neck, which allows the head to swivel to practically any position in an instant. An owl enjoys all-round vision, for it can turn its head through nearly 180 degrees on each side."   Y

DEAD AS A DOORNAIL   16 April 1987

 Birds do die of natural causes too. Say, a heart attack. At any rate, there he was lying on his back, wings half open, his ridiculous white claws clutching moss and grass, and dead as a doornail. Not a sign of violence, from shot or beak or claw. Just dead and cold. And he was (or she was) a short-eared owl, a miracle of aeronautics when alive, a brilliant pattern of brown and fawn and white in death. No clues, as it has been said, as to death, but did the tightly clutched fragments indicate perhaps that nesting was in mind? It's a ground nester according to the books.

Tom Murray of Kells, whose tackle and gun shop is much more than a tackle and gun shop – it's a major source of information and chat – says that it probably can be stuffed and mounted. Apart from the breathtaking colour patterns, the amazing thing about it is the tiny body and the slight weight of the whole. Yet in flight it seems a big bird.   Y

BLACKBIRD GUERRILLA   7 April 2000

It's dangerous to attribute human reactions or feelings to birds and animals in the wild. Home-based pets such as pussy-cats and parrots may be thought by their owners to respond in a human fashion to the right sounds and actions with gratitude, or in some cases with disdain, and surely do, but you won't find so many to believe that a bird out in your garden would react similarly. It might eagerly and instantly leap on food you put out, but don't expect any cooing or kindly whistling or purring. On the other hand, surely it is possible for a creature out there to turn nasty, to take a scunner against a person or a house. Here is a possible example. We have been through all the stories of birds pecking at their own image in the side-mirrors of cars, or in windows. We have heard how a bird approaching a window in a house and seeing through the room another window in exactly the same line, will assume (we think) that there is clear space between, and will dash itself against the pane and kill itself.

But here is a blackbird who, for about four months, has kept up a daily pattern of aggression against a house, often starting before it is light. Now there are three rooms where thickish branches of rose trees cross the panes from about a foot away and one other where there is a rail less than a foot from the glass. When he first started his campaign of pecking at the glass, all sorts of devices were arranged so that he wouldn't break his beak or scramble his brains – cardboard to spoil the image he could otherwise see reflected, white streamers just to make things difficult for him. All in vain. From morning to late afternoon he has his fun. The inhabitants don't get cross about it. They regard it as a comedy act, out of which they get as much as he does. For example, if you approach the window from inside and wave, he goes off without fuss but lurks behind a big pot or bush. But if you open the door and shout "Gwan outa that you cod," he takes off majestically towards the heavens, crosses a high wall with *élan* and looks as if he is not due to land for a couple of hundred yards. He is the only bird to peck at the window, and God knows there are enough about,

43

especially in the afternoon bathing time, when the queue for a dip can be formidable. Incidentally, the most quarrelsome of all are the blackbirds, often flying at each other like gamecocks. Thrushes stand quietly by, as this goes on.

So is our man malevolent or just a bird with a sense of mischief? Or humour? Someone wrote a book on animal psychology about 20 years or more ago. Does anyone know the name of the author and book? It should be a good read just now.   Y

MIRROR, MIRROR   26 April 1988

Odd sight in a quiet corner of a Dublin suburb: a row of cars, each adorned with a pair of plastic bags over the side-mirrors. Just the ordinary supermarket bags, roughly tied on. What for? To keep small birds like blue tits from pecking endlessly at their image in the mirrors – bad enough in itself – but, more to the point, splashing mirror and car door intensively with their dirt. Which, as everyone knows, destroys the paint. Birds pecking at windows are common enough, but is this a characteristic only of south Dublin tits? Never seen it before.   Y

WHAT COLOUR IS AN EGG?   8 April 1989

You'll be finding bits of egg-shells from nesting birds from time to time. Why are they coloured as they are – some white, some dull in camouflage, some brilliant? There may be a full explanation in every case. Anyone can see why the eggs of birds that nest on the ground should be unobtrusive, brownish, speckled maybe, fitting in with the nest colour or the colour of the ground cover. Then, an expert pointed out in a recent article, eggs laid in holes in trees or in burrows don't need protective colouring. So they can be white. But then you have, say, the song thrush with its brilliant sky blue background, and black spots. If one of the parents is not sitting on the nest the eggs must be very visible from, say, a magpie above.

Could it be that tens of thousands of years ago thrushes laid their eggs against some blue background?

Pheasants, though nesting on the ground, lay eggs which are pale in colour. That may have been OK in their original homes in eastern marshland, but not great cover in our present conditions. So they can cover the eggs when they leave the nest, as ducks do? You know it all.   Y

KEEP FEEDING THEM   17 April 1999

 Feed the birds all the year round? Yes, of course. For even in summer, as a writer in *The Countryman* reminded us, there come wet spells when insects and grubs get washed off the leaves and odd spells where caterpillars may not be so easily picked up. Some birds can have problems in feeding themselves and their young when it is assumed that all is well with them. There is always the argument that a whole peanut, say, could choke a nestling. But modern birdfeeding devices are such that no bird can extract more than a small portion of any kind of nut from them. You do not leave out on the table or on the ground whole peanuts. Better still, don't have a table. As well as nuts by the way, feeders with easy access to the interior should carry a lump of fat, such as one of the cooking brands of lard. You would be surprised how often it is availed of.

The presence of a set of feeding devices often draws the attention of sparrowhawks. One such rather lavish set is on a river edge, overlooked by a pair of tall willows. From the topmost branches there is a strategic view of the coal tits, greenfinches (very busy just now), blue tits, great tits and at times chaffinches. Long-tailed tits are temperamental and clannish. Earlier in the year, they would come in parties of six or more. And, of course, with small fragments of nuts falling, as they inevitably do, many birds which do not or cannot cling and eat at the same time pick up a reasonable amount of titbits. As for the sparrowhawk, there used often to be a floating feather or two in the air, now and then, and you would find the feeding hangers empty. Things have improved since an ingenious friend rigged up a curtain of small-gauge chicken-wire, about three feet by two, which swings gently between the sparrowhawks' perch and the feeders. It does not prevent the occasional fatality, as the birds leave the protected area, but gives them a bit more security than they had.

They are 100 per cent safe while they eat, for all the food is in a tangle of branches of three slim, old hawthorn trees. The only unwelcome guests are the grey squirrels, but they no longer disturb the birds. And the latter know that the dog is not after them when she comes around.   Y

HAREM STYLE   23 April 1987

It seems all day long that the call of the cock pheasant, which has so much of the smoker's cough in it, rings out. A knowledgeable neighbour explains it thus. He will have a small harem of nesting females in the area. This is his reminder to them that he is on duty and his warning to them that they had better stick with the job – sit on those eggs no matter who or what passes close by. Right enough, the calls come now from up river, now from down river, now on this side of the road, now on the other. He is not only doing his duty, he is making a public declaration of it. Something like 50 per cent of the readers of this piece are already saying: how masculine.   Y

CUCKOO GAMES   14 May 1988

 The steady call of the cuckoo, to the point where you don't bother to comment on her, is the one sound to crown a May day with perfection. The notes come as if muffled in a blanket of sun-heat, when the bird is three fields away in Cuckoo Valley in Achill. The first birds were sighted on 7 April and one pair paired off and were together fairly constantly up to 25 April when one dropped from a power line, followed by the other, the first swooping and banking as the second bird followed. But there were no song notes heard.   H

DEATH IN THE GARDEN   7 May 1988

The cruellest hunters of all, of course, may be wild creatures themselves, furred or feathered. Thus, a nestful of young thrushes, already fairly well-feathered, is found scattered on the ground nearby – all decapitated. The neighbour says she saw the magpie descend on the nest. Would she have been justified in shooting it with her air-gun, if she had one? Would she be allowed under the current legislation? There is some logic, after all, in say-ing that the less we do to interfere with the balance of nature, the better. There may be some inscrutable reason why magpies have been sent into overproduction just now, some reason not discernible to us.

Similarly, what looks like an infestation of certain insects in a garden or a crop may be wiped out with chemicals and yet a worse plague succeed them. "Sit it out," was the advice of a wise horticulturist to an ama-teur tree-grower who was infested with weevils. "The trees, after all," he said, "always survive. And sooner or later those bugs will simply die out. In a few years. Patience." Have you that sort of patience? With bugs? With magpies?   Y

BUSIEST BIRD   25 May 1988

Surely the busiest bird parents must be the blue tits. Anyone with a nest in a wall near a kitchen or sitting room can have a lot of fun with a stop-watch, checking the number of flights the parents make in any five-minute segment. An ordinary watch will do just as well, timing the flights over 60 seconds. If the nest is near trees with insects, the trips will obviously be more frequent: if they have to "travel" for the food the number of flights drops.

The young are never more than a few seconds with-out attention. As the hen flies off, the cock is on his way back. Best "score" to date for flights was six and the "worst", three. At 6.30 am the parents were already working and their last flight of the day was logged at 10.10 in the third week of May. It seems they keep going right up to the edge of darkness. Could the meadow or reed warblers who get "landed" with a cuckoo be busier, remembering the hulk of the bird compared with foster parents.   H

BIRD BIRTH CONTROL   18 May 1998

Have you, too, been frustrated by putting out nest box after nest box and never finding any tenant to occupy them? You wonder if you have them facing the wrong way, say into the wind, or is it just that there is so much good natural cover that they don't need to bother with your nice little bit of carpentry, even when it's cunningly covered with real bark. Or you think it's cunningly covered. You may get the odd feather in it, as indicating maybe that birds occasionally use it as a night shelter, but no obvious little brood of blue tits or robins or whatever.

A woman wrote to the BBC *Wildlife* magazine in dismay. "Throughout April and May," she wrote [that would be last year], "a blue tit visited our bird box, apparently building a nest and then feeding chicks. But when it stopped visiting, we found no sign of a nest ever having been there. What had it been doing?" Chris Mead, an ornithologist, replied that his guess was that that particular bird did not have any chicks that year, but continued to check out potential nest sites – such as the nest box in question. For, and this may come as a surprise to many of us, he said that even short-lived birds such as blue tits, do not necessarily try to breed every year. "Taking a break every now and then can be a sensible strategy, as raising a brood is an exhausting business."

He goes on to say that birds who try to breed every year are likely to produce small broods of weaklings, and may get so worn out that they jeopardise their own survival over winter. Further, he points out that gardens can be a particularly tricky habitat in which to raise young: for, he says, there are often few native trees around to supply the chicks with their staple diet of caterpillars. And by missing a season, the adults can stay in better condition, have more chance of surviving the winter to breed in successive years and produce healthier offspring when they do.

And he says finally that, in the case of blue tits it's usually easy to tell whether nestlings are inside or not, for, when the adults bring food back to the nest, it is carried very visibly in their beaks. What if the nest boxes are in a rural setting with no reason to believe that there is any shortage of caterpillars and other nursery food? Just inability to position the boxes correctly? Too exposed to raids by grey crows or other killers? Boxes that for some reason look too much like a trap? Or just that there are so many other, better places?   Y

POOR, UNLOVED BIRD   8 April 1999

 Nobody loves the cormorant. Unkempt-looking when it stands on a rock with its wings out-spread – digesting its food, maybe – vaguely sinister, and it probably smells awful. Not only is the cormorant unloved, but anglers and sometimes sea-fishermen seem to be always planning its demise. You can understand how they would be feared by owners of private fisheries or by those who run fishfarms. In eastern France there is a place called Les Dombes where huge fishfarming work goes on and, it is believed, the rule that you must have a licence to shoot these birds is often treated lightly.

But David Cabot in a new book, *Ireland, a Natural History* (Harper Collins £17.99), gives us a good, balanced view. In Lough Ramor, County Cavan, a reasonably good trout lake, an examination of undigested remains in cormorant pellets showed that coarse fish, roach and perch were the main species taken, with few or no brown trout, eels or pike recorded. "The increasing spread and abundance of roach is certainly linked to the growth and expansion of parts of the national cormorant population so clearly witnessed at some colonies."

It is comparatively easy for naturalists to keep track of them, writes Cabot, because so many get caught in nets or fish traps. They are big and easily seen. Still, there are a lot of them about. For example, 1,827 pairs on Lambay Island, near Dublin, and lesser, but significant, colonies in islands all around our coasts. Do they eat a lot of our favourite sea fish? A study of regurgitated food around the Little Saltee colony showed that 76 per cent of the catch comprised wrasse, three kinds named, one unidentified. A Dublin fish shop was asked if they sold wrasse. "Never heard of it", was the reply.

Now, of course, if a cormorant suddenly appears on your favourite trout stream, you know that he can only get trout and maybe salmon parr – so, bad news. But generally the impression you get from Cabot is that it is not nearly as destructive of the fish we like to eat, sea or freshwater, as some believe. The French hunting magazines, for example, go into fits at the increase of cormorant population that they believe to be taking place in their country.

And, in the case of a small trout stream, as mentioned above, you would not be human if you did not grudge it a meal and hastened its departure to other feeding grounds. And those of you with long memories will recall the case of the author of *The Fowler in Ireland* who reported that he shot a cormorant which could not fly – because it had swallowed or half-swallowed a three-pound trout.   Y

HERON'S DIET   13 April 1985

Herons and human anglers are much admired for their patience. As far as anglers are concerned, the attribution of patience is nonsense. Anglers are far from patient. They palpitate, they shiver with expectancy, they are keyed up, their blood pressure must rise with every cast, for each time their line shoots out they see in their mind's eye a lovely trout rise from the bottom to take their fly. No one knows what goes through the heron's mind; and, unlike the angler, he freezes as his eye searches the water. He can stand without rolling an eyeball – if bird eyeballs do roll – for many minutes on end.

And it is not always fish that the heron chases. Frogs are a good part of the diet; and now Phil Drabble, whom everyone knows from television, writes in the English *Field*, that the heron's diet includes a lot of fur as well as scale. He has examined the pellets of undigestible matter which they regurgitate and has found that they eat moles and shrews and voles. In spite of all that, if you've a pool with goldfish or anything else in your garden, be prepared. A small Dublin suburban garden pool which was stocked on a whim with a dozen or so rainbow trout had a visit from a heron within days.   Y

TADPOLES BUT NO FROGS   24 April 1999

 "What happens to tadpoles?" he asked, knowing well that they grow into frogs – if they are not eaten by some enemy in the water or even fished out by a heron or other bird. He asked, he said, because for some years a small artificial pond in a garden he used to have in Dublin nearly always got a quota of frogspawn, yet never, he swore, did he see one of the tadpoles evolve into a frog. No. Once he saw a tiny frog come out and then vanish. He remembered from his schooldays, when a teacher of nature studies used to have a large glass tank in the classroom with frogspawn brought in in January or February. The tadpoles duly emerged and were eye-catchingly wriggly. Needless to say, there were pond weeds in the tank and a rock on which an emergent frog might climb. But come the Easter holidays or some later half-term break and the tank and all vanished, the wrigglies returned to the wild.

A copy of the *Field Book of Country Queries* (1954, Michael Joseph) tells of an experiment in which two lots of tadpoles were taken from the same pond. One lot, kept under glass in the house, developed normally into frogs. The other lot, kept in a shallow six-foot stone trough containing water lilies, remained in the tadpole stage. Normal time for the egg-to-frog state, the article says, is about the 85th day after egg-laying. But to come back to that garden pool. If a heron had made raids on it, you could understand the lack of froglets, but no heron ever came. And the blackbirds and other birds doing their evening ablutions in the water hardly got them. Of course, as Cabot tells us in his new *Ireland, a Natural History*, while a high percentage of eggs hatch into tadpoles, fewer than one per cent survive to young froglets. And there will be plenty of enemies out there.

Another aquatic creature which small boys would come across in the years before the present conservation laws came into being was the newt. One friend says he remembers, as a very small boy, visiting a nearby pond in search of frogspawn and seeing a wonderful sinuous creature in the water, a sort of water-lizard, which he was able to identify later as a newt. He described it as having a crest and a lovely reddish speckled breast. It was a long time ago, the pond has vanished under houses. Back to the first question. Why did the original questioner never see a tadpole grow into a frog, save one? Anyway, in the bogs and marshes outside the urban scene, frogs are aplenty, it seems. Y

RIVER   7 March 1998

"Everyone should have a river in his life," an old friend used to say. He was thinking primarily of trout, it may be, but even on a blank, fishless day, he never ceased to be curious about the various whirls and depths, the colours of the stones, the animals in the fields and the birds – perhaps, above all, of the trees and hedges. Many a tree that subsequently flourished, came from his gathering of pine cones, acorns or beech mast, as he sauntered along, rod in hand, with always enough time to stop and chat with someone mending a fence or just wandering, as he was.

Southside Dubliners can experience some of the same delights in a new printing of Christopher Moriarty's *Down the Dodder*. And down the Dodder is a full, or surprisingly short to some, 18 miles. And from Kippure to Ringsend it runs through change after change. He is optimistic about the future of the river, even as more and more housing enters the valley. He tells us that he has purposely refrained from dwelling on the negative side of "certain dismal parts of the river", meaning the bits of old cars, the abandoned trolleys from shops and the general rubbish that festoons hanging willow branches and banks. Optimistically, he argues that rubbish can be removed if there is a mind to do it. And he reminds us that in the past, in the 19th century and even in the first half of the 20th, the Dodder was a good deal worse than it is today. Factories, sewers, made of the river a very unsalubrious place at times. Today, you may sit at the window of a well-known hostelry at Milltown and, as you eat your smoked salmon or curried lamb, keep your eye on the river, just below you, and expect to see a duck cruising or a dipper bobbing. Certainly a wagtail is likely. There are, to be sure, a few cartons or tins or rags on the bank opposite. With luck this problem will eventually be dealt with by a more enlightened generation.

The concept of a footpath all the way along the river bank has not been realised, but there are green stretches of some magnitude in quite a few places. Dr Moriarty gives great credit to voluntary organisations and special mention to the Dodder Anglers' Club, founded in 1958. And on that note, somewhere between 1910 and the early 1920s, a reputable, honest man used to tell of getting white trout around Milltown. Came up in a flood? Was this unusual? This is merely a local glimpse of a lovely adjunct to life on the south side of Dublin. But the book covers the river from source to the sea. Splendid photographs.   Y

FOR LIFE   23 February 1999

 Some people have a lifelong passion for birds. Watching them, admiring them, waiting each spring and summer for the return from mid-Africa or South Africa of certain familiar visitors, marvelling at the homing instinct of those who can find the same house or barn, and marvelling, too, at each generation which builds the nests to the same pattern and of the same materials. And note the dexterity which rooks, for example, show in balancing their twigs and weaving them into a firm nest. Other people are fascinated by wild animals: the regal, disdainful pace of a fox across even a suburban lawn; the friendly look of three white-striped badger faces approaching up the drive, then, suddenly taking fright and leaving at electrifying speed. It's a wonderful world, indeed, but of all creatures there is one species which lodges in the human mind to the point of addiction: the fish.

From the day your young boy, standing in his bare feet in a little stream, catching sticklebacks or spricks in his cupped hands, from the moment he espies, peeping out from under a stone, a three-inch fish, even, with red spots – he is gone. After that first glimpse he may move from brown trout to sea trout, to salmon, and the miracle 3,000-mile journey across the Atlantic and back to

Ireland to spawn and reproduce. Or the boy may stay with the brown trout of our rivers and lakes. Hooked. The March issue of the English magazine *The Field* is marked "Irish Number" and has, as its colourful cover, three large trout: gillaroo, sonaghan and ferox. Inside is an article devoted to the trout of Lough Melvin and Lough Neagh. Ireland, runs the text by Colin McKelvie (illustrations are by Rod Sutterby), "is lavishly endowed with rivers and loughs, the vast majority of which hold trout, and wild trout at that".

And he goes on to Lough Melvin, and particularly refers to work carried out on it by Professor Andrew Ferguson of QUB in the seventies. Lough Melvin is a glacial trench, deeply gouged, of about 9,000 acres and he lists the four types of trout which local people have known for a long time: brown trout as normal; ferox trout, which preys on smaller trout and arctic char, which may live long and grow very big; sonaghan, small, dark, which feeds on daphnia, midge larvae, etc., and the gillaroo, vividly coloured and with a thickened stomach to cope with a diet of shrimps, snails and other crustaceans. Then Lough Neagh has dollaghan, the buddagh and the black buddagh.

Sounds too good to be true, but you can always try. Fine tourist publicity anyway.   Y

KING SALMON   15 April 1998

"Fresh, farmed salmon." Was that TV or radio advertisement heard correctly? Soon, perhaps, everything finned will be farmed. Was there not farmed bass recently on sale? And did not someone speak of the possibility of farming char (*Salmo salvelinus*) – a splendid fish when it comes from northern chilly waters, but not to be sneezed at when it comes from lakes, as in Geneva and sometimes in Ireland. But, to salmon again. So many of the products we now ingest give the details of the contents on the label or container, such as "no added sugar", and/or "no artificial colourants".

Is there a hint for salmon farmers here? They feed their fish on several kinds of pellets, it is believed, and the beef experience is not reassuring to customers. The salmon farmer might be able to tell us, by advertisement, say, just what substances he gives to his fish. You can't expect this with every salmon steak you buy (and it all goes down well and often) but, for example, a little label on the side of the smoked salmon you buy at the airport? It is good business to give the customer as much information as is reasonable.

The salmon comes to mind on looking through a colourful brochure from the Eastern Fisheries Regional Board, entitled *The Boyne Valley Fishery*. Lovely cover photograph and a few lines from Francis Ledwidge: "Where the jewelled trout are leaping/And the heron flings his spear."

Great clarity of presentation and details of not only the hundreds of miles of river but also separate sheets on various lakes all around. You can have it in English, French, Dutch, and maybe more languages.

One message is hammered home: it's a brown trout fishery. They do admit: "The River Boyne holds some stocks of salmon and sea trout [!] and anglers must obtain the necessary permission before fishing. A State licence is required to fish for salmon and sea trout." Some stocks, note. You wonder if the salmon is holding its own. Certainly they don't, to public knowledge, appear to be under siege from sea-lice as are so many waters in the west and in Scotland. Jobs are jobs, but the problem in the west is a funked issue.

One solution suggested for a Scottish river in decline was a catch-and-return system, an ignoble end for such a mighty fish. To be hauled onto the bank, then probably weighed, and chucked back. Better to stop salmon angling for a few years, combined with intensive patrolling of spawning areas. And in the west, experiment with putting salmon farms a couple of miles out to sea, away from river estuaries.   Y

FARMING ALL FISH?   5 March 1998

 After Tree Week, what about Fish Week? Especially salmon and sea trout week, or just all trout. Can one always tell farmed fish from the wild fish? There was a worthy two-and-a-half pounder trout from the Corrib donated by a kindly legal eagle. Anyone who could not tell this magnificent and delectable fish from a farmed version would be certifiable. And now it is clear that the world is moving into the farming of sea fish in a big way. A writer in the *Financial Times*, while declaring that she had mixed views on fishfarming, nevertheless declared that if everyone who wants to eat fish insists on having the wild creature, already depleted stocks are liable to be wiped out.

Farming fish "with intelligent care", she saw as the future. And that means, among other things, not crowding them like sardines in a can. If their numbers are kept reasonable in their cages, if they are given a natural diet, space to range freely in their confines (and these should be located in seas where currents will scour the cages), then those would be some of the necessary conditions for the future, she prophesies, God help us. The writer here is concerned primarily with bass, or sea bass, which is now, apparently widely farmed. It must suit chefs that, using farmed fish they can get what they want, more or less, in terms of weight – a pound weight being, according to Philippa Davenport, the writer, something like a "greedy single helping" or at twice that weight – or more.

Bass is a good example. Was the catching of bass by anglers in Ireland recently limited? It may still be. That may all be far in the future for us. We need still to worry about our salmon and sea trout resources – as they do in Scotland. The chief preoccupation of those who wish to save these fish is the closeness of the farms to rivers which have a salmon and sea trout run, and the contamination of sea-lice, which stems, anglers claim, from the salmon farms.

The feed given to these caged fish must also be a concern to a country which has had such scares on the fodder and the stimulants given to cattle. We'll see.   Y

AND MORE FISH   5 April 1989

Netting on the high seas; netting on a vast scale inshore; gang-poaching; pollution – and we still hope to have salmon galore. There is fishfarming to help out, but what a pity that we are not as geographically well placed as Iceland. For there, it is said, they ranch, not farm. You plant out your smolts into the river system; they migrate naturally and then you pick them up as they come in back over the estuary. This year, according to reports, they will release about two-and-a-half million smolts. There is normally a return of about 15 per cent, so that makes 370,000 salmon coming home to be harvested.

All right. That presupposes a few things: no netting on the high seas, no poaching, no netting on the estuaries. Furthermore, Iceland is near to the spawning grounds and the fish thus face fewer risks in their shorter run. It's a lovely thought. There must be a flaw somewhere.   Y

TO THE BEACHES   28 March 1986

Easter and harvest were the old times of festival, and beaches were often the places for the festivities. What place more deeply planted in the folk memory than the seashore? The first arrivals on this island landed (naturally) on the beaches, and for generations, perhaps thousands of years, many of them remained close to that bountiful source of food: fish, shellfish, sea birds' eggs, edible seaweed. Around the coast middens, mostly shellfish come regularly to light.

The more enterprising spirits, in due course, will have gone up the rivers to become eventually farmers, but the coast was the safe source of supply. Later, in Christian times, and especially in Lent, the shore gave suitable nourishment. Tomás Ó Criomhtháin writes in *The Islandman*: "It has always been the custom here to go and get kitchen from the strand to eat on Good Friday."   Y

FISH SOUP
25 April 1986

"For fish soup" reads the legend on the fisherman's slab in a small town in south-west France. The miserable little creatures with big heads, bulging eyes and very spiny backs don't even merit being given the name. But they must make good soup, because French shoppers in this sharp society are not easily fobbed off with second best. This is a fishing district.

Now, a bucketful of perch or other coarse fish – such as English anglers catch, weigh and then put back into the Irish water, or which so many here simply leave on the bottom of the boat – would be something precious in this part of France. It wouldn't, of course, be worth transporting. Too costly. But suppose we, our own selves, complaining about depression and the price of food, made more of our own, easily culled "national resources". Tony O'Reilly's oil is another thing altogether.   Y

NEVER EATEN ONE
27 March 1998

 Razorshell fish or razor shell-fish or razorshellfish, said to be so-called because it resembled an old cut-throat handle; the French call it *manche de couteau* or knife-handle and in Irish, says Fergal Nolan of Bord Iascaigh Mhara, it is *scian na mara*. You see its shell (empty) on sandy beaches; about six inches long and an inch wide, hinged down one side. The shells are used in more than one house for ladling out the salt from the big jar, or flour. Inside the shell is, or was, muscular flesh. Does it taste like or have the consistency of scallop, you ask, and Mr Nolan gives his opinion that it's more like squid.

Now it seems to be a growing business for export. Trawlers using hydraulic dredges are active along the sandy east coast, pumping up the sand and mud and with it the shellfish. The exporting, it is said, is largely to Spain; also to Hong Kong. But do we eat it here? Well it may not be in the shops, but Mr Nolan says it used to be the custom at Easter for the people around Carna to go collecting the razorfish between the tides. You just brought some salt with you, put it down the hole made by the fish, and waited for it to surface, which it did.

Since learning of this a friend who knows the Omey region says the same was done there, whether at Easter or not, he couldn't remember.

But how do you tell the little hole, now closed over, with just a hint of indentation, from the hole made by, say, a lugworm? There are other methods of digging out the razorfish, with a hook of very strong wire or, as suggested in *Wildlife in Britain*, a fortnightly series, by dropping a barbed metal rod down the hole (pushing, likely) and drawing the animal up after it has closed its valves over the rod. Surely the creature would be mangled.

The dredgers on the east coast, it is believed, get something like £2.25 per kilo and very many tons are said to be harvested. What restaurant will be first to give us a taste? Mr Nolan recommends frying in olive oil with a little garlic. A friend who visits the fish market almost daily, just for family use, says he has never seen our razorfish for sale there.   Y

IT'S RAINING EELS   18 March 2000

We talk of it raining cats and dogs, and every now and then someone comes along with a story of a shower of herrings or sardines caught up in a whirlwind and deposited on a startled population. That fairly staid publication *Scientific American* presents an issue devoted entirely to weather – what we can and cannot do about it, and, dammit isn't there a huge heading "It's Raining EELS". And many stories of like occurrences. We'll work backwards from the more recent, for you might not give serious credit to something dated 1780. Anyway, the latest is 9 July 1995, with the heading "No Safety Anywhere". It tells us that lightning from a storm in Bristol, Florida, struck a tree, sending a power surge through the water in a nearby septic tank. The exploding water catapulted a 69-year-old man sitting on his toilet into the air. A hospital treated and released the man, who suffered only elevated blood pressure and tingling in his lower extremities. "More Ways To Pluck A Bird Than One" is dated 8 June 1858, and tells how a tornado tore off the feathers of a chick in Flint, Michigan, and the local paper showed a photo of it pecking around a truck that has been twisted by the same tornado "like a steel pretzel". The National Severe Storms Forecast Centre remarks on the story: "While it is not our mission . . . to record tornados which deplumed fowls, enough events of this phenomenon have been documented over the past 140 years to warrant its acceptance."

But to the shower of eels? It happened in 1892. An enormous number of eels fell during a rainstorm in Coalburg, Alabama. Farmers quickly drove into town with carts and took the eels away to use as fertilisers for their fields. "The eel deluge," says the article, "may have resulted from a waterspout lifting and jettisoning the fishes." Odd use of very good eating was it not? A friend in Paris used to plead with his Irish colleagues not to bring smoked salmon as a present, but smoked eel. Much superior, he always maintained. In March 1876, the magazine reports that many witnesses in Bath County in north-east Kentucky observed "flakes of meat" drifting down from a clear sky. One investigator declared that the flakes tasted like mutton or venison. The cause? Lightning may have struck a flock of birds and roasted them. And lightning in the Wasatch National Forest in Utah apparently killed, by a single stroke, more than 500 sheep (1918). No mention of pennies from heaven anywhere, but such oddities as snowflakes in Montana "measuring as much as 15 by 8 inches". And we complain about our weather!   Y

RIVER TRAFFIC   18 May 1995

"The river is going nearly bone-dry," he said with pardonable exaggeration. "Since arterial drainage it is either a roaring, bank-high torrent in winter, or a poor, flat, trickly thing in a dry spring or summer. And to think that children used to have a wonderful long, deep pool in which they could swim – and even dive – on a summer's evening. But still one can't deny that there is considerable, non-human river traffic. On Sunday last a wild duck swung around the bend with seven chicks paddling easily behind her. They can hardly have been more than a day or two old. Later, the heron appeared, for the second time that day. A waterhen has a nest somewhere nearby. They are more shy this year. There are still grey

wagtails, as they are called. Yellow more than grey, in fact. A robin has built behind a big stone on the bank. The kingfisher goes past, though less frequently this year. The flycatchers have just appeared. Wrens are all over this river. One has built somewhere up in the roof. We can't find the nest without danger of scaring them off.

"The sparrow-hawk flashes by occasionally, taking with him, usually, one of the birds around the feeding cages. And leaving a few feathers on the grass. There must be a couple of blackbird pairs around. They are everywhere. A song thrush appeared. We thought they had gone. What else? Lots of finches including, not too welcome, a bullfinch. Eats too many buds off the trees and bushes. We don't see much of the pigeons which nest in the ivy top of a tall hawthorn hedge. But there's a white egg often enough on the lawn. The swans have left us, after the female died.

"Needless to say, the otter, which appears only once in a while, still leaves his and/or her trademark at various points, including on a big stone in the river. The mink does the usual trick of pretending that there is only one of them. That's all we see. That's our river traffic. A few years ago it would have included many leaping, rising and rolling trout." Say no more.   Y

RESTLESS   16 March 1985

Hares are endlessly unpredictable, endlessly fidgety. A quartet, watched over a long sunny day, never seem to eat for more than two seconds from the one spot, but settle and nibble a few blades to the left, a few blades to their front and a few to the right, then move on, either a yard or two or maybe a half-mile. They are shy and yet get used to having humans around them; a path mowed through rough ground near the house to make strolling in the sun a pleasure for young children is now adopted by the hares which come trundling along at a steady pace and past the window and the snoozing dog.

In slow motion their movements are awkward and kangarooish, at speed they show their grace, as they also do in their gentle, brief coupling. No boxing or rough stuff.   Y

HARE TIME   26 March 1986

Hares are at it with vigour and assiduity. "It" being sex. The thinking used to be that mad March hares were males boxing for the favours of the females. Today the idea is that the boxing is done between male and female – it is foreplay, in other words, to the mating. The naturalists tell us that we have two species of hare in this country: the brown and the Irish hare. The Irish one is more social than the brown and is often seen in groups, says James Fairley in *An Irish Beast Book*. Largest grouping of hares seen by this corner has been 12, though eight and 10 are common. But the mating is not communal.

Debatable point: during the mating season hares seem to jink and dodge and weave less than they do for the rest of the year. They run and canter in straight lines as if the adrenalin or something else had put purpose into their criss-crossing of the fields and ditches.   Y

DAYS HUNTING WITH A RAT PACK   22 March 1999

There are various ways of dealing with rats around farms. The most obvious is to lay poison, but this could cause death to creatures for which it is not intended. Even the corpses of poisoned rats could be attractive to carrion-eaters for which it was not intended. Anyway, in north Yorkshire a syndicate of shooting people organised a rat hunt. Well organised; a pub booked, drinks and hampers packed and the right weapons chosen, a fortnight after the end of the shooting season. Rosie Nickerson tells us about the day in the English *Field*. The rat pack, as she calls them, met at the inn at 8.30 in the morning to eat huge plates of "fried things" and at 9.30 were off, armed with spades, sticks, ferrets and terriers. At the first hedge the ground was riddled with rat holes. Nothing doing. "And there we stood: 16 ratters and one journalist, weapons and ballpoint poised in readiness for absolutely nothing." But at the other end of the hedge, terriers were released and a long-haired German pointer.

Then a chainsaw, minus the saw bit, but trailing a long tube from its exhaust, poured smoke down the holes.

Rats came out in plenty, and the terriers with a shake of a rat broke its neck. If a rat was by chance missed by the terriers, the swing of a spade, stick or bat from the hunters did the job. After an hour the score was 30 rats. Then to a field of stubble where, according to the writer, the ground nearly collapsed, so riddled was it with rat holes. One intrepid hunter would even plunge his arm shoulder deep into a hole and haul out a live rat by the tail. Within an hour the haul was so big and the plastic rubbish bin of corpses was so heavy that it took two to lift it. Some rats were 10 inches from nose to tail "and rather rotund".

Writes Rosie: "Despite my revulsion for rats . . . I did catch myself silently urging 'Run ratty, run, run, run,' as each one tried to dodge terriers and sticks to escape. Very few did." At the end of the hunt a sweepstake was run on the number killed. It was 220. But, she remarks, it was a cull, and she is only too aware of the vile diseases rats carry as well as their propensity to eat eggs and nestlings. A traditional photograph with hunters and their trophies laid at their feet, then back to the inn, "with the last ratter staggering home at 2 am". All this near Rievaulx, Yorkshire.   Y

RATS IN THE SPUDS   30 April 1986

 It's only a small patch of early potatoes, and the weather has been enough of a handicap. Now, suddenly, huge lumps have been taken out of several drills. It looks like rats. Mice tend to go in through small, neat holes. What to do? Too many birds and other creatures around to put out rat poison – even in a pipe. As it's only a small area, some of these animal repellents like soot or even pepper could be tried. The most ingenious counter-attack ever come across was published in *Field* magazine not long ago. A man who kept ferrets simply put out the sweepings of his cage in the plot and that highly discouraged mice that were attacking his beans. Fortunate the ferret fancier. Presumably the contents of a cat litter tray would do.   Y

RATS AND CATS   24 April 1998

You may have doubts about using some of those anti-rodent poisons around your house or working farm. It was suggested here recently that in earlier times, cats, which lived in the outhouses and barns and were looked after by the farmer's wife, could keep rats and mice under control, even at harvest time when a lot of oats or wheat might be spilled around the yard. Anyway, in the course of a diverting letter a couple of weeks ago, Anthony Lowry, from his place Bachelor's Lodge Stud, on the road from Navan to Kells, which incorporates farm and riding school, has a relevant anecdote:

"I set out to tidy up a section of one of our hay barns. Almost immediately my son unearthed a very well and snugly concealed nest of kittens – six little mites about two days old. The cat who bore them belongs to our daughter, Naomi, who is in France for a few weeks; nevertheless she is phoning nightly for news of her pet. We knew the cat had kittened but had no inkling where. So we were delighted and calculated that this would bring our cat numbers up to 18. Yes, Anthony Lowry (senior) has a bit of a weakness for cats and so tends to see that they are well fed, etc. However, we do have the scope.

"Now, very interestingly, ten minutes later my son then unearthed a rat nursing 11 ratlings. Again, almost new-born, quite naked and rather pathetic looking. We stepped the distance from nest to nest – six paces. So the picture I'm painting shows that we have 12 adult cats – yet the above phenomenon can and did, occur. How now those of us, relying on cats to keep the rodents under control?" (Maybe a pair of barn owls?)

Non-farmers who live where rats are a constant, as, for example, near a river, may nevertheless still have qualms about laying down poisons which, no matter what the manufacturers say, are dangerous if they happen to get into water for human consumption. For many people still rely on their own well for drinking water.   Y

EVER EAT A HEDGEHOG?   4 March 1996

There seems to be a big campaign against grey squirrels coming up this season in England. For, says a report in the London *Times*, there is concern about the damage they do to trees by eating the bark during spring and summer – the growing seasons. So what are they going to do? They are going to put down Warfarin, better known as a rat poison. The animals die bleeding to death, from memory. So that other wildlife will not be affected, the report says, the Warfarin will be placed in feed hoppers that other wildlife cannot enter. That would be an ingenious device. Can these authorities be certain? The permission to use the poison came from the British Forestry Minister Lord Lindsay. He said that the damage to beech and oak in some areas is such, according to the Minister, that it is proving a disincentive to new tree-planting. People who own land just wouldn't invest in woodlands simply to have them destroyed in the first years.

Yes, a friend had a beech planting severely damaged a few years ago. That was in Ireland. Not so long ago, driving into his fields, about a dozen grey squirrels were seen, on their hind legs, munching something, or running up and down tree-trunks. Our friend is a philosopher and a noted arboriculturist.

What other animal must be stamped out? Not the otter. We used to hunt them to death. Now protected. Now, the badger: it's not quite open season on him, you need official permission to kill him, or the services of an official. We wouldn't have to do that if we could clean up bovine TB, but it appears we can't. Anyone remember, by the way, that a Young Irelander on the run in Kerry was fed badger ham for his breakfast in the safe house?

The fox you can't kill off. The more you do, the more they breed. They will outlive humankind. Who wants to kill the hedgehog? George Borrow was it, perhaps in Lavengro, said that gypsies baked them in mud to get rid of the quills, and found them delicious.

Have we stopped shooting mink? Trout anglers used to do it. Some people now think mink have been absorbed into the wildlife system, without much harm. And, fortunately, no one has yet found a reason for going after the pine marten. Legally or otherwise.

You will remember that squirrel pie is a recognised dish in parts of North America. Could Lord Lindsay have the grey squirrels trapped and marketed, and set off a posh foodie fashion in London? Y

UNLIKELY EDIBLES   28 April 1998

Grey squirrels have been around in this island for only about a century and probably just a decade or so earlier in the next island. One thing about them that is new to this quarter is that they have been known to take and eat small birds, also to take and eat their eggs and nestlings. You learn something new every day. To see them landing on the bird-feeders gives no clue, for while birds already at that particular contraption will move to the next one, they do so with no appearance of fright, just go on eating at the next available source of monkey nuts or whatever. Red squirrels are said to do the same, but the greys, being bigger, can take larger prey. And, it seems the taking of flesh occurs mostly at times when the normal fare of nuts, etc., in the wild is scarce.

As has been noted here before, a landowner in Scotland or northern England some time ago encouraged his gamekeepers to make it widely known that grey squirrels are good for eating. In stews or barbecues, much superior to rabbit. This is well known in the United States. And a long-ago correspondent to the English *Field*, dated only as 1930, wrote to that journal encouraging not only the killing and consumption of these tree-rats, but also of starlings, both on the grounds of their being pests of the countryside. "Undoubted edible qualities" were possessed by both, argued the reader.

He referred to the American experience with grey squirrels; English friends of his had pronounced them excellent eating. As for starlings, the reader had tried them himself and found them "to my surprise, neither musky nor bitter, and but a little inferior to sparrows". If they, meaning their corpses, could be distributed in numbers in our larger towns, "they would provide a palatable meal for many poor people, while the task of securing them would provide very fair sport, especially for young people and for those with limited opportunities of obtaining nobler game". Isn't that a good one: "nobler game"?

The most famous starling in literary history, many of us will have read of in school, in Laurence Sterne's *A Sentimental Journey*. He passes a starling in a cage on the stairs of an abode in Paris and hears a voice say clearly, "I can't get out, I can't get out." It was the starling. So they can talk, too!   Y

URBAN FOXES   14 March 2000

 Yes, they are handsome creatures. There is one of them on top of the 10-foot wall as our friend goes off to work in the morning, debonair, innocent-looking. And how lightly they step across your lawn, forelegs lifted as elegantly as trotting ponies or those schooled horses from Vienna (Lipizzaners, is it?). And brazen, some will say, who have suffered loss from the same. For there is a woman in south Dublin whose picture of the fox is simply that of a ruthless raider who twice at least got into her henhouse and killed every bird – except for the bantams who could fly up into the trees. To say it again – twice a fox or foxes slaughtered every one of her two dozen or so hens and left a trail of mangled bodies from the henhouse up the garden on the way back to the lair or whatever.

Even today, six years or more after, foxes still patrol this house. Not the same ones, because a fox's life is, from expert reckoning, not more than four or five years, but their descendants perhaps. The other morning the lady of the house, having a quiet cup of coffee, looked out the window to see one slowly and observantly circling around the house – in which, by the way, were two dogs. No haste on the fox's part. A confirmation to her that she was wise to give up the hens – otherwise, with obviously a big fox population in the area, she would always be worried. They are a fact of life in south Dublin, even in as far as Harold's Cross, where an active young gardener – excellent fruit, vegetables and flowers – buried some over-ripe fish as compost. Foxes obviously have great noses, so next morning he found a hole where he had deposited his over-ripe fish – the ubiquitous fox. And not more than a hundred yards from there, his sister saw a handsome face nosing around the glass cat-hole in her dining-room door. No, he couldn't get in.

With their young being born about this time of year, they are on the lookout more than ever. Any food put out for the friendly badgers, who are still sluggish enough at this time of year, is likely, if they are not punctual, to be spotted or rather scented by the same red devil. There is another, and sentimental view. In *The Countryman Wild Life Book*, published years ago in the Pan series, a woman tells of efforts to set up a relationship with a vixen. After studying the animals for seven years she had "found them to be charming creatures and by no means the rogues others would have us think them".

Tell that to the woman who lost her hens to them.   Y

FOXES ARE EXPERT AT BIRTH CONTROL   6 April 1995

Not all the thundering cavalcades of horsey folk with their attendant hounds, not all the night raids by hunters armed with searchlights and shotguns, have the slightest effect on the ultimate population of foxes, according to a long feature in a French sporting magazine. Basically, it says, the more you try to wipe out foxes, the more they produce. But leave them alone, and their numbers stabilise. For this, the magazine quotes examples from various parts of the world. A lot was learned from a study in a defined zone, the arboretum of Chevreloup near the château of Versailles, which was not hunted over. Naturalists caught and marked foxes, giving some a tiny transmitter radio that would send back information. The investigation over the four years of observation established that from 16 to 18 foxes lived on or used the 250 hectares from the end of winter through the spring. Each fox would cover from 30 to 40 hectares during night movements. The average life span was around ten years. (How did they find out?) They extrapolated from all their studies the conclusion that a population of foxes which was actually hunted could renew itself in four years. One female out of four gave birth each year. This regulation of births was, says the magazine, as if the predators kept breeding only according to food available in the territory. Defenders of the fox sometimes claim, the article reads, that while he will take the odd young rabbit or pheasant, its diet is mostly of voles and such like, and worms and berries and other fruits. On the other hand, a huge list is given of farmers who have lost chickens, geese, lambs and often in considerable numbers. Say 43 chickens in one case. So the Irish farmer who lets off a gunshot at a fox which has raided his yard (that is if Irish farmers still keep chickens around) may be rid of one marauder and get some satisfaction himself, but if he shot forty foxes, he mightn't be making the slightest dent in the overall population. The vixens would outbreed the threat. So it says, with some qualifications, in *Le Chasseur Français.*   Y

MARK OF THE DOG 11 April 1988

 In a glossy English magazine, a full-page advertisement for a gorgeous house somewhere in a fashionable county: nearly a couple of hundred acres, parkland, lake, the mansion dating back three centuries, the trees stately, the lawn beautifully manicured. And, of course, the interiors – treasures galore, all in colour.

One very homely touch. In the foreground of one interior picture is a blue sofa, back to the camera. The unerring woman's eye seizes on three yellow circles about six or eight inches from the floor. It's hard to look after every detail in such a stately edifice. And it's good to know that other people have a problem too, with a dog that now and then cannot resist lifting its leg, even at home. For the three patches, says the expert, on that lovely sofa in that exquisite house in that splendid estate, are undoubtedly dog pee. It can happen in the best of circles.   Y

TIGER DUNG?   9 April 1996

"How did that badger get into my back garden?" asked a Dublin suburban dweller. "The walls are quite perpendicular." The answer, presumably, is that the badger has powerful claws and can get a grip on most surfaces. Also, in spite of its apparent lumbering activity, it is in fact, extremely sinuous and springy. Though it hardly took a running jump. Just climbed. And this was not the first suburbanite to note the phenomenon.

And foxes have been able to climb into trees. Whatever hope you have of keeping badgers out of your garden, you have practically none with the fox. Unless, maybe, you have a Doberman constantly on the loose within the confines. And why, if you don't keep chickens, should you be so inhospitable to the fox? They are lovely animals to watch as with the badger. (Beats watching blue tits any day.) And it's not unusual to see a couple of foxes, a badger or two, and one of the local cats, all feeding from food put out, side by side.

If you have a bowling-green type of lawn, right enough, you might resent the badger's habit, in hard times especially, of making little holes to get at worms and whatever. And, especially if there is no food left out for the night, you should make sure the lids of your bins are well screwed on.

Anyway, a man came into a garden shop recently and asked if he could buy a repellent for foxes. There are indeed preparations sold which, in pellet or dissolved form, are recommended to keep unwanted animals away from your vegetables or flower beds, maybe. Tried once to keep mice from digging up acorns planted in a bed, didn't work. Some of these preparations are believed to keep cats and dogs away, even.

But this customer had a different idea. He wanted a repellent against foxes. The proprietor didn't know of one specifically advertised for that purpose. He asked a friend who was something in the pharmaceutical or general chemical business. "Only one remedy," he said, "and it's tiger dung." Where was that to be got? "From the zoo of course. Don't tell them I told you." Now this was on 3 April, not 1 April. When it was mentioned to a woman who gardens well, she said that of course everyone knew that. Would you have the nerve to approach the zoo? Could you, never mind the fox, live with the smell?   Y

LEAVE THE OTTER ALONE   5 March 1988

 It will be news to many that the otter may still be hunted in this country. Yet Mr Pat Phelan of the Irish Council Against Blood Sports has written to the Minister of State for the Office of Public Works, Mr Noel Treacy, asking him not to issue licences for hunting otters. Apparently there are still some hunts in existence, and visiting otter hunters have been known to come here on the trail of this most evasive of mammals. The otter is extinct over many parts of England and great efforts are being made to replace the loss by breeding in farms and releasing the young into the wild.

In Ireland, as James Fairley has pointed out in his *An Irish Beast Book*, there is a surprisingly satisfactory population of the animals. They are seldom seen – unless you are Éamon de Buitléar – but they are there. A fishing friend who lives on a river tells how nearly every day he finds tracks or spraints (faeces) to prove their existence, yet he and his family have in 20 years seen an otter on less than half a dozen occasions. They do take a salmon now and then. They chew up trout and crayfish, but not on a scale to upset the anglers, who regard them as local inhabitants like themselves. If otter hunters are part of the new, selective tourism, we might be better without them, decent people as they may be in other respects.   Y

OTTER SHELTER   15 April 2000

If your interest is more in leaving otters to get on with their own life than in chasing them, and you live on or near a river bank, Gerald and Lee Durrell have a suggestion. It is to build a shelter, one of the oddest shelters you can imagine. But, they say, it works. On one of their recent television programmes they simply piled up what looked like the makings of a Twelfth of July bonfire. It was five or six feet high and made up of quite substantial tree lengths, some of them three or four inches in diameter. All just piled up in a wigwam shape. Supposedly, it imitated a complicated tree-root system and therefore would be particularly appropriate on a river which has been drained and therefore, and perversely, deprived of all its bank-holding tree root systems.

Of course, otter-hound followers could easily dismantle it if the prey took refuge there, but Durrell and wife were talking in a country where otter-hunting has been banned. Other means of keeping the otter population going, he said, was to leave growth on the river banks uncut. Otters like moving under cover.   Y

FURRY DEATH ON THE ROAD   22 April 1996

The Swiss are a fine people: different languages, different religions, different races. And yet they can live together without territorial disputes. And, of course, without murdering each other. Their careful way of doing things spreads into some interesting details of living together. Take a very odd one: the death of animals on the road.

At this time of the year in Ireland you will notice here a dead young badger, there a dead fox, or a rabbit, perhaps even a hedgehog. In one case, a badger, killed on the middle of a main road, lay there, slowly being pulverised for nearly two weeks until there was nothing left. The Swiss, according to an article in one of their papers, reckon that annually on the 70,000 kilometres of national roads, cantonal roads and others, there are 7,500 accidents involving animals. One to two per cent of the human beings involved are injured or die.

The article explains that each animal has a different reaction to coming into contact with a road. The hare, it seems, can be petrified. Anyone who comes across a hare at night on an Irish road, will have noticed a regular pattern. The hare runs in front of the lights on the same side on which he has been picked out by the headlights. And he seems to know nothing other than to keep on that course. If you stop, he may dive into the hedge, but if you keep on going so will he. That's just one example.

This article urges motorists to slow down when they

come to a wood, or to an area where signs show that game may be about. Slow down and now and then sound the horn. And remember that dusk and dawn light is a time when animals are on the move. Flash your lights up and down. And remember, an animal running for cover may lose its sense of direction. We hear, in our own country, of passages under roads being built for badgers, animals which may have been padding the same tracks for centuries. The Swiss go further. This article gives the dimensions needed for both underground and overground passages for all game. It points out, too, that underground passages are used by frogs, reptiles of one sort and another and small rodents. And, an interesting legal point, if you brake suddenly and cause a collision, are you to blame?

In 1989 the Federal high court (Tribunal) acquitted a woman driver who had caused a collision by braking to avoid a fox. "To demand of a driver that he should simply run over animals which appear suddenly in front of him or her is incompatible with the respect which mankind owes to the animal world, respect which is expressed by the duty to maintain the animal world and not to destroy it."

And the documentation centre for the study of game can tell us that in 1994 there were 710 hares, 6,400 foxes and 1,700 badgers killed on their roads.   Y

"ATE WITH THE WOLVES"   3 April 1999

Boars, we read recently, are becoming a nuisance in such a prize town as Nice; bears have been imported from Slovenia to make up for falling numbers in the Pyrenees, with mixed reaction; wolves have penetrated France from Italy, are spreading across the country, causing some havoc among sheep farmers, and now a judge in Oslo, according to the *New Scientist*, has forbidden sheep farmers in southern Norway from shooting a pair of wolves which are among the last in Scandinavia. Environmental campaigners in Norway have hailed the judge's verdict "as an important re-affirmation of the country's commitment to protecting endangered species". Yet the very day after the judge's ruling, a wolf from another pack was killed by a train. Some people suspected that the victim had been killed illegally, then left on the line to cover up their deed, according to a spokesman for the World Wide Fund for Nature in Oslo. But the train driver says that the wolf ran onto the tracks and thus met his death. It wasn't a lone wolf, by the way. There is a pack of nine which lives about 150 kilometres south of Oslo. It is officially protected. But when another mated pair formed a new pack by settling west of the river, i.e. on the other side from the nine already mentioned, farmers who are afraid for the safety of their sheep asked permission to kill them. And it seems that such action would be illegal according to the World Wide Fund for Nature, and, writes the *New Scientist*, it appears the courts have agreed.

How would we feel in Ireland if by some accident (hardly possible) or a deliberate introduction, news spread of a couple of wolves being on the loose in our country – even in its bleakest spots? We know what the farmers would say, and even the most jaded of city cynics could hardly see any virtue in such an addition to our wildlife. Mind you, there has been some (urban) welcome for the return to France of this animal, which spread naturally, it seems.

But the last wolf in Ireland was long ago, and writers can't even agree when it disappeared. There are many "last wolves" – from Antrim to Kerry and Connemara, which Fairley lists in his *An Irish Beast Book*.

He quotes William Thompson, the famous naturalist, as listing Glenarm as one of the three likely last (1712) spots. And a slapstick account of an escape by a horseman in Kildare, by a pack which wounded his steed. As he got to his door: "Oh, James, James let me in – my horse is ate with the wolves."   Y

SETTING WOLVES ON US? 4 May 1998

The EU is accused of doing the oddest things, but officials there will hardly compel us to re-introduce the wolf to Ireland. They have done just that in France, according to an article in a reputable journal. So far the wolves seem to be concentrated around the

National Park of Mercantour, high in the Alps of Provence – north of Nice, more or less. "Wolves also kill for fun," said a woman shepherd, Cathy Delpath, as she and her interviewer sat on a rock near this same park, having lunch. Suddenly a flock of crows swooped down nearby. The wolf doesn't distinguish between the National Park and surroundings. "Wolves kill in the night and next day the vultures and I find the carcasses." The shepherd and interviewer were in an area "now controlled by 40 to 50 wolves".

Locals haven't a good word to say for the machine that made the re-introduction of wolves a priority – the French Environment Ministry backed by the EU. Life has been made easy for the wolves and hard for the sheep-rearers, locals say. Michel Barengo, the farmer for whom Cathy Delpath works, says that instead of looking after his sheep, she counts carcasses for the bureaucrats in Paris and Brussels. "If I tell you that I have lost 14 sheep this week and that it comes to more than 275 sheep in five years, would that make sense to a . . . Greenpeace journalist like you?" Money is paid out in compensation, of course.

Barengo had bought a Pyreneean sheepdog (big, shambling, white creatures). It had been with the flocks from the age of seven weeks. One night a pack of wolves attacked the house. There was clamour for a long time. Eventually the shepherd found the dog, now three years old, dying. The farmer got 5,000 French francs compensation (say £590) "from the Environment Ministry in Paris or was it the EU . . . anyway the dog was dead". Local people are enraged at the wolf experiment. They have taken thousands of sheep into Nice to make their point and the National Park is regularly vandalised. The farmer Barengo says his business is going down the tubes.

And all this for an EU-funded study of wolves under the EU Wildlife Programme called LIFE – which "seeks eventually to ensure a lasting return of the wolf to French territory and to favour its social acceptance". (Social acceptance is good.)

This article by Mogens Cuber of Denmark is from *EUROP* magazine of the wonderful Journalistes en Europe Programme, founded by Philippe Viannay with

Beuve-Mery of *Le Monde*. Viannay also founded the Glenans Sailing Club, well known here.   Y

BEAR COUNTRY   22 April 1986

If we had bears in Ireland, would some people treat them as they do badgers: dig them out of their lairs, put them in a trench or a barrel in a closed yard and set dogs on them? In the Pyrenees there are still brown bears and the French Government is trying to preserve the species. In 1972 hunting or shooting them was forbidden, but there are now only about 20 of them left. Tourism and creeping urbanisation deprived them of cover, of peace; even afforestation, with its attendant noisy machines, adds to the forces working against them. It is said that they are 95 per cent vegetarian; but early in spring, after hibernation, they need protein and go for meat – carrion or fresh prey. Same thing as autumn ends and fruit and other food goes scarce. In the valley of the Aspe, in mid-Pyrenees, it is said that about 50 sheep per year are lost to bears. But the farmers are compensated.

Shooting is forbidden, but as an official remarked to a local magazine: with beaters doing a drive in a normal game expedition, and all the noise and excitement, the man with the gun might just mistake a bear for a boar and let fly. "Every year," he said, "some shooting man mistakes his brother-in-law or a hiker for a fleeing animal. Why not a bear?" And, locally, it is admitted that anyone who shoots a bear is "un monsieur dans le village". Somebody special.   Y

SECRETS IN TURF   27 April 1987

 Turf preserves. Human bodies buried in it, many centuries ago, have been dug up in a remarkable state of preservation. Everyone has heard of firkins of butter which have lain in storage for long periods. Here's a short-term use of the same substance, mentioned recently by the novelist Ian Niall in the English *Country Life* magazine. A Welsh farmer told him that when his family went up the mountain to the bogs to cut the turf, they came down each year without the spades. The work

tired them. They took the easy way – simply buried the tools in the turf and, each spring, found them in perfect condition.

Even more surprising, a scythe used to cut a small field in the same area was permanently kept in the turf. It would cut, the Welshman told Niall, each year, without being sharpened with the stone. Yet down below at the farm, the same would rust in the toolshed. That's what is says in *Country Life*. And nobody can say it's all a bit Irish.   Y

SILENT SPRING AND ALL THAT   26 April 1999

Looking at the abundant, beautiful blossoms on a sole apple tree in a suburban garden, the old schoolboy joke came to mind. Which is: "What's worse than biting into an apple and finding a maggot in there?" Answer, "biting into an apple and finding half a maggot." You are unlikely to find maggots or odd creatures in any apple you buy in the shops today. Their super-glossy skin is unbroken or unpocked, the inside, all too often, of an impossibly tough and tasteless nature. You may be lucky enough to buy locally-grown apples, just as unflawed as the stiff, frozen foreigners but tasting, in most cases, so much better. In a way, we shouldn't be too supercilious about all of this. To be able to get, at all times of the year, imported cherries or strawberries or paw-paws or mangos is a great advance in living standards. But at what a price? Rachel Carson, some forty years ago, startled the consumers and certainly the manufacturers of chemicals for crop-spraying with her book *Silent Spring*. In an introduction to the Penguin edition published this side of the Atlantic, Julian Huxley wrote: "It is almost certainly impossible to exterminate an abundant-insect pest but quite easy to exterminate non-abundant non-pests in the process." He does also write: "though chemical control can be very useful, it, too, needs to be controlled".

We have seen, since those early days, various chemicals banned or dropped out of favour, but when you read that apples, for example, may be sprayed ten or fifteen times or whatever, are you sure that by peeling them before eating, you are getting rid of all traces of the sprays? We live in dangerous times, and chemical spraying of crops may not be the greatest hazard in the atomic energy age, but there is no doubt that the move to organic farming is no longer regarded as a somewhat crankish or far-out solution. It is, after all, a return to older practices. Young people lucky enough to have gardens are in so many cases taking courses in The Organic Centre, Rossinver, County Leitrim. Day courses, and some two-day.

It's possible to be too scared of chemicals. One friend won't even spray cleevers (goosegrass, *Galium aparine*), that awful sticky weed, which can grow to ten feet. He just doggedly rakes it out, and rakes it out, and rakes it out; and it just grows and grows and grows again.   Y

LATE SPRING   21 May 1998

 "What a wonderful world", Louis Armstrong sang. And suddenly, last weekend it was. After the blasts which stopped spring in its first blossoming, which cut leaves to shrivelled tatters, which blasted flowers, everything burst out. It was as if the wise trees and shrubs had been holding back and then, pouring forth that pent-up energy, showed us a May that lived up to all the poets' expectations. Fields in Meath bordered in white, as if the hawthorn was covered in clean sheets of linen. And more: some of the bigger fields had half a dozen plump bushes, all white, scattered across their acres, all clad to the ground. And some roadsides, especially where bordered with trees, were four feet or so deep in the white, fragile blooms of wild parsley and other plants. Most surprising of all, a young oak, about twenty or twenty-one years old, which had borne, recently, one or two measly acorns, had, in a few days, burst out in the most prolific and golden blossoms of all. In a couple of days, it seemed. Dripping, the tree was, with them.

The beech this year, as always, seem to have the most delicate green of all, and they are many. Bird life: marital peace is disturbed when one partner insists on setting the alarm clock (an unusually quiet one) to enjoy the

dawn chorus. And speaking of birds, the same partner says she spent some minutes beside a sparsely-leafed bush in which she counted up to a dozen tiny, young wrens. Now this is a puzzle. For Cabot tells us the wren lays five to six eggs. Another source says five to eight. We are also told that the male wren builds two nests, and moves the first brood to the second nest while the female in the original nest incubates the second brood. Could these be the two broods already hatched and fledged?

Anyway, while the kingfisher is still on the river there are, for the first year, no wagtails. No flycatchers arrived yet. The swallows have so far not taken to work on their old nests. And, of course, the wild duck has vanished. No fire needed in the grate for the first time, and the lovely ash logs wait for another day.

"There is no time like Spring/When life's alive in everything", wrote Christina Rossetti. Of course, it's really summer, isn't it? Anyway: "What a wonderful world." Y

SUMMER

THE SOUND OF SUMMER   18 June 1998

 "I'll admit it's summer when I hear a corncrake," he said with some exaggeration. Where will he hear one? Birdwatch Ireland told him. Said Annemarie McDevitt, the project officer, speaking from Banagher: "At the bridge here you should be lucky and at Shannonbridge . . . after ten o'clock at night." As everyone knows, the bird has been disappearing from the scene at an alarming rate. Helpful measures have been taken in this country and elsewhere. Perhaps the fall may be checked or even a revival started. The French expert Joël Broyer puts the decisive period here in Ireland at 1900. It accelerated around 1939.

Broyer estimates that Russia, Byelorussia, Ukraine, the three Baltic states with Poland, Romania and Bulgaria may have from 80,000 to more than 200,000 singing males. The rest of Europe adds up to at most 10,000. He writes that more precise information is needed from Russia, Byelorussia and Ukraine.

Very versatile and resourceful birds they are. Reapers uncovered a corncrake's nest containing seven eggs. The female was able to escape. A naturalist observer hid nearby when the harvesters had gone. The mother came back and almost without hesitation sat onto the nest again and looked around. She quickly seems to have realised that it was impossible to stay, and took her decision. Using her beak, she managed to place one egg under her wing, then did the same for the other side. Finally, she took one in her beak and disappeared into nearby reeds. Soon she was back for the others and so the clutch was saved (J. Kunstler 1908, *Account from the Biological Society* [of France presumably] vol XIV p. 105).

We now and then see corncrakes on television. In still pictures, such as in Broyer's book *Le Râle des Genêts*, the delicacy and grace of the bird when on the ground comes home to you. And the colours. Most of us know it's a brownish creature but, seen close, the chocolate specks on the back and the bright red around the wings give an altogether more distinguished effect. There is a story of corncrakes in the Val de Saône in France. One year floods in its favourite nesting places lasted longer than usual. They seemed to find other hides. Then the floods went down and, weeks late, the majority moved into their old haunts.

What do they eat? During reproduction: insects, molluscs, worms, spiders, the odd egg, the odd nestling maybe. Our other term for corncrake is landrail.   Y

DRUMMING, HUMMING, BLEATING?   30 June 1995

"It's one of the most haunting sounds of early summer," he declared, "and fortunately, it won't follow that of the corncrake to near oblivion, for you'll never beat the snipe out of Ireland or drain them out. It is the drumming of the snipe, I'm talking of. You are gliding idly around in your boat, pretending to be making an effort after the trout, but in fact just listening to the tinkle of the water against your oar or the odd churring sound made by one of those little warbler things in the reeds, when you hear the sound you are really waiting for. Drumming is the most common word for it, though humming and even bleating have been used, too. It comes, apparently, from the outer tail feathers which the bird spreads when it is showing off in display flights. You can almost feel it beating against your ears. And my main memory of it is from lazy June nights on Mount Dalton lake, out there beyond Mullingar, and you see the dive of the bird as well as getting an earful. Are they still doing their stuff down there on that lovely, tucked-away stretch of water?

"When that fine observer of (and slaughterer of) birds, Sir Ralph Payne-Gallwey, was writing his famous book *The Fowler in Ireland* around 1880, there were apparently some people who favoured the view that it was a vocal sound.

Anyway. "There is another sound which comes into the same context," our friend went on. "You have a small river. As you know, long after the sun has gone down, there is still enough light from the sky to let you crouch down and see, along the surface, the slightest dimple or splash, from trout or fly. And that brings me to the second sound of this time of year: the audible gulp as a cautious trout pulls down a fly. And you hope it is yours. That, of course, is after the last wren has stopped chattering (always very vocal) or the heron has finally croaked and gone off. Just quiet, and you and the trout."   Y

BIRDS BRING IT UP   29 May 1985

 Most people who are aware at all of the bird life around them have heard of the owl's habit of disgorging pellets of indigestible matter. It is usually mouse fur and hairs and bits and pieces of his various kinds of prey which come up in an oval pellet when the rest of the matter is digested or digesting. But it is not only owls which have this habit. Most birds of prey apparently do it, and in fact very many others.

Thus, the other day, the balcony of a house was found to be heavily splashed with bird droppings and, in addition, a dozen oozy pellets, about the size of an almond shell and not unlike that in shape. They all looked black, and, on inspection, were heavily peppered with bits of shiny beetles. Inside were hairs and shards of what might be grit or shells and ends of grass and roots. Crows, it was hazarded, the grey kind which haunt this particular stretch, or maybe something else which has taken up residence in the chimneys which were recently cleared of jackdaws.   Y

REVERSING EMIGRATION   21 June 1986

Can migratory birds be induced to stay on in our northern climate and not return to their African abodes? (And for their own good, as man sees it.) The experiment is being tried in Europe with storks. The stork spends September to April in Africa, and the desertification of the Sahel is taking its toll on the birds. One of the chief items of nourishment is the locust – and man is already annihilating these insects. Then, too, the stork is regarded in the Sudan as a legitimate game bird, to be eaten. There are dangers in Europe, too (though only in Portugal may they be shot). Electricity wires kill many.

So conservationists in Europe have encouraged the storks to make their home full-time in the countries where they have traditionally nested. And, it is said, the stork acclimatises itself very well to the colder regions. You just have to stop him (and her) getting itchy feet. In Alsace, it is said, 23 couples chose to stay on in an arranged environment. After two years, it is claimed, the stork no longer wants to do its migratory tour. Near Bordeaux, a marsh of 250 hectares, developed as a conservation zone, though surrounded by industrial estates, has welcomed a pair. The first ever. What about Ireland? Could anyone divert a pair of corncrakes to a boggy, flag-ridden river bank where they would be most welcome and where winter quarters might be arranged? Or a cuckoo pair? Food for thought.   Y

PUGNACITY IN BIRDS   25 June 1998

It has started up again. Early in the morning there is a thump, thump, thump from the window above. It's that blackbird doing what the experts call image-fighting. It goes on until you go out and wave it off. A chance turning up of a small paperback printed 30 years ago (*The Countryman Wild Life Book*) shows that it takes many forms: on hubcaps, for instance, which 30 years ago must have been very reflective, shiny polished things. One morning, finding the hubcap smeared with red, the owner feared the worst, but was soon surprised to find the bird returning with a morello cherry in his beak, evidently trying to feed his alter ego in the reflection. One woman wrote of the most persistent case surely on record: "In April 1963 I first noticed a male house sparrow banging against a bedroom window of my neighbour's house. It kept up its attacks from early morning until late evening except when, at my suggestion, the curtains were drawn." (One might ask, what was left of the poor bird's beak?) "But it went on, sometimes at another of the windows but, with a break of five or six weeks in autumn, it continued its visits until the following June. Then it disappeared, coming back at the end of March this year to the same window. It kept up its attacks for a month before vanishing again."

A bird described as a bookmerie shrike attacked a workshop window in East London, South Africa, until it so fouled the glass that no reflection could be seen. One small bird attacked a window so often and so fiercely that it was found dead underneath it. "And the habit is not confined to the smaller birds. One pair of crows attacked the French window of a house near Cardiff, rapped sharply on the glass several times (and they have heavy beaks), then flew up and scratched the pane with their claws. On the ledge, they set to fighting each other; feathers flew and the window became smeared with dirt and drops of blood. The pattern changed. The crows would perch on a branch about 20 yards from the window, then launch themselves together, both striking on the pane." With a good bang. "Then dropping to the ground to fight each other." Could all this be a form of overcoming boredom?   Y

PHEASANT VELOCITY   26 June 1987

The velocity of a pheasant is something to be eludicated, perhaps, by an artillery man. At any rate, when a young angler was heard to shout in surprise, and a splashing sound indicated that he had fallen into the river, it turned out that he had been propelled there by a pheasant. Not frightened or surprised into falling on the rolling stony bottom, but actually knocked over. He had backed up towards the scraggy bank of the river as he cast his flies, not being aware that at that point, covered with reeds and seldom walked by anyone, pheasants tended to congregate and to nest. He stepped back, an explosion sounded at his ear and a pheasant at muzzle velocity hit his left shoulder and tumbled him over. Fortunately the water was no more than a foot deep.

Anyone who walks over pheasant territory knows the heart-stopping detonation that resounds under your feet – yes, sometimes literally underfoot – when a pheasant sets off. The loudest noise in a day, apart from the sound of gunfire.   Y

DUCK DAYS   5 August 1987

Sometimes you would think that there are more birds on the surface of the river than there are fish under the surface. Mallard, this year, are in abundance. Within a few hundred yards, three broods have so far been raised. Weekly the numbers drop. For they have formidable enemies, perhaps chiefly mink, rats, foxes, predator birds. One brood of what seemed like a dozen is now down to two plus the mother. Another is three hefty ducklings and mother and, suddenly, in the same area, nine rose from the river all together, presumably mother and eight almost fully-grown young.

Assuming that the original number in each brood was a dozen – one Collins book gives the optimum at 17 eggs – so far 13 have survived out of 36.

There is still some time to go before the shooting season, but they are well on their way. Then, of course, according to one authority, mallard sometimes have a second brood. And among the losses to raw nature you may well count some nests ravaged by crows, foxes, mink and whatnot.   Y

FREE RANGE BUGS   30 August 1989

When you buy game, your mind is not principally fixed on the hygiene of the transaction. For, after a few days hanging if you are a real game buff and think that the older the better, your bird, admit it, smells like a sewer. All sorts of biological processes are going on in the little bundle of feathers, bones and blood. Which shows that either you've never worked out the implications of the decaying process or that you don't give a hoot. The latter probably, for eating game is surrounded by ritual and myth. It seems that all this is not good enough in the modern world, where listeria scares, salmonella scares and the like are, rightly, material for newspaper headlines and genuine public concern. Should not game be as subject to the food inspector as the chicken?

Apparently rules and regulations were drawn up for all EC members but, under British pressure, they are being amended on the side of exemption in certain cases.

A newspaper report, anyway, says that British landowners and sportsmen felt that the rules would have serious
consequences for some remote areas which depend to a
great extent on shooting for income. And elsewhere also
for the pheasant season, which depends so much on
farmed birds. The question hasn't so far made much stir
in the general press. It's ironic that the high-class food-
ies and eat-fish-not-red-meat advocates so often urge
you to eat game. David Bellamy was seen on TV tucking
into roast pheasant – "free range" as he said, and therefore, presumably, good.   Y

BIRDSONG AND BIRD SOUND   15 July 1998

 We call it birdsong, but how much of it
is song in the sense that humans
employ? How much of it is declaration of
territorial rights, and not necessarily melodious. Or a sort
of early morning bugle-call to announce another day? (The
dawn chorus.) And warning cries at the approach of a hos-
tile being: a cat, say, or a feathered predator. The dawn
chorus may be easing off now, with birds well into the
rearing of their young. But still, in the early hours there
are stirrings and soundings off – and pure melody to be
heard. A friend used to creep out with his recorder early
on spring and early summer mornings to listen to a thrush,
whose ringing notes seemed, in addition to being a greet-
ing to the new day, also to contain a lovely melodious
theme, along with a running up and down scale.

This friend convinced himself that he could whistle a
few bars in imitation of the thrush, and the bird, after a
pause would send the same notes back to him. He says
he has a few recordings to prove this. Lewis Thomas, in
The Lives of a Cell, has it that the robin "sings flexible
songs, containing a variety of motifs that he arranges to
his liking". The same writer attributes to the nightingale
24 basic songs, but the bird varies the arrangement of
phrases and the length of pauses. Gilbert White in his
Natural History of Selbourne notes the changing calls of
birds according to the seasons. Some utter notes all the
year round for the purpose of keeping together, but many
have cries "peculiar to the love season", which are

uttered to summon the mate or as a cry of distress when the breeding grounds are invaded.

He then lists "singing birds strictly so called" which continue in full song till after midsummer. They include song thrush, wren, redbreast, hedge sparrow, blackbird, goldfinch. Among those who cease full song before that date are the chaffinch and nightingale. He makes a point of using the word "sing".

The poets are in no doubt, as with Ferguson's elation: "as I hear the sweet lark sing,/In the clear air of the day". While Shelley's skylark is addressed: "And singing still dost soar, and soaring ever singest."   Y

MATERNAL BLACKBIRD   25 July 1986

In the bird world the hen blackbird must surely be the most attentive mother in the business. For weeks now we've watched her fly beakfuls of food to the nest. The three survivors of the brood have now broken nest but still the maternal instinct to feed continues. She leads all three to a feeding patch where there is a mixture of crumbs and flake meal and, one after the other, she feeds them. The chicks seem as big as the mother: it is only their brownish breast feathers which mark them as young birds. After a week, two of the young birds shift for themselves but the third, obviously the peata, is still being fed. The peata stabs uncertainly at the flakes and succeeds in spearing one but still relies on mother for his main meals.   H

UNOBSERVANT HUMANS   13 August 1987

 Every year, birds remind us how unobservant we humans are. Didn't Edward Lear have a rhyme about a bird which built in a man's beard? It could happen – almost. A pair of blackbirds – fairly substantial and noisy they are – can spend weeks building a nest under your nose, can sit on the eggs and only when they have to cast caution to the winds in their pell-mell feeding of the gawping young nestlings, making hundreds of journeys daily to the nest, are you aware of what is going on.

This particular nest was built on a window ledge, tucked in at the end of a long flower-container. Some of

the greenery hung down to conceal the nest. So no one observed the hundreds, no, the thousands of journeys that must have been made, stealthily, while the haven for the eggs and nestlings was being constructed, out of plaited and woven grasses and finally of mud plaster inside. All this in a busy garden with windows on two sides. And next year they will do the same. And there are probably two or three nests of smaller birds which will only be discovered when the leaves fall.   Y

WHEN NESTLINGS GO ON A DIET   29 August 1997

You can go so far in applying human traits to animals or birds, but here is a great opening line to a piece from the *New Scientist.* "Before leaving the nest, some birds decide to go on a crash diet and do press-ups to make sure that their wings will be able to carry them." So reasons a zoologist in Scotland. Common swifts feed on insects, and in bad weather there may be a gap in their food source for a day or two. So, to protect themselves, the nestlings put on extra fat – presumably by over-eating beyond hunger.

But this could be a problem when the time comes to fly; so the birds lose that weight again before they leave the nest. Some theorists believe that the parents stop supplying the food, so that the young will lose their excess weight. Then again, could the young diet of their own will? In the University of Stirling, Thaïs Martins thinks that young swifts and perhaps other species do just this. She reaches this conclusion after two years study of common swifts in different weather conditions. Birds from twelve days old are weighed and measured. She also – hard to believe this – mixed up broods to make sure that a chick's weight was not just due to having good parents.

She found that the birds always leave the nest when the ratio of their wing area, known as the wing-load, lowers to a certain point. Also surprising is that the chicks took the same time to shed the extra weight, regardless of how fat they were when they started to slim. How do you know when a young swift is sulky? Well, she tells us that, when preparing to leave the nest, they sit sulkily on the edge of the nest entrance and won't take food. When they can balance on their wings for ten seconds or more "in a kind of avian press-up", they know they can leave.

It's good to think that when all sorts of machines of destruction are being produced and refined, humanity can put its mind also to some of the insignificant, but nevertheless intricate problems in the wonderful world of nature.   Y

OF BEE STINGS   13 July 1998

 A woman stung by a bee in her own kitchen was fortunate to have the antidote spray handy. The bee kept buzzing around dodging in and out of the electric iron, the accumulated letters and newspapers of the day, and hiding up in the tubular light. At least, it was said, a bee dies after stinging because its sting is barbed, and wounds it mortally when withdrawn after attack. The books were looked up to see if this was true and no more stinging was to be expected. Oracle (*The Field Book of Country Queries*) said flatly that the sting of the bumble-bee differs, in that it is not barbed, and so can be withdrawn easily or used again, up to two or three times in quite a short period.

It goes on to lay down that there is a difference of opinion as to whether the sting of a bumble-bee or a honey-bee is worse. It states that bumble-bees may be provoked to sting by unfavourable weather conditions – particularly, perhaps, as when a heatwave breaks up in a thunderstorm (indeed a thundery rain came down a few minutes afterwards), but less was known about the venom of the same bumbles than about honey-bees. In Britain, according to the *Field* book there are nineteen species of bumble-bee and they vary in readiness to use their stings. Drone bumble-bees have no sting. While bumble-bees often bite their way into flowers, it is said, it is hardly possible for them to bite quickly through clothing. That depends, you may think, on what is meant by clothing. A summer dress for women?

In this case, anyway, the bumble just ran into the woman and stung her on the finger. And, if you're going after one of them with a fly-swat, *Field* tells us that they have a certain ability to withstand crushing, due, possibly, to the thick hairs on their body! And did you remember that there are birds called bee-eaters? Mostly found in southern parts of Europe and the Middle East. A friend recently came across them in Majorca, maybe passing through, though there is an account of bee-eaters found actually nesting in Sussex. And it mentions how *they* deal with the sting. Y

THANK GOD FOR THE BEES   22 August 1997

What is honey for? Enjoyment, sheer pleasure. You can, of course, go the whole way with some people who believe it is an elixir of life – like the famous Vermont Dr Jarvis who wrote *Folk Medicine*, a book "that swept America" according to the blurb. He argued that bacteria cannot live in the presence of honey, for the potassium in honey withdraws from bacteria the moisture essential to their existence. And he quotes a bacteriologist of Colorado Agricultural College, at first a non-believer, who put honey to the test and was convinced of Jarvis's argument.

Jarvis gives nine telling points in favour of honey: "But for me the crowning glory of honey is its medicinal value. Being a medical man, I would naturally be interested in a substance which study and experimentation have convinced me is a help in living this life literally from the cradle to the grave." A doctor in Dublin, asked his opinion of honey, said it was sugar in a different form. No more.

Well you don't have to go to the extremes of some continental enthusiasts who make even more ambitious claims for it than Dr Jarvis, but it is a versatile item of diet. To put in your coffee or unmilked tea, or in yoghurt, or over fruit salad; or just a couple of teaspoonfuls before going to bed. Said to help you rest, and also quoted as a mild laxative. Cooks use it in baking: biscuits or cakes, etc. Generally, it's just one of the good things of life. That's it.

First of this year's honey tasted came from Sean Cronin. His Irish Woodland Honey from Woodtown, Rathfarnham, surprised him in its quantity. He had feared the bad weather would have hit hard, but believes that his good crop came because the hawthorn, chestnut and sycamore were blossoming at the time of the good weather. He doesn't have it in sufficient quantity for commercial use, but The Gourmet Shop in Rathgar, Dublin, run by his brother Tom and himself, always has good honey along with all the other gourmet requirements including good wine and cheese.

A friend, as well as relishing Irish honey, orders, direct from a part of France he knows, several varieties from very high upland valleys to Mediterranean scrub produce. And remember, bees are needed to pollinate fruit and other produce. "Honey bees," writes one authority, "are the only insects present *in sufficient number in the Spring* to carry out effective fertilisation of the blossoms."   Y

BATTERY HENS NO MORE   16 July 1999

Will battery cages for laying hens be banned by the year 2000? The European Parliament agreed this in January, but the decision has to go to the Council of Agriculture Ministers for decision. The hen used to be a creature that ran about farmyards and fields, scratching at the ground, uttering throaty sounds and coming in to lay its eggs in a nest in a shed, or, now and then, "laying out", so that the farmer's wife and children often had to go searching the hedges for the impromptu nest with its eggs. All changed by the battery system. An Irish publication, *Organic Matters*, bought in the organic butchers O'Toole's of Terenure, Dublin, gives us some of the distressing details of today's methods. Sometimes, goes this article by Aoife Ní Fhearghail, up to five hens are confined in a cage so small that one hen alone cannot even fully stretch her wings. In the Republic, 1.8 million hens spend their entire productive lives confined in such cages, deprived, the article goes on, of fresh air, exercise, sunshine and freedom. No scratching the ground, no dust-baths, no perch at night or even a nest for the eggs. Each hen, she calculates, has less individual space than an A4 sheet of paper (say, eight inches by 12). As hens are peckers of the ground and food, they might peck each other in confined spaces, so, it appears, they are often de-beaked at a young age.

The egg industry, according to this article, holds that there isn't enough land to keep all our hens free-range and that free-range eggs are too dear. A ban on battery cages would spell ruin for egg production, the operators argue. But the writer quotes the case of Switzerland, which banned battery cages in 1992 without cutting down the sale of eggs. In fact, the sale of Swiss-produced eggs increased from 62 per cent in 1981 to 72 per cent by 1997. Which admittedly could be due to increasing prosperity or other causes. Still, it is said here that the demand for organically-produced eggs far out-strips supply. Seems to be reasonable, though if there is a big difference in price, people of lesser means may be deprived of healthy nutrition in a battery-less poultry and egg market.

The writer of the article in *Organic Matters* is Campaigns Officer with Compassion in World Farming, Ireland. Now we have to wait for the decision of the Council of Agriculture Ministers in Brussels, including, of course, our own man. There is price to bear in mind, but also our own standards of morality in exploiting the creatures around us for our own uses. And so thinks the European Parliament.   Y

MOYNALTY'S DAY   7 August 1987

"What's this Moynalty place?" asked the crowd who had driven down from Belfast. "There were notices about it all the way from the border." No wonder. The "Moynalty place" is a village near Kells, County Meath, and the site of this coming Sunday's Steam Threshing Festival – the twelfth the village has held. It's a big day for Meath people and many farther afield. In a vast undulating field, on the banks of a lovely little river, you can see us as we were a couple of generations ago, with huge, roaring, smoke-emitting steam engines bringing home the harvest and much else on the same theme. There will be a horse thresher, a pedal thresher and a hand thresher. The river will be harnessed to turn a churn. There are stalls of all kinds, and oatcakes will be made at an open hearth.   Y

IRELAND CONVERGES ON MOYNALTY   17 July 1999

 Moynalty, County Meath, is a few miles from Kells, or maybe in some eyes Kells is a few miles from Moynalty. For nearly a quarter of a century this lovely little village has been the site of the magnificent Steam Threshing Fair or Festival. Don't ask what goes on there, apart from the threshing, which alone must be the chief draw in its evocation of a romantic past, with huge engines bellowing out clouds of smoke as the people of today's computer, digital age watch in awe. This is the heart of the matter, but there are always other reminders of skills in the fields which intrigue today's folk, city and country people alike. For example, the committee have this year engaged the skills of some Fermanagh people to demonstrate the sickle and scythe method of cutting barley. And it is not just an occasion which pulls in people from neighbouring districts. Last year, says Sean Sheridan, the public relations man for the occasion, a busload of people came from Cork and a minibus from Mayo. Only magnificent stewarding can deal with a crowd of visitors which numbers around 25,000.

The location is a great undulating field which runs down from what may be a motte of Norman origin (they were very strong in all this area), to the clear waters of the Borora river. The main purpose of the day is, of course, to keep reminding us of our history on the land, but aside from the engines and, this year the scythe and sickle men, and some interesting agricultural implements and machines of another age, there are, from year to year, magnificent dray horses, all a-jingle with brass ornamentations and whatnot. Vintage motorcars, too. Besides this, more or less the heart of the matter, there is always the huge variety of normal fun-fair entertainments with its hurdy-gurdy music. It is not all concerned with the past. And there is sustenance to be had, bread baked in the open by women from the area, and various tea-tents. Valentine Farrell wrote a book on Moynalty, "the plain of the flocks", meaning flocks of birds, maybe swans, in 1964. Unfortunately, it is out of print. Mostly pronounced Minaulty. The achievement of the commit-

Summer

tee in making this such a great event in the calendar, the achievement of the people as a whole in giving it such support, shows what heart there still is in our country-side.   Y

SPECTRE AT THE LAMMAS FAIR   24 August 1990

Yellow Man is all right if your teeth are strong and if you are partial to a rock-like sweet. If you have fillings, you may lose them. But Yellow Man lives on as one of the specialities of the Ould Lammas Fair at Ballycastle, County Antrim. And dulse, of course, or dilisk, the chewable seaweed. These two delicacies are annually boosted as part of the fair, which this year is to be held on Monday and Tuesday next, 27 and 28 August. Like many another such occasion, the fair has grown and become "a tourist attraction". Moyle District Council – and the sea of Moyle, just beyond, is a restless presence off that far northeast coast – announces that over 600 stalls will be on display. The oldest known attender says he remembers the day when 30 stalls would have been good. And to add to the picture, Moyle Council is, not for the first time, putting up £400 for a competition for street entertainers. And you have a Heavy Horse Show, a Duck Race and other larks.

This is also the territory of the Grey Man. What werewolves and vampires are to Eastern Europe, the Grey Man is to that coast.

> "For the ship that nears that ghostly form
> Shall wrecked and riven lie,
> While the mangled forms of her hapless crew
> Shall strew the shore hard by.
> And woe betide the peasant lone
> Who meets him on the shore,
> For he shall see his cottage home
> Or family nevermore."

Watch out for him on Monday and Tuesday nights. (The verses are by James Stoddard Moore, the Glens of Antrim poet.)   Y

RIGHT OF WAY   15 August 1988

 "Right of Way" is not a sign you come across everyday. But there it was, on the lefthand side of the road out of Oughterard going towards Clifden. "Waterfall: public right of way." So you take it and find a narrow path bounded partly by wall and partly by fence and shrubs; not much more than a yard wide in places and even then further, though not seriously, occluded by large individual trees. A sort of crazy walk leading towards, on one day this week anyway, a thunderous sound.

At the end of the path you stand on a slender iron bridge above a mighty rush of water as it bounds over huge rocks. The hope was to see a salmon leap and slither its way up the obstacle course. None came in our time, but it's a happy aside in a tour of the area. "No fishing", says a notice. If you don't see a salmon you can count the trees and shrubs around you . . . ash, holly, whitebeam, cotoneaster, sycamore, beech, bilberry, bramble, strawberry and leycesteria. And you wonder what generous gift to the public or what struggle, maybe, lies behind the notice.   Y

KEEP DIGGING PLEASE   10 August 1995

What an exciting story was told the other night in the film on RTÉ by Michael and Ethna Viney – the story behind the Céide fields centre. It goes back a long way, with Seamus Caulfield, now Professor of Archaeology, at the centre, and, as he said himself, heroic teams of students. But to put the present mighty structure where it is took enormous local persistence and enterprise. They have created something. Nearly twenty years ago Louis Marcus filmed Seamus and some students working on Bronze Age cultivation ridges or lazy-beds at Belderg, four to five miles from the present centre. Seamus's father, the local schoolteacher, had kept on noting stones sticking up out of the bog and was curious. Seamus followed his example. As knowledge increased and digs went on, it became apparent that this discovery extended far beyond Belderg. In fact, they said the other night, something like eight square miles was included in the vast Stone Age settlement extending around the Céide centre.

It will never all be uncovered, but Seamus gave us a fascinating – and visual – eyeful of a multiple sandwich of soils: first the Stone Age layer, then the layer of bog which enveloped it, either because of climate change or because these Stone Agers, for some other reason, upped and left. Then along came Bronze Age people. Bog in turn covered the land again. Of course, as Seamus pointed out, the Stone Age folk had first to clear the site of trees. Mark you, with stone axes, though some burning would have helped. This is not surmise or speculation. For example, the roots of a pine tree were sent, a long time ago, to the Smithsonian Institute to be carbon-dated at about 2,700 BC. Give a bit, say 5,000 years ago.

It is a certainty that more than archaeologists will come to the Céide centre to marvel, and perhaps to wander over the surrounding bog and rough grassland, knowing that under their feet there flourished, a long time ago, a vibrant, inventive farming community about which we will, no doubt, learn more and more.

This is the age of the archaeologist. To Seamus and his late father, the country's thanks.   Y

IN A KERRY WOOD   27 May 1996

 On some of the more difficult stretches of the Ring of Kerry roads you come across a huge notice: "DANGER". It warns you to be careful of the upcoming bends and squiggles, and you might think it was because of cattle crossing or sheep or wandering goats. Not at all. It is to keep you on your toes against being squashed by an oncoming bus. And even as this is written, in the third wet week of May, the buses are out in marauding bands: French buses, German buses, Irish buses and buses from God-knows-where. So you take to the woods for the greater part.

Lovely, ancient, almost primeval woods. In Eastern Poland there is a famous woodland where visitors are allowed entry only on the understanding that they never leave the paths, much less pluck a flower. If a tree falls, it is left lying and, eventually sinks back into the earth, enriching it again. So it seems in parts of these Kerry woods. In the remains of the Bland properties around Parknasilla, for example, outside, that is, the strictly planted environs of the original castle, now only a sketchy ruin. Trees, we normally think of as reaching for the sky. Upwards, straight or moderately so. Here they often seem to conform more to the slope of the ground. Almost crawling up them like giant crabs. That is when they are old and sagging. And not just oaks, or those of them which reach out long arms. But birch, many of multiple trunks. And hollies. And others. Everywhere the older trees are covered in moss.

Moss so thick and rich that, thirty feet up a tree, there will be ferns growing out of it. And where a tree is blown over in a storm, it tends to be left thus, its roots like a little roof over a cave entrance, and, as long as there is penetration by some strands, it goes on growing. Holly, beech, birch, lime, ash, willow or whatever. And where there has been lopping, there is the tendency to let the cut wood, in its turn, decay to enrich the wood floor.

And the flowers: bluebells, violets and yellows and whites that you can't identify. Above all, that invasive rhododendron which may yet change utterly the wood as we know it. Not so many birds. Or they keep out of the way. Thrushes, a few; blackbirds, around a lot; robins in the hotel area; one heron plodding along; a rook or two; a whimbrel, someone said.

Hard to tell what the odour of the wood is: is it the moss? the composing whole, mixed with the nearby seaweed?   Y

BONES ON THE BEACH   1 June 1995

Sand, sea and, hopefully, sun are in the minds of many people just now. Including archaeologists, though for different reasons. They want to dig more and learn more of our past. And, oddly, in an article in the current *Archaeology Ireland*, the statement is made that 75 per cent of our dunes are to be found in the north of this island. Mind you, it stretches the point by including in "the

North" Mayo and Sligo; the others are Donegal, Derry, Antrim and Down. (And some of the more interesting sandy finds of recent years have been by the Gibbonses in County Galway.) We have long been accustomed to read of interesting archaeological finds in our peat bogs and elsewhere in the ground. Now sand is being investigated on a wide scale. Dr Peter Wilson of the University of Ulster, Coleraine, in the article mentioned, tells us that the oldest coastal dunes in Ireland, *circa* 4,000 BC, occur at Portstewart and Grangemore, respectively east and west of the estuary of the river Bann.

Dunes are, by their nature, shifting things, but here and there are overlays of soil, or sand of different quality, which help the experts to date such artefacts as are found. Sand presents more difficulty to the researchers than soil. It can be altered by wind and weather generally. It is, at times, easier for illegal dealers to get at valuable material for export. Then, the well-intentioned conservation of sand by such methods as planting marram grass may be in the general interest, but not all archaeologists can be pleased by it. There is, as said before, also natural erosion, but nearer and nearer comes the threat of rising sea levels as a result of global warming.

So you never know, walking along your holiday beach, when you might come across a scattering of bones or seashells, the detritus of a suddenly revealed battlefield, cemetery or kitchen midden. (*Archaeology Ireland,* Summer 1995 issue; £3.95.)   Y

UNDER ONE ROOF   17 June 1987

 Live and let live, tolerance demands when, not for the first time, a grey squirrel comes down to wreck a few trays which contain small oak seedlings. He digs up the residue of the acorns and scatters the rest. That's his nature. So you don't shoot him when he comes to finish the job, just scare him off. The next day you notice that the pair of blackbirds which have been industriously, even furiously, feeding a nest full of gaping beaks high up on the same wall, are nowhere to be seen. Squirrels are known to eat small birds. Still, live and let live.

And when you find that the rustling behind the corner of the ceiling is not a rat or two, but just a pair of starlings under the slates raising a noisy brood, you act the philosopher again. After all, the jackdaws have been in the unused chimney since God's time and no obvious harm done. And the blue tits are so discreet you'd never realise they were there, under the slates at the other corner of the room. Live and let live, indeed.   Y

GLASS FOR HEAT   9 May 1985

People in glass houses – have a great time. The very fact that our sunshine is intermittent should constrain us to make the most of what we have. Ideally, if you can't afford or don't want to be bothered with solar panels, a veranda covered in by glass, a greenhouse attached to the living room, or even a small glass porch can do a lot for your life. The obvious advantage to gardeners need not be stressed.

You can have shrubs and delicate plants that will not live at all out of doors. Various flowers and herbs you can have all the year round. By leaving the connecting door open in sunlight you can improve the temperature in the neighbouring room. You have a playroom for your children. There is in fact no valid argument against local authorities and private builders incorporating into every house a room or annexe in glass. It helps save oil bills too.   Y

GREEN DEMONS   10 June 1987

The fiercest destroyer of the foliage of young trees and shrubs is on the march. If he doesn't exist in your area, you are very lucky. He is the green leaf weevil. Every year in this eastern part of Ireland, hands are wrung and comfort is sought from foresters, landscapers and savants of the green kind. And every year the wise ones are helpful with details of the whole, complex life-cycle of the creatures, which emerge in swarms in early summer to wreak devastation for three weeks to a month. But nobody has yet given the formula to prevent them emerging at all. You can, of course, descend on them with malathion and that wipes out one wave of the troops. They come on again. In some years the whole first growth of scores of young trees is consumed before your eyes, the branches and twigs dripping with turquoise blue-green devils.

"Let it pass," say the good conservationists. "They'll be gone in a few weeks and if you go at them with sprays, you may kill other valuable insects." And they do disappear. And your bare branches do sprout leaves again. But no one has yet satisfactorily answered the question: how to prevent them over-wintering successfully. You're lucky indeed if you don't have them. They go for oaks especially, but young birch will do them; probably other fresh shoots.   Y

SPIDER TROUBLE   27 June 1987

If you have tried to grow peaches in your greenhouse and have given up, it's almost certainly because you have been plagued by red spider, which flourishes in warm conditions. The most successful growth of peaches, year after year, known to this corner was throughout two decades entirely free of the pest. No doubt because the roof leaked, the door was permanently jammed half shut and the site was on an exposed bluff, torn by the prevailing wind. Red spider, no matter what measures are taken against it, seems to be the most persistent pest and the better built and the better maintained your greenhouse is, the more your red spider flourishes.

One peach grower has thrown out the prized plants in disgust and is now going to try kiwi fruit. It flourishes in the open in southern France, where it now often takes the place of vines which are being phased out under government direction, and does well. Probably would even get by in the open in good conditions in Ireland.   Y

WHEN IS A TREE DEAD?   18 June 1986

You can never be sure that a tree is dead. Certain species such as willow and poplar seem to have a touch of immortality about them. One poplar which grew out of a river bank fell across and formed a bridge to the other bank. After a few years it was dragged back by the riparian owner of the rooted side and left there. Not for any purpose; just left there. Moss grew over the trunk. A couple of elder shrubs sprouted from its heart. Birds and beasts dug into its dying wood for grubs. A spread of branches, peeled off their bark, bleached until they showed white as bones on the seashore.

At that stage they were judged so handsome, so graveyard bleak that it was decided not to cut them. They were a thing of beauty: dead and beautiful. Then, out of the shiny, metallic hard white surface of the branches – about four inches in diameter – there shoots new life. The shoot, within a few weeks, is an inch thick, the leaves are the usual early bronze and the corpse is reaching out gratefully towards the sun. No roots appear to be connected with the ground at all.   Y

SPARKS   19 June 1985

Elm wood is traditionally good for coffins, not for firing. Having stood, dead, for two years, an elm which is soon to be taken down will be put to the test of burning – after life, so to speak. It would be better than a cut-up tree trunk which promised much because it had lain across a river for several years, was cut into rings and has been drying out and maturing for nearly a decade. It is poplar. It burns merrily enough, but with loud reports and flying sparks. Even with the fireguard up, it's not worth the racket. A holly stump which was taken down, dead from the ground apparently, but sending up suckers of great vitality, burns like a dream. Of course, these days you'd need the central heating more than a fire.   Y

FIRE   19 June 1987

Fire is going out of fashion as a means of getting rid of rubbish. In cities, there are rules against outdoor burnings, but out on the farms you seldom see a fire for anything other than incinerating the croppings from hedges. Even in remote parts, the plastic bag with its rotting food leftovers smells away outside the back door or at the gate. And old lino and bits of decaying wood, too awkward for the indoor grate, and so much of the detritus of today's living demand a cleansing end. A good, quick outdoor fire every week would do wonders for many a place.

Isn't there a bit of a fire worshipper – pyromaniac even – in all of us? Fire, in our cave-dwelling days brought the greatest revolution in human life. In lighting a fire, even for the hell of it, we are making an obeisance to what was, maybe, the secondary deity after the sun. Also, it's fun and smells good with the right wood. Let's have a fire. Let's have a party.   Y

FIGHT FOR TURF   8 July 1986

In common with most other crops on the smallholdings in the west, the turf men are having a rough year of it. In Achill where there is great competition to have the banks cut by Patrick's Day and the turf "saved" by June, families were struggling in the first week of July on sodden banks to break out the footings to refoot them again in an effort to catch any bit of wind and sun needed to dry the turf. Normally Achill families who are on the bog in July are generally saving a second crop of turf but there'll be very few second cuttings this year unless there is a heatwave in August.   H

ALL RIGHT IN THE END? NO   6 July 1995

 Everyone who gardens or dabbles in the growing of trees, has his or her failures. Persistent in some cases, and apparently insoluble. Blame the climate, or the soil. Curse the people you bought the tree or bushes from. But go on, year in, year out, hoping that it will all come right in the end. Take mulberries, for instance. The huge purple things that splatter down on your deck-chair as you sit outside your hotel on the Mediterranean. All over the place. And it's not that they can't grow in Ireland. In the old days, many of the big houses had mulberries in their walled gardens, or even on the lawns. In recent times – well, say a decade or two ago – there were old, fallen, but still productive mulberry trees encountered, one in Tipperary, one in Mayo.

And while your own two trees are struggling along – the last to come into leaf, well behind even the ash – you

read in the London *Times* of the lush crops of other folks. And the books will tell you that any two-foot length cut from the tree after leaf-fall, and pushed two-thirds into the ground, is bound to succeed. "Fruiting will begin in eight to ten years." Oh no, it won't, not for this patient grower. For his black mulberry stands in a sheltered spot, which yet gets plenty of sun. And all he gets from it, after twenty years, are a few groups of pinheads, barely covered in pinky flesh, which never mature to purple or to eating consistency.

It's an odd year anyway. Never has there been such a crop of cuckoo-spittle which, as you know, is not spat out, but comes from the other end of the little frog-hopper which produces it. And then there is the hugely advanced "Lammas growth", where lovely new orange-to-copper coloured leaves and healthy, speedy-growing shoots appear on the oaks, well before their expected time. And in one midland area, the flowers of the elder are still in their prime. Delicious with your fried bacon, and so easy to pop in and pick up by their stems.   Y

"HERE WE GO ROUND THE MULBERRY TREE"
4 August 1997

You can buy homegrown raspberries in the shops, and often loganberries, blackberries, even; but a fruit which resembles a cross between the last two is not available. It is probably a climatic matter. For, though the tree which produces them grows well, the fruit seldom comes to anything like full maturity. So, while it is a pleasure to have around you, the mulberry tree does not earn its keep if it's the fruit you want. A friend had told of a mulberry tree growing in the grounds of Breaffy House Hotel, Castlebar. He had seen it on a visit about 30 years ago, and was impressed by the fact that, though it had fallen, the roots remained attached to the trunk and the tree was not only in leaf but actually fruiting.

The impression had been given that the trunk was fairly long and straight, with some of the limbs flourishing vertically. A small watercolour behind the front door shows Breaffy as it was "*circa* 1900", and in front of it is a modest enough tree, not of any great height, but already being propped up by stays or posts. (Perhaps it was bigger but the artist had to show more of the then house.)

Anyway, you look for this fallen mulberry and find what looks more like a shrubbery. Lovely big shining leaves, a stout trunk with branches all in a fine tangle. Have one or two of the branches actually rooted as they lay on the ground? Anyway, a splendid wreck, though wreck is hardly the word, for it is a characteristic of the mulberry to be at its best when of some age. One item in the *Field Book of Country Queries* tells us that the tree must be long past its youth before it becomes a regular bearer of fruit. So the young trees, being poor bearers, are, you suppose, cut down.

King James I of England was a fan; he encouraged their planting in the early 17th century. In southern England and maybe even in Kerry and Cork here, the good eating variety may be successful, that is *Morus nigra*, but in, say, Meath the fruit is small, interesting, but a conversation piece rather than a crop. The Breaffy tree or trees had some fruit, much of it still green, but a few red. Breaffy House, by the way, has a Mulberry Bar. Mrs Beeton gives Preserved Mulberries in her book, i.e. jam.   Y

MAKING PORT WINE WITH SLOES   6 August 1997

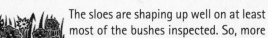
The sloes are shaping up well on at least most of the bushes inspected. So, more sloe gin this year. Or a more expansive liqueur which includes, as well as sloes, blackberries, elderberries and crab apples. And very welcome, too. And then, by chance, you come across another use for the sloe, practised a couple of centuries ago, according to William Cobbett: to make port wine.

First he gives a little disquisition on the qualities of sloes. They have "a little plum-like pulp, which covers a little roundish stone, pretty near as hard as iron, with a small kernel in the inside of it. This pulp, which I have eaten many times as a boy until my tongue clove to the roof of my mouth and my lips were pretty nearly glued together, is astringent beyond the powers of plum. The juice expressed from this pulp is of a greenish black, and mixed with water, in which a due proportion of longwood has been steeped, receiving, in addition, a sufficient pro-portion of cheap French brandy, makes the finest Port Wine in the world, makes the whiskered bucks, while they are picking their teeth after dinner, smack their lips observing that the wine is beautifully rough and that they like a *dry wine* that has a good *body*."

Well, you wouldn't doubt William Cobbett, but apart from anything else, how do you get cheap French brandy? But Cobbett is mainly interested in blackthorn plants as the best possible hedging. He says, and this was in a book called *The Woodlands* (1825), that, however, while you may then have bought a sack of hawthorn seed for a shilling or half-a-crown at the most, to get a number of blackthorn sloes, equal in number to the hawthorn berries in the sack, would "in almost any part of the kingdom cost five, ten, nay twenty pounds".

It may well be, as a landscaper friend maintains, that you get successful propagation only by suckering the blackthorn. Certainly if you buy a set of thorn quicks, asking for a mixture of hawthorn and blackthorn, you may find that you get ten of the former for one of the latter. But blackthorn makes a fine hedge, particularly because of its long, tough thorns.

(Quotations from *The Oxford Book of Nature Writing*, edited by Richard Mabey (£8.25).)   Y

HOW MANY TREES DOES A BIRD PLANT?
23 July 1998

One of the loveliest bushes of all is leycesteria. The more usual type is *Leycesteria formosa*, hardy, strong-growing, almost bamboo-like, of up to six feet and sometimes more. It is particularly attractive in summer and autumn, when its long flowers hang down, white and claret, in a tubular shape. Up to four inches. Deep purple berries, not edible by humans. It is not a tender plant.

Now this is all largely because, by pure chance, sev-eral times these big, lanky creations have appeared on top of walls and stone gateposts of neighbours. Your nurseryman, by the way, may have added a flourish by calling it the Pheasant Bush. And indeed, droppings from these birds have been found around them in places where the odd pheasant is not unknown. But when the familiar purple and white dangling flowers appear on top of a ten-foot wall in a Dublin garden, near which no living pheasant has been seen in a lifetime, you begin to wonder. Where is the nearest leycesteria? What bird deposited the seed (voided is a word often used) just where it is potentially most harmful – for the wall is up against a greenhouse, and the same wall is no recent erection.

Moreover, the plant is now about six feet and must have been lurking for several years, concealed by other foliage. To dislodge it is going to be a tricky business. Which brings us to the point; how many of the shrubs and trees around us, always excepting the well-barbered garden, are planted by birds? An old oak carries a promising elder in one of its great joints. The seed could not possibly be airborne. An ancient willow has several trees flourishing quietly in its great span.

And then think of the stores of acorns which some birds lay up for winter and do not take up because they have died in the meantime or just forgotten where the cache is. Life goes on. And how many of the hawthorn and crab apples and rowans and other trees and shrubs owe their spread to birds? Brambles don't need birds to help them; they crawl and crawl without help.   Y

"NO LETTUCE, THANKS" SAYS THE DOCTOR
27 June 1995

 "I could live on bread and butter and herbs. Well, with a little cheese."

"You mean that, in good weather, you fancy that sort of thing for lunch now and then."

"More than now and then."

"We'll leave it at that."

Certainly, the sort of advice you often get when herbs are mentioned – namely that you use them sparingly, to enhance the flavour, not to dominate it – is nonsense. So much that we eat today has no flavour at all, unless you liven it up with lots of herbs or whatever. Lettuce, for example, in a salad, tastes only of the oil and vinegar and other condiments you add. To make a lively salad you should add about a handful of good, spicy stuff. Say a mixture of winter savory (the king of them all, and an all-the-year-rounder), chervil, parsley, woodruff, salad burnet, borage, lovage, hyssop and some weaker element like lemon balm. If you fancy sage and rosemary, keep them for another day. And, of course, with any mixture of herbs, you can put in chives. Then, when some guest rolls a mouthful of salad around and asks just what the flavour is, you have a whole conversation in front of you. If they don't ask, you need not have them back.

Incidentally, the medical correspondent of the London *Times*, talking about diet and how he watches his calories, recommended, as well as fish, "lots of green vegetables". But told his interviewer he had learned that lettuce "has no food value at all". So he gave it up. Needless to say, all these herbs should be grown by yourself. Some perhaps from seed, but many come on easily if repotted from the little plastic containers you get in garden centres. You need little space for a pot-herbery.

That's by no means a full list given above. A woman in England deals in 300 herbs. She gives two words of advice. More than an ounce of nasturtium leaves could be toxic! And hyssop, safe as a flavouring, could be bad for you if made into an infusion.   Y

FEAR OF FUNGI   8 August 1997

The great rule about eating fungi collected by yourself in this country is: don't. That is, not unless you have an expert with you or have a friendly expert whom you can consult. On the continent, in France particularly, there is a great cult of the wild fungi. Chemist's shops, in many parts, show huge illustrations in their windows and many types are to be bought in the market. The taste for them is growing here, but most people prefer to buy from reliable fruit and vegetable dealers.

A friend who is also a landscaper rang the other day with the news that he was eating his way through a huge puffball he had found. About 10 inches across. He fries thick slices in butter or oil, preferring butter. He gave half to a neighbour. Apparently the puffball can be eaten if the flesh is still white. Pure white. Not if it is turning yellowish at all. Later, as you know, the inside turns to a dusty brown. But if you're sure, it is a good, tasty thing, says our friend. In a way, not unlike chicken!

That splendid book by the authoritative Roger Phillips, *Wild Food*, illustrated as no cookbook you have seen before (it's all photographed in the open, on grass, or beach pebbles, or attached to a tree trunk and so on), gives a recipe for those who know their puffballs. You make fresh breadcrumbs and toast them. You whip an egg with a little water and mix in two ounces of flour. Pepper and salt. Leave 20 minutes, he says, for flour to swell. Now, you've already fried some bacon. You dip your slices of puffball (he recommends one quarter-inch thick, our friend goes for the thicker slice) in batter and then bread-crumbs, and fry in the juices of the bacon. So, bacon and puffball, fired until they are golden brown for breakfast. Phillips gives this as Crunchy Puff Ball. He has another for Savoury Puff Ball with beef, onions, courgettes. Puffball, he says, comes from Puck or Poukball. The Irish, he gives as Pooks-foot. De Bhaldraithe gives bolgán beíche. The book is a *tour de force* – large softback £13.99, Macmillan. Phillips is assisted by Jacqui Hurst.   Y

PORRIDGE AGAIN   20 August 1988

 In hotels nowadays at breakfast they tell you to take your pick from the cereals on the side table. They have the full range of all those well-televised sweet things. Not all hotels offer you the alternative of porridge. Yet, with the potato, porridge may be making a big comeback. It deserves to. An udated book, *Irish Country Recipes* by Florence Irwin, reminds us that, before the introduction of the potato, the staple food of the people was a stirabout or porridge. Mostly it was of oatmeal but that made with wheatmeal was better. Sheep's milk porridge, says the author, was a great delicacy.

Her formula for three varieties: (1) 1 quart water, 3 oz oatmeal plus salt. (2) 1 quart new milk, 2½ oz oatmeal plus salt. (3) 1 quart buttermilk, 2½ oz oatmeal plus salt. You put whatever liquid you choose into a saucepan (or

double saucepan), bring to the boil, sprinkle in the meal. Boil till well cooked. With modern flake meal, she says, this takes about 25–30 minutes. Add more liquid if required thinner. But, in the old days, the right consistency was: enough for the spoon to stand up in it. Porridge, it is said, sticks you together in the morning. If you've ever scrubbed out a porridge pot you'll agree, for it's like glue.   Y

SEEN ANY WORMS LATELY? 19 July 1999

Do you think there are fewer worms around than there used to be? Or is it that, in the case of the gardener rather than the farmer, you are using so much manufactured compost and working mostly in pots and small beds? Or is it that you are using pesticides with a heavy hand? For, surely, worms couldn't live through a barrage of chemicals. There never seems to be any shortage of slaters (or woodlice, if you must), and slugs and snails do very well at this time of year. (So much so that a garden path where seed is put down for pigeons and other birds, of which a portion is always left in the evening, suddenly crawls with slugs and snails. Or did, until the master of the house saw a great opportunity, and swept up from the concrete 80 huge examples which he fed to his nightly badgers. The next dusk, he got only 40 and then 20.) Anyway, back to worms. Charles Darwin seems to have been the first to examine in detail the life of the earthworm. He wrote: "Worms prepare the ground in an excellent manner for the growth of fibrous-rooted plants and for seedlings of all kinds. They periodically expose the mould to the air and sift it so that no stones larger than the particles which they can swallow – are left in it . . . worms likewise drag an infinite number of dead leaves and other parts of plants into their burrows, partly for the sake of plugging them up and partly for food."

There are five different sorts – apart from that awful illegal import, the roundworm, which many of us have not seen. Dr D G Hessayon in his *Armchair Book of the Garden*, names and illustrates five different sorts. To the untrained eye, not so very different, except in size, but the good doctor dismisses something most of us believe about worms – that, if cut in half, the two live on. Not so. They generally die. On the other hand, when the tail end is severed, new segments are formed and soon the worm is "as good as new". When the head is severed, the injured worm stays immobile for about a couple of months, by which time a new head is regenerated. It then wiggles away. There is a new word about – new here anyway – vermicomposting. In this, worms are added to your compost heap or preferably bin.

And you can buy a kilo of them, it appears, containing about one thousand to four thousand of mixed size – and after you buy them, they work for free, as Michael Lynch of Irish Earthworm Company, Farnivale, Bandon, puts it, turning waste into a valuable soil conditioner. This is, again, taken from the magazine *Organic Matters*.　Y

SILAGE AND VIDEOTAPES　　　　　　22 July 1998

 Any old videotapes? The request came on the phone. The tapes were not for viewing, but for good farming reasons. This was explained in patient detail for the uncomprehending one. You know those huge black rolls of plastic you see in the fields now? Yes. Well, they are expensive enough but a great help to the farmer, as he can keep some of his silage rolled up in them in this field and that field, and near the house itself, according to where the animals are at any time. Very practical and labour-saving. But there is one big snag. Snails get in among the rolls, and birds soon get to know this. So they peck and grub around the heap on the lookout for the snails. Naturally they tear holes in the plastic and thus the silage can seep out, or rather its juices. God knows what creatures could follow in. Anyway, to keep the birds away at least one known farmer has constructed a sort of line you hang out the washing on. But between the two poles, just over the rolled-up piles of silage, he stretches a line of videotape film.

Loose and flapping, you ask? No, in fact quite taut, but it still moves, and probably glitters, and may even make an unusual noise and thus additionally add to the menace – as the birds see it. So some videotapes were to

hand and we'll hear word about their success or otherwise in due course.

This was on a trip into County Kildare, and you wonder how it is possible that the Naas road could for so long remain the atrocity that it is. Bump, bump, weave here, weave there, and most of the time pursued by monsters whose drivers at times seem determined to carry out a cruelty-to-private-motorists campaign. They loom up behind you so close that if, heaven forfend, your motor died or even checked, you would be flat as a pancake on the road. And how is it that the first couple of hundred yards of the road to Blessington from Lawlor's Hotel in Naas are surely the most pockmarked in the country? It's not great at all times until you reach Blessington, but viable. Then, of course, you come onto the luxury of a Tour de France stretch on the way back to Dublin.

Anyway, must take a good look at any other farm that has its piles of black plastic rolls, and see if this device is universal or even common.   Y

NINETEEN ACRES   2 August 1997

It is always better driving from east to west across the island. Last Saturday there were buckets of rain against the car for a couple of hours, but once over the Shannon the road rises with you and the stone walls become the norm. The gardens of the roadside houses everywhere keep you admiring – perhaps especially those older, smaller houses with their front doors often not more than five yards from the roadside.

The old regulars still thrive. Mallow, cheerful and lasting. Roses, honeysuckle; buddleia, of course, spilling over the wall, and, as you go farther west, that semi-domesticated stunner: montbretia. The more modern houses often go for variegated poplar. No comment. Mercifully, the verges are unsprayed and all sorts of plant life flourish. The fields are, this year, carpeted with the greatest show ever of meadowsweet. Is it the wet season? Then there is, on verges and in fields, the yellow horror, ragwort – one of the noxious weeds that in your parents' or grandparents' day would bring the sergeant on his bicycle to warn them of the penalty for not cutting the offending plant. And along the way, too, runs of brilliant purple loosestrife.

The John Healy Forest Park on your left after Carra-castle and before Charlestown, in Mayo, carries on a plaque set into a giant stone the opening words of his splendid book *Nineteen Acres*: "It isn't much of a road and it doesn't lead to much of a holding. The road is clay-topped and rutted. The other half, above the house on the hill, is lean and rock-ribbed . . ." And it is on the lower half, running down to the road, that the trees in memory of John are planted: oak, ash, cedar, birch, beech, Norway spruce and others.

The summer grasses and wild plants grow luxuriantly now, but the trees stand out well above them – in so few years. John Healy was widely thought of as primarily a political writer, but he had a broad view of life, and trees became almost a passion with him. A fitting memorial. *Nineteen Acres* tells a story which could be repeated in France, Germany and other European countries. Brendan Kennelly wrote: "It is both vigorous social history and imaginative creation . . . *Nineteen Acres* will be read a long time from now by people yet unborn."   Y

TREES FOR SMOKE-STACKS   12 August 1997

In 1996 the Forest of Belfast saw 10,000 trees planted. The year before, it was over 8,000. The Forest of Belfast? Well, it's not one big planting or even two or three. It's an urban enterprise to comprise every tree in and around the city, both naturally growing and planted, set in pub-lic and in private land, in parks, woods, housing estates, along roadsides and river banks, even in gardens and school grounds.

There was a time when, the cynic might say, Belfast's forest consisted of a concentration of tall smoking chim-ney stacks, of shipyard gantries and cranes. They had their day. Belfast, if short of trees, has a lovely sickle of hills around its northern and western sides, including some woodland along the Cave Hill and on the County Down side. But this Forest of Belfast initiative of several official bodies, Government and local, also voluntary organisations and the private sector, is making a mark. Some of the plantings have been of 400 and 500 and many of 300. The biggest appears to be of 1,608 in the Colin Glen area of west Belfast. And over 1,000 along the motorway. Jordanstown University will have nearly a hectare of new trees.

There was a Forest of Belfast Fair and woodturners, basketmakers and wood sculptors gave demonstrations. And – this is the real turn – the Traditional Bow Society, who make yew bows and ash arrows, demonstrated their skills. There is a great deal of information in two well-turned out reports kindly sent here by Dennis Kennedy. A good range of trees is being planted, but the oak makes up only 2.6 per cent of the total. "However, oak is being planted in increasing numbers mainly in the south and east Belfast zones. It is a desirable tree . . ." On the cover of the 1996 report is a representation of the Wesley Tree, Ballyskeagh, Lisburn. It is a beech, or in the words of the caption "reputedly two trees twined together by John Wesley, who visited Chrome Hill on Sunday 10th June 1787. Protected by a Tree Preservation Order since 1981." It looks a bit battered, but intriguingly shaped.   Y

BISMARCK'S INSPIRATION   15 August 1997

One of the loveliest effects of the wet, humid weather has been the unusually dramatic Lammas burst or Lammas spurt, or whatever you like to call it, in oak trees. Suddenly you find new shoots, with delicate orange-gold leaves breaking out all over the trees. A wonderful contrast to the deep green of the older leaves. The oak gives good value to the tree watcher. Slow, slow this year in producing and swelling its acorns – here in the east anyway – and once again afflicted with that wretched knopper gall.

Everyone knows from childhood up of the round gall which in autumn turns brown. It's the marble gall, not to be confused with the oak apple. There is a fat grub at the centre which is pleasing to tits and other birds which choose to break it open – not difficult. Not much harm to the tree. But the knopper gall, which covers the whole acorn with a whirly green heavy excrescence in shape not unlike the whirl of cream on top of your ice or cake, kills that one acorn. The tree goes on, but any number of acorns may be affected.

The gall comes from an only recently known gall-fly, which has one remarkable factor in its cycle. That is, that some part of its development must be spent in a Turkey oak. There may not be a Turkey oak within 10 miles, but this gall-fly will find it out. So the experts tell us. But oak can endure a lot. There are many sorts of galls and yet the tree survives. As some put it, the oak "plays host" to many insects and animals and birds. Not to mention fungi and humans. According to Ralph Whitlock, author of a book on the subject, when Bismarck felt low, he would stand for half-an-hour with his back against the trunk of a great oak, apparently absorbing something of its strength. North Americans, too, used the oak in the same manner, writes Whitlock. And, some sensitive people claim they have heard the oak singing, much as telegraph wires are heard to do.

Back to those lovely, long pinky-orange Lammas shoots, some of them a yard long already. This warm weather may brink mildew to their tender tips. But the philosopher says: "Mildew must be part of the scheme of things." Be grateful that you have oaks, and growing well. They are survivors.   Y

TO THE STAKE   2 August 1988

 The advocates of non-staking of young trees will have had a busy time in the wake of last week's high winds. The persistent gusts over several days took more toll than did some of the storms of the past few years. In one open planting, a whole group of ornamental conifers now stands at a slight angle to the upright, and many were found to have gouged out an opening the size of a rabbit-hole around the base, due to rolling around for several days. Anything not put in at whip stage or alternately well staked had to be examined. Many ties were broken. A friend points out that a diagonally planted stake has advantages over the upright. There is no danger of the tree moving and rubbing against it as there can be contact only at the one point. Also, it may be shorter and perhaps takes the strain of wind better. Easier to trip over, however, if you are using many in the one area. Try it. You can use shorter and thus cheaper stakes.   Y

WOODSMOKE   10 August 1987

Wood fires, which last only an hour or two, are pleasant at this time of year. Not so much for the heat as the smell and the cheerful colour and the crackle. And someone the other day mentioned all the dead elms around the country and how useful they should be as an auxiliary. Then someone else said they were deadly to try to saw up. Indeed, only a chainsaw will do the job. Any wood that has long been dead tends to tighten up – that is, before it grows fungus and gently returns to dust.

Elms always had the name of being funereal and a slow, surly burner. So it is in normal times. But elm that has been dead for some time, if difficult to cut without a chainsaw, is fine fuel. And like all wood, burns out entirely. You get the last ounce of energy. Not like coal, which leaves cinders.   Y

"LEAVE US OUR MESSY BEACHES"   31 July 1998

 "We need more seaweed on the beach and more sewage in the water." That's just one of the more startling lines in an interview with Paul Llewellyn, a biologist at the University of Wales, Swansea. And he paints a word-picture of tractors hitting the local beaches. "Fuelled by a distaste for anything smelly, rotting or creepy-crawly, they sweep back and forth across the sands, taking away detritus from the last high tide. By the time the first holiday-makers unpack their towels, swathes of shoreline or high-tide line that should be nurturing dynamic ecosystems, have become sterile no-go areas for wildlife." And the sea itself suffers, from this biologist's point of view.

The water companies, he says, "are working so hard to provide pristine bathing water for tourists that marine worms are going hungry and birds are taking off for more nutritious shores". Llewellyn admits to conversion from

being a campaigner in the 1980s for cleaning up the beaches. The campaigners have gone too far and "people are now frightened of things like seaweed which they see as dirty and harbouring disease". The key to beach ecosystems is, apparently, the strandline or high-tide mark, where all sorts of flotsam and jetsam wash up.

This repository, as the article puts it, of dead dogs and timber, algae and plastic bottles, used condoms and rusty cans, is a dynamic, ephemeral and ever-changing habitat. Unique. Its residents are invertebrates such as flies, beetles, nematodes (wormy things), woodlice and centipedes; feeding on them are oystercatchers, ringed plovers, crows and finches. This high-tide line is becoming, with its debris, "perhaps our most ignored natural habitat". Fifteen years ago a large part of this beach was designated as a Site of Special Scientific Interest because of its bird population. Today, bird numbers are down by more than three-quarters. The ecologist has found virtually none of the small crustaceans such as sandhoppers, but, where the beach is not cleaned, he found an average of 2,500 in each 25-centimetre sampling square, and therefore a thriving bird population.

Reassuringly, a consultant explains that 95 per cent of the Welsh coastline is not cleaned at all. This from a fine article by Fred Pearce in *New Scientist* for 25 July. Moral: don't try to rearrange nature too much. Or?   Y

BACK TO THE WATER BARREL   3 August 1995

The tropical heat of recent weeks has brought home to us the value of water. We don't know how to take care of it – individually and collectively. Read the local newspapers and you will find, time and again, complaints of dirty tap water, of rivers polluted by inefficient sewage works, as well, of course, as the injections of silage and slurry from some of the more careless farmers. We don't realise that water is a resource of a very precious kind and, if the globe is warming up, and this summer is an indication of what is to come, we had better get smart about it. Many of us will be thinking again of the water barrel that used to stand under the gutters. Some, even today, needing to depend on their own supplies, not being on any scheme, not having a ready tap supply, have to be more enterprising.

One westerner, for example, whose house was built against a steep slope, had that slope excavated and there installed a huge concrete tank, almost as big as the house, which supplied her, by gravity, all the year round. In a very hot season, she used a nearby well of great repute for drinking water, for herself and guests. But for the most part, the water from her giant tank sufficed the small household. You think back to the days when your finely built superior house in the country had only one tap – the kitchen tap, which was fed from the cistern on the roof of the outhouse. For washing of clothes or dishes, you heated the water on the stove. The bathroom? Don't be silly. No such place. And although the house was well furnished and pleasantly laid out inside, the dry lavatory was out at the back. Emptied each morning by the farmer himself, if there were holiday lodgers, not so often when the family was alone. Then daily, or twice daily, there was the journey down the hill with two white enamel buckets to fetch the drinking and tea-making water. Not so long ago, maybe still in some places.

The ability to turn a tap when you wanted may well have been one of the greatest attractions to the cities for many of the young of rural Ireland.   Y

NOT-SO-COMMON FROG   11 June 1998

 Surprise, surprise, a day or two ago a young frog was seen hopping into cover in a garden which is entirely enclosed by stone walls and the walls of the house itself. How did it get there? This year there were no visible clumps of frogspawn in the pool. Probably it came in with a lot of compost from the heap or with some plants on the barrow. Where is it now? It hasn't been seen since. This incident came to mind after reading through a longish article, or rather a series of questions and answers in *BBC Wildlife* magazine for May. Jim Foster is the authority, and tells you much you'd like to know about this creature.

How long do frogs live? He says there is no simple answer, but tells us that the vast majority of eggs laid

will never make it to adulthood. Some embryos never hatch. The tadpoles have a host of enemies. They are very tasty. "Frogs that reach six years deserve a medal." Who or what eats frogs? His answer is more or less: Who doesn't? At the spawn stage, newts, moorhens, ducks. At the tadpole stage, thrushes, herons, just name it. On land, young frogs and adults can fall prey to foxes, crows, some rodents perhaps, and even dogs who may just kill and leave or . . .

What do frogs eat? Your tadpole feeds mainly on algae, but will also devour tiny pond creatures, and will nibble away at corpses of fish and even of adult frogs. When it emerges from the pond, the adult frog is entirely carnivorous, most common items being slugs, snails, worms, beetles, flies, moths and woodlice. Do frogs live in ponds all the year round? No. Most of them become land creatures, favouring a moist environment and also spending much time in good shade and long grass away from the sun, lurking under small trees and plants, or rotting logs, which give not only shelter but creepies to feast on at night.

Modern farming techniques work against the frog. Firstly, in that damp places and pools are drained; and secondly, says our expert, frogs must suffer from the use of fertilisers absorbed through the skin. And then possible poisoning from eating slugs that have taken anti-slug pellets. Is, then, the common frog appropriately named? No, he is less common in Britain for reasons given above, and other reasons including increased levels of ultra-violet radiation.   Y

SENT FOR OUR CHASTISEMENT   25 June 1998

This woman was going about her garden (partly paved), picking up something carefully with a plastic bag, without touching the object with her bare hands, popping it into her bag, and moving on. It became clear that she was collecting snail and slugs. Mostly dead, it appeared. Yes, she said, the pests were so fierce this year that she had sprayed some of her most precious plants such as peonies and foxgloves and certain lilies. The nightly predators are attacking, this year, plants they barely touched previously. And in herbs, she said, she had never seen such visitations among some of the stronger-smelling, such as chives and winter savory. (These she did not spray.) She picks up the dead slugs and snails, hammers the bag with a stone in case some are still alive. Then the bag is put into the bin.

She believes that this preparation she uses contains a bird-repellent and that no thrush or blackbird is going to be poisoned if it did pick up a corpse or still living creature, but she is being very careful. For seedlings of chervil or other herbs in the cold frame, it is safe to use the little blue pellets. No bird will get at them, and no predatory slug or snail can get out by penetrating mole-like under the wood. The woman doesn't believe she has ever seen such a proliferation of the pests.

Pests? One William Derham, quoted in Richard Mabey's *Nature Writing*, an Oxford paperback, takes the presence of such creatures philosophically: "The fierce, poisonous and noxious creatures serve as rods and scourges to chastise us, as means to excite our wisdom, care and industry . . . The wise author of nature, having denied feet and claws to enable snails to creep and climb, hath made them amends in a way more commodious for their state of life, by the broad skin along each side of the belly, and the undulating motion observable there. By this latter it is they creep; by the former, assisted with glutinous slime emitted from the snail's body, they adhere firmly and securely to all kinds of superficies, partly by the tenacity of their slime, and partly by the pressure of the atmosphere. (From "The Great Variety and Quantity of all Things", *Physico-Theology*, 1713, 1754.)

Field once airily advised keeping snails in check in the greenhouse by procuring a couple of toads. Said also to keep down woodlice.   Y

LOCAL SCAMPI   12 June 1985

 Every now and then, someone, usually an angler, discovers crayfish. The midland streams and lakes, it will be said, are crawling with them. There are certainly a lot and they are easily caught. Is it worth the trouble? From experience, they are as good as the sauce you make to go with them; rather tasteless in themselves.

But here is the English *Field* suggesting that any of its readers who have a pond filled with "reasonably fresh water" and bordered by reasonably steep banks will have a pleasant and easy way to make money. (That's in England.)

The breeding stock will cost £50 but the crayfish are self-perpetuating and self-feeding. There will be, in these ideal conditions, a twice weekly lorry service to London. The current price is, says *Field*, £11 per kilo and there is a rapidly growing restaurant market for them. Maybe they taste different in England or are bigger than ours.   Y

MINNOW ON THE MENU   24 June 1986

If you eat whitebait in restaurants, why not minnows? Whitebait is defined in the dictionary as "a small, silvery-white fish, the fry of various fishes, chiefly herring and sprat . . . and esteemed as a delicacy". Anglers know minnows largely as live or dead bait for trout – that is, non-purist anglers. But, to answer the first question, people do eat minnows as whitebait, according to the learned contributors to the English *Field*. In a recent issue one of their experts even gave a recipe for a minnow/whitebait dish called "minnow tansies". This is a mixture of minnow, well-beaten egg yolks, with cowslip or primrose flowers and a little tansy "all finely chopped, fried in butter and served with vinegar or a butter sauce".

No one has yet come up with the answer to a question posed here more than once: of all wild eggs, is frogspawn nowhere cherished as a delicacy? Probably forbidden here, but someone, some time, must have tried it. Might be preferable to minnow.   Y

THEIR EYE ON YOU   1 August 1988

Whitebait is one of those macho items of food, like maggoty cheese with port, which men like to consume in their clubs. Fork them down with your own eyes closed, for the eyes of the little fish – abnormally, disproportionately large – rebuke you at every mouthful. The dictionary says: "Whitebait, so-called from its former use as bait." That explains the second part of the word, but why white? Is there brown or grey bait? Such as lugworm? No, the white would refer to the white fish of which the whitebait are fry – herring and sprat mostly. Indeed, it is possible that minnow could serve the purpose. According to the *Oxford*, whitebait is (or are) caught in large numbers in the estuary of the Thames and elsewhere, "and esteemed as a delicacy".

All the cookery books tell you that, having floured them, you keep shaking the wire basket in which you suspend them (it) during the three or four minutes you fry them in deep fat or oil. The trimmings are important. You must drain after frying and then, having dusted them with rock salt and cayenne pepper, serve on a folded napkin, with lemon and bread and butter.   Y

HAPPY DAYS   20 June 1986

It has been the unpopular thing to suggest throughout the long, wet months that it was not all disadvantage. The rain, it was maintained by a few zealots, was good for trees and trout. And was it, in fact, the oxygenating rain that has made this such a bumper year for the angler? So far, anyway. One who volunteered his age as being in the mid-seventies, claimed that it has been the best year for trout he remembers; and he had fished many Irish waters. Sheelin is booming. May its reawakening draws visitors from across the water, and from home territory, to help out the hoteliers and guesthouse keepers.

There are repeated stories of big catches, but a simple, physical demonstration is often most effective. "How is the fishing going?" a customer enquired in Tom Murray's rod and gun shop in Kells. Tom reached behind him and presented a plastic tray with two trout on it, large as battleships. Well, about 4 lb each. Happy days are here again.   Y

FISH FOR TOURISTS AND OTHERS   24 June 1987

 John Wilson, Minister for Tourism, could do himself a good turn by calling in to Kells on his way to Dublin from the Cavan constituency, there to collogue with Tom Murray. Tom not only runs a fine fishing tackle and sporting gear shop, he is a mine of information on the fishing all round the country. Legions of people tell him of their exploits, legions ask him for advice. He can tell you how many fish were caught the day before yesterday in Delphi or on the Bush, never mind in Meath and Cavan waters. He knows.

And he will report to the minister – as did a very good letter on this page on Monday – that Sheelin, after a great year in 1986, is getting dosed again with pollution. He put his hand in the water the other day and said afterwards that it was like lifting the skin off a pot of paint that had been left open. There is no reason why pigs and good fishing cannot live side by side. A Cavan minister will be particularly aware. And, says Tom, there are fine fish still in it. But is the lake on the downward turn again? The minister has spoken firmly and confidently about making a big push on tourism. Fishing tourism is a useful part of that whole. And Irish anglers like to have the best of conditions, too.   Y

TOO MUCH SALMON   13 June 1987

Salmon are said to be running in the west, at last, after all that rain. They'll be running in other parts of Europe too, and everywhere they are prized and everywhere the same legends seem to surround them. Our *Salmo salar* has a short enough run in most of our rivers. What about those that return to their native Loire and its tributary the Allier? They have to make a run of something like 800 kilometres. The magazine *Parcours* which is handed out by Air Inter has an article which declares, good gourmet style, that the salmon that has made its way up the Loire and into the Allier has had time to lose fat and, apparently, then takes on a flavour of almond.

The numbers are declining, of course. In a good season you might see from 10,000 to 15,000, whereas three centuries ago (ah well!) according to the article, one fishery alone at Puy-de-Dôme – and that's very far up – would give 20,000 to 30,000 fish per year. And, yes, they too have the story about the workers or apprentices stipulating that they must not have to eat salmon more than twice a week. A century ago, it is stated, the salmon, in some parts, was like the pig in the yard and some people ate it every day.   Y

DUSK TROUT   4 July 1986

 July is not the greatest month for the river angler for trout. The weeds are high and water summer low and generally low enough in oxygen to make the fish lethargic so they lie up in holding pools and holes, coming on to feed at dusk. It is not given to the majority of anglers to be able to indulge in dusk-fishing. If you have travelled 50 or 80 miles to a favoured river, the long drive home after a day in the fresh air demands a departure with the evening sun. For two hours after sunset those living on the river bank get great fishing in the dusk. A big bushy dry sedge floated down the throat of a run into a holding pool will bring a rise and a splash and, if you strike quickly enough, a pound trout. No need to be delicate or to worry about disturbing the pool: another fish will be on station within three minutes.   H

HEAVY WEEDS   14 July 1986

The July growth of weeds in east coast trout rivers, or in those in the south like the Little Brosna, can make life difficult for wet-fly anglers fishing in the wake of a flood. Most anglers use a cast with three flies and when fished at dusk it is really asking for trouble.

Your veteran wet-fly man knows better and, in a heavy weed situation, cuts his flies back to one. This reduces his chances of losing a good fish for, when a good trout takes and the hook is set, he will invariably dive for the weeds.

It is a far easier task to extract a hooked fish from a clump of weeds than if you had to contend with a further pair of hooks stuck in the bed.   H

LITTLE FISH, BIG FISH   17 August 1987

There they were, laid neatly in a row on the riverbank, shining and silvery and the pride of the visiting angler: eight salmon smolts, arrested, cut off in their prime on the way down to the sea. That was some weeks ago. A local man explained slowly, in basic English, to the delighted predator that these fish, if spared, would come back to the river in a year or two "like this" and he stretched out his arms to demonstrate length.

The same man has a good idea: every tourist entering the country, professed angler or not, might be issued with a coloured sheet portraying what fish may or may not be taken. There have been stories around the same area of one stranger boasting about a bucketful of the same fish, salmon smolts, to the number of 88. And, of course, most visitors claim to have been told that all fishing in Ireland is free. Local clubs are not amused. But, whatever the statistics say, every stretch of river, every lough and pool in Connemara, seems to have its complement of French, Belgian, Dutch or Germans, joyfully swinging their spinning rods. Someone, somewhere, must be getting something out of all this frenzy.   Y

RESTOCKING WITH WHAT?   15 August 1989

"Complete restocking of the river will be necessary", it is often said after a major fish kill. (Is there such a thing as a minor ditto?) But that's nonsense. There is no such thing as a complete restocking. For a fish kill will often not only dispose of the fish, but also of the creatures on which they feed: the flies, the nymphs from which they emerge; the eggs, the crayfish, the hosts of tiny creatures in being or to come, and plant life too. You cannot replace the full life of a river. If you put in fish in restocking, you may be condemning them to starvation, for it could take many years for the whole of the river to come into existence again. A fish kill, as it is termed, is a blow

127

to a whole, unseen universe as well as being the slaughter of trout and other fish. That should be borne in on any people or bodies who think that money can mend anything.   Y

LESS FISH WITH THE CHIPS   22 May 1998

 Eat more fish. While you can get them. And get the right sort. Michael Wigan, in a recent article in the *Financial Times*, paints a gloomy picture. "There is a vague idea that we can outsmart nature by replacing natural management with the fish farm and the battery trout. We have domesticated the salmon as we did the cow, with ruthlessly intensive farming, and so the words 'wild salmon' are a marketing novelty on the plastic pack." He goes on to give the prediction that there may never be a mad salmon disease, but tells us that until a decade ago pigs' blood was on their diet and that the salmon "are still tossed a blend of fish meal that they would be unlikely to ingest in their natural habitat".

But mostly he deals with the at-sea fisheries. Fish, he tells us, is no longer synonymous with cod, herring and mackerel – the largest catches are now of low-grade species: anchovies, pollack and jack mackerel. And as stocks shrink, more sophisticated ways of seeking out fish are devised. "Deepwater species, alien creatures of gothic strangeness are being jerked into unfamiliar light from hitherto inconceivable depths." In some cases a third of the catch is jettisoned as being of wrong species or size. A cavalier disregard for scarce resources. And "the chances of a North Sea cod dying a natural death are almost non-existent". And the demand goes on rising.

He hasn't a good word for seals. They often destroy a fish by taking one bite out of it. "But seals have an important role as cuddly fundraisers for environmental groups . . ." He says that aquaculture, as practised now, with its benefit to governments in giving regional employment has boom and bust cycles "that have cost bankers and local environments dear". In Norway, a leader in this, a third of the rivers have lost their native stocks, "in part because of parasite proliferation on the farms".

What does he propose? "Estuaries and accessible brackish waters are critical areas for wild fish, which seek protection to breed and leave their eggs. The challenge is to farm fish in an environmentally neutral way, and to enhance wild stocks to see at what point we can hand the lead back to nature. But aquaculture's potential is Lilliputian compared with nature's abundance and workable policies will not be achieved without the fellows in oilskins."

It's not easy. Fisheries management must be marshalled; markets should be allowed to sell discarded fish; wasteful discarding should be penalised. Migration routes must be respected. If you want more, Michael Wigan has a book *The Last of the Hunter Gatherers*, Swan Hill (£19.95 stg).   Y

THOSE-DARING-HARPOON-MEN   23 June 2000

Anyone who has seen Robert Flaherty's great film *Man of Aran* knows the dangers and hardships of the men who, in their frail boats, went after the basking sharks with harpoons. As far back as 1737, fishermen of the west had gone after what is also widely known as the sun-fish. A verse of that year urged western fishermen to equip their boats with harpoon and lance and: "So shall returning Gold reward our toil. When London lamps shall glow with Irish oil." Getting oil from other fish was a part-time occupation too, in the west. In 1765 government bounties of 30 shillings per ton for fish oil were offered and in 1774 the Dublin Society (RDS of today) announced premiums of £3 per ton for oil "extracted from fish without fire". Herrings were rendered down for oil in a glut year: it was sold for 10 pence per gallon. Lord Sheffield, writing in 1785, suggested herrings, seals, dogfish and sun-fish as good sources.

"But sun-fish or basking shark was already becoming a major industry in the West and was the biggest source of all, already in the second half of the 18th century. All the fishermen there reckon it a day's sail out of sight of the land." They were brave and adventurous, these western fishermen.

Other oils were coming onto the market: colza or

coleseed; paraffin was extracted from coal and, of course, petroleum was discovered in Pennsylvania. Not the end of the sun-fish, which lives on in such excellent accounts as this (well illustrated with maps and contemporary advertisements, etc.). A great read.   Y

"HOW HIGH CAN A HARE LEPP?"   1 June 1999

Here in Meath where, not so many years ago, at mating time, you might see 10 or a dozen across the river while you were fishing, now even an individual hare is news, in spite of many signs saying "No Hunting Dogs Here" and words to that effect. They exist elsewhere, says a correspondent, who recently came across a pair in County Mayo. On an idle weekend this couple went to an old country house to which are attached two walled gardens, now being farmed organically. Approaching the entrance gate to the gardens through a bluebell wood, they disturbed a pair of hares who responded by entering the gardens and making a circuit of the inner walls. Initially amused by this, our two visitors began to realise that the hares were alarmed and, to avoid distress, they hid themselves. Rather than escaping by the entrance through which they had come, one of the hares tried to jump the perimeter wall, eight or nine times; it could leap vertically about six feet as though on springs – not unexpectedly in a creature with such ample rear legs.

Are there any records of hares' ability to jump vertically such a height as was demanded? We know how they can leap ditches and streams, though sometimes they prefer to swim, even swimming salt water to nibble some grass and herbs on a small islet. But no; these hares did not succeed in the great escape by leaping, but eventually exited by the way in which they had entered. And, incidentally, they didn't get any of the organic produce, which was guarded by a trusty sheepdog. But this drew a reminder of something in *The Experienced Huntsman* by Arthur Stringer, first published in 1714 and more recently by Blackstaff. Stringer was a huntsman to Viscount Conway's estates at Portmore on Lough Neagh, and in his book ascribed to some authors on hunting the fact that, when pursued, hares may run along the top of a hedgerow and even climb a stone wall six feet from the ground.

Anyone ever see a hare climb a wall? On the other hand, Stringer thinks that if a hare were so crafty, hounds would never be able to kill her "by fair hunting" – i.e. by man on horses, with hounds. The hare he describes as "the most noble little creature for gentlemen's sport"!   Y

ANIMALS KNOW BEST?   9 June 1998

Do you believe that horses and cats and birds and even domestic fowl (if such a creature exists around you) react to coming changes in the weather, and are always more sensitive in this than is the average human? The writer, Ian Niall, in an old issue of *Country Life*, admits that old men, "and those of us with old wounds or scars, get warnings of change and look to the barometer to confirm the information", but cows out in the fields lie down before the rain comes, horses become frisky and, he says, when a severe storm is threatening, find a more sheltered place and turn their backs to the wind. He goes on to tell us that goats come downhill well before the deluge, though you'd think the wild ones stay put. He brings birds into it, in stating that many of the smaller kinds come to the seaboard before frosts catch up with them, and certainly it has been noted that kingfishers in winter make for the estuary of the Boyne, and possibly the same happens on other rivers.

The most sensitive animal, to him, was, however, a pet called Topsy, presumably a dog rather than a cat, which suddenly seems possessed with an urge to race at high speed all around the house, upstairs and down. "She becomes quite mad and we know that it will soon be raining." When it does rain, she settles down at the window to watch. Sometimes, apparently bored by the view from one side of the house, she moves to the other side, asking for the other door to be opened "as though expecting that here the weather will be different".

What about the effect of bad weather on wild creatures? We know that a severe winter kills very many of our small birds. (Hence, feed the birds as best you can.) Gilbert White, author of *The Natural History of Selbourne*, gives a picture of the effect on many wild creatures of a prolonged period of frost and snow. "Tamed by the season, skylarks settled in the streets of towns because they saw the ground was bare; crows watched horses as they passed and greedily devoured what fell from them; hares now came into mews' gardens, and, scraping away the snow, devoured such plants as they could find."

This was 1776. And of 1768 he notes that after the cold, the first signs of a turn in the weather came: "roost-cocks, which had been silent began to sound their clarions, and crows to clamour, as prognostic of milder weather; and moreover moles began to heave and work and a manifest thaw took place". From that, White concluded that thaws originate from underground warm vapours!   Y

BADGERDOM   23 May 1985

Among the corpses along the roadsides, badgers loom large. It is said, with what authority is not known here, that badgers stick to traditional paths and even when a concrete road is laid down over those paths, they cannot break the habit and thus are slaughtered by motorcars. However, the news these creatures make these days is mostly as disease carriers. In England there is a furious controversy as officialdom declares total war on them in certain areas because they carry TB germs and infect cattle.

The Wildlife Fund in Britain points out that other mammals such as deer, foxes and shrews also become infected and that it may in the long run be necessary to put up with a low-level incidence of disease in these animals rather than resort to general slaughter. In Ireland there seems to be no big official campaign over badgers. Sometimes it is as if mankind becomes more jealous of its stature and wants to eliminate every form of animate life.   Y

BADGERS   15 June 1999

When that good man Andy Barclay sent a veritable anthology of cuttings, book excerpts and many, many ideas, some time ago, there was included an item from a book published, he thinks, about 1945, in which Brian Vesey Fitzgerald, a name well known to many, wrote about a badger's funeral, one that he had actually witnessed. It was a fine clear night in June and he settled down behind a bush to observe the comings and goings of a badger family he knew to inhabit the nearby sett. Unusually, he thought, it was the sow who first came out. The observer immediately knew she was excited, for the hair of her back was "running up and down, forming tiny wavelets" and the hair of the back, he tells us, is the barometer of the animal's emotions. She raised her head and uttered a cry – "the first real sound I have ever heard from a badger". A weird half-whimper, half-howl. Then she moved to a disused rabbit warren about 20 yards away and he could hear her grunting and digging. She came and went several times after. Suddenly another badger came into view, smallish, definitely not the male that Vesey Fitzgerald had seen often with the now agitated female. And then she uttered a thin sound, a kind of whistling, raising her head and bringing her nose back to the ground. Then the male, exactly opposite her, went through the same performance. This was repeated until the two noses were touching.

Then both went down into the sett and the male soon came up, dragging the body of the old male across to the rabbit warren. Soon sounds of scratching were heard, confirming the writer's guesses: "Father was being buried." Our watcher had taken up his station about nine o'clock and it was now after 4 am. But how, he asked himself, did the young badger know? Had he been summoned by that first great cry of the female? The human ear, anyway, he reckoned, could not hear it at any such distance as the nearest sett, which was five miles away. And the female was certainly expecting him. Had she been to his home to tell him? It seemed unlikely for more than one reason. But *how* had her helper learned? "Was it sound, or scent, or instinct, that indefinable quality?" Two mornings later our man was at the sett. He went to the rabbit burrow and shovelled the earth away. The badger was there and crawling over his body were thousands of ants. The smell was bad. "I pushed back the earth."   Y

HUNT THE MINK   5 August 1989

It will have surprised many readers to find in yesterday's *Irish Times* that last year in the Republic there were 115 legal otter hunted, mostly, if not all, it appears, in Munster. The report does not say how many otters were killed. Now the clubs have agreed to suspend hunting during the dry season. Fishermen and others who haunt riverbanks must wonder how it is that the legal hunting period is from May to October. Now, in early August, there are still broods of young birds – mallard, waterhen, and smaller birds – being reared in the reeds and on riverbanks. Hounds ploughing through the cover could cause great damage. In May, June and July much greater havoc could be caused. It seems an odd and arbitrary date-setting.

In Britain, it is frequently reported, former otter hounds are going over to mink-hunting. There is even an Association of Mink Hounds, with 16 members. Some of these are former otter hounds. You may be against hunting of any kind, but there has to be a difference made between an animal which lives only from its natural diet of fish and water creatures generally, and an animal that destroys as well as kills for food. Slaughter, by mink, of hens, for example, is well enough documented, in addition to game birds and wild fowl in general. In some parts of England, the magazine *Country Times* reports, moorhens (waterhens) and coots have been wiped out. Anglers and other interested parties have made up mink shoots in this country. Probably the more effective control.   Y

HUNGRY BADGERS, BOOZY FOXES   18 August 1997

Our Dublin suburban badger-and-fox watcher came across some advice given long ago in an English magazine about rearing a badger. Though who would want to keep such a lively creature in captivity? Anyway, as feeding, it suggested household scraps – bread crusts, boiled potatoes and bits of fat and pastry together with green foods cooked or raw. But the finest food of all is milk and raw eggs. For the tame badger the advice is, one meal only – at night. And water should always be available.

So far, so good. Then we look at James Fairley's *An Irish Beast Book*. He tells us that badgers, indeed, usually come out at dusk to feed and, he writes, "their menu is decidedly *à la carte*". For Irish badgers, according to research, "the single most important item is earthworms. But they also take young rabbits, mice and birds (possibly as carrion), slugs, snails, insects, fruits, seeds, and even fungi are known to be eaten, too". So, our badger man in Dublin, who has been putting out bread scraps and monkey nuts, mostly for his badgers – though the foxes, just now, frequently get in first – reading about the slugs and snails had an idea. He noticed one night that the overspill of seed from the bird-table had attracted a huge number of snails. Sooner or later they would be picked up by birds, in the morning, for they seemed sated, if not a bit muzzy from the rich diet.

So he scooped them up and added them to the badgers' fare at the other side of the house. About 40 of them. Nature in the raw. He did it more than once, and fancies that more badgers are coming than normal. Maybe not. Foxes are increasing in the area – south Dublin. Even gardens right down in Rathmines have them hopping over their walls. And, just off the Harold's Cross Road one was seen tripping nimbly along the top of the wall, making, it was thought, for the overripe pears which had dropped to the ground.

Could foxes become addicts of alcohol? One family, to cope with slugs, put scooped-out grapefruit halves filled with beer here and there. The theory is that slugs love beer, drink it and expire or at least become comatose. One night the couple looked out and saw, lapping away at their beer, Brer Fox. They should carry on the experiment. What does a drunken fox do? Science awaits the answer.   Y

MINK ALL OVER HIM 28 August 1998

From foxes to another prey. The current stir in England about mink is, for press people, a good summer story. An item on page one of the *Daily Telegraph* was headed "Mink Mug Angler For His Bait". This chap was sitting by the River Avon with an open can of dog food, his bait, between his feet when, at darkness, there came "a high-pitched squeaking" and out of the bushes about four shapes hurled themselves at him. "They were all over me . . . I was screaming." He tried to beat them off with his net, but they were fearless. He ran away but was brought back by a fellow angler. The report doesn't say if the mink ate all his dog food.

These would have been among the 7,000 released from a mink farm by animal rights activists, no doubt. It is thought that about 1,000 may still be at liberty, the rest captured or killed. It's not so long since anglers and bird-lovers in Ireland expressed worries about the spread of the same animal, the American mink, from farms here. Fairley tells us in his *An Irish Beast Book* that at one time in the 1950s and 1960s there were 40 mink farms here. Two of them contained over 10,000 and one was thought to be housing over 50,000. The number of farms were much reduced when Fairley's book came out, revised in 1984.

One river in the east had for some years a problem with mink; it was a good spawning river, well stocked with trout and crayfish. Today there may not be one mink left. Some shot; many shot perhaps, but they may have moved westward or are just dying out, or even blending into the natural population and not much noted. Possibly the lack of waterhens on one stretch may be due to them. They like eggs, and will even climb a tree to get them, for ducks sometimes build in a handy fork of, say, a bank-side willow.

In Britain, there are plenty of people who get a kick out of hunting the mink, with 19 mink-hunting packs. A recent *Country Life* article showed about 100 people with shaggy dogs, three mink-hunting packs combined. "Two brace of mink proved wily quarry, one of the animals was caught midstream, but the others escaped." The Kent and Sussex Mink Hounds met on a recent summer evening and according to a writer in *Field*, three mink were dispatched, in a pond by one crossbred puppy. For the rest, the writer summed up, "Mink hunting really is a glorious way to spend a summer's day or evening. It is a wonderful opportunity to explore the country at leisure without that added bother of a horse that pulls or trying to avoid the one in front that kicks."   Y

FOX: THE UNEATABLE; WILD BOAR: VERY TASTY
20 August 1997

How far will the British Labour government's inclination – it is hardly more than that – to ban fox-hunting go? If the ban went on, wouldn't the gentry on the grouse moor be next? And what about the village bobby and his pals going after a few woodpigeons at the weekend? And then the patient line of fishermen along the canal with their keep-nets and maggots?

As far as keeping the fox population down, the hunting crowd can't be very effective. In fact, genetically educated naturalists tell us that the more foxes you kill, shoot or otherwise, the more the remainder bring up the population again. They have the ability to exercise real birth control. Anyway the Terror of the Henhouse is a thing of the past. Fowl, nowadays, sit behind wire cages in huge concentration camps. The bets surely are that the banning idea will drag on to a slow kill.

But if it comes to a wild animal that really does damage crops and fences and generally causes disruption it's the wild boar, subject of a series of articles in a French hunting magazine. In 1996 compensation for damage to crops and otherwise, was paid out to the tune of £30 million – well, 155 million francs. Damage done, that is by wild animals, of which 80 per cent was attributed to boars. The rest to deer and other game. It's not clear how this sum is divided between the hunting federations and the government, but there must be some governmental backing. And the thing is, that the wild boar is increasing in numbers and very rapidly. Six-fold in the last 20 years, the magazine states.

Last year there were 250,000 of them; the previous year 230,000. The boar is big enough and tough enough to have no predators, isn't put out by bad climatic conditions and, in short, is thriving. For, while you might think that shooting young females might keep the numbers down, in fact the older females produce twice as many young. Hunting the boar of course, is by shooting. It is said that the cost of leasing a piece of boar-rich forest is rising, which means the gun-clubs have to increase their membership fees. They also, in some bad cases, have to put up electric fences for farmers.

Shooting in forest can be tricky. On the first day of the season, in particular, regular accidents are recorded. One thing you can say for boar-hunting, as against the fox crowd, is that the boar makes tasty eating. Elizabeth David gives a recipe.   Y

HOW DO YOU LIKE YOUR STEAK?   11 May 1999

 You may have read about the new campaign to use all our technology and experience to create what at least one newspaper called a "designer steak", or rather steaks and beef generally, for the foreign market. Teagasc recently revealed new plans to make our beef conform more to what the continental consumer wants. And it is not the same in every country. Not only do our farmers have to manipulate the diet of the cattle, but also new techniques have to be employed at the processing level. It has been found, for example, that beef from animals finished on a diet of concentrates is more tender than from animals finished on grass alone. And if they are fed on maize silage, they produce whiter fat than animals fed on grass silage. White fat is preferred in some countries to cream fat. (The things you learn from reading *The Meath Chronicle*!) And research, it appears, shows that if the producer hangs carcasses from the hip, they are more tender than the usual hanging from the hook.

Big steaks are surely a macho thing – the sort of food that athletes train on. That idea has probably been at least modified. And how many men know the difference between fillet steak and other versions – rump steak, chuck

steak – to begin with? The women will. And everyone knows that steak tartare is raw, minced fillet with raw onions and raw egg yolk. But when we go abroad, do we not tend rather to explore the great world of fish and shellfish, and other delights? Foreign holidays are surely changing our eating habits as we modify our food for export.

One steak you haven't heard of: whin steak. Whin refers to the method of cooking rather than to the shape or content. You may prefer the word gorse or furze. You can lay the steak on wire mesh or chickenwire over the burning whins – preferably, or of necessity, out of doors. Or simply hold it over the burning whin fire on a graip or fork – we are getting very rural. And, of course, barbecues could take this on board, though smaller bits and pieces would be more usual.

The originator of whin steak – as far as this corner is concerned – is Basil Blackshaw, whose recent query about the value of feeding whins to horses got this plant into the discourse. He says the whins give a wonderful flavour to the steak and, of course, there are no prickles left to pierce your tongue.   Y

ORF   10 July 1986

The word sounds like Cockney slang. No one knows the derivation of it or whether it is a Gaelic word. In the Achill Galltacht and Gaeltacht this year there is no doubting the damage it is doing to lambs and yearling sheep just as there is no mistaking the disease. It is like a foot and mouth disease in that the lamb with orf can barely stand on swollen, bleeding legs. The lips of the mouth swell up painfully. The disease flourishes in wet, cold weather and if caught in time the lamb can be treated with a drench and tablets.

Mountain lambs can go five or six days without being "seen" and when they are inspected the orf has got in on them. Over 25 per cent of the lamb crop of this spring have succumbed to the disease, the worst spring for many years. The cattlemen had it hard but they got government aid for fodder. The moutainy sheepmen are not as well organised but suffer financial losses comparatively as great.   H

THE DOG OF DOGS   24 August 1998

 Often they used to be called alsatians. Now they are German shepherd dogs. A French writer on sporting topics tells us that a century ago a Prussian Captain von Stephanitz thought he should synthesise the shepherd dogs of various provinces; his dream was to produce the ideal dog. He laid down draconian rules of selection for the breeders in order to produce this most perfect dog. The colour or texture of the coat was not important to him. He was interested only in the dog's working ability.

The breed developed into a dog that could do anything and everything. Originally a guardian of flocks of sheep, it retained, from its original function, the instinct of defending what was entrusted to it, even at peril of its own life. So this is the dog most used by the army, the police, the customs service. The dog has an excellent memory and is most adaptable. It plays a big role in detecting mines and explosives generally; also in finding drugs and in tracking people who have disappeared or wrongdoers who have fled. German shepherds are to the fore in searching ruins after earthquakes, or under snow when skiers are engulfed in an avalanche. The dog often shows itself more effective than modern techniques of detection. Dogs working after an avalanche, this article declares, can find a person buried under six metres of snow, or two metres if it is compacted. It takes a team of 20 men 20 hours to probe one hectare of snow – the dog can do the same in one hour.

The dog, it has said, has a remarkable olfactory system. It has 180 to 220 million olfactory cells – if that's the correct term – compared with 5 million in humans. In Sweden, Finland and Russia the dogs are trained to detect copper and nickel, in which, it is claimed, they can outdo a geologist equipped with technical devices. They are trained in America, the writer tells us, to detect escapes of gas or petrol and even to know when cows are coming into heat! Only labradors or golden retrievers can be compared with them as guide dogs for the blind.

The dog needs to be exercised, to run, to be played with. While it is good with the members of the family, the German shepherd is basically a one-person dog. The formula, according to this article, is that it be brought up from an early age with an iron hand in a velvet glove, in justice and co-operation. "As the master is, so is the dog."   Y

LE BORDER COLLIE   7 August 1998

There can be few TV viewers who have not been captivated by those sheepdog trials, with the whistlings and odd calls of the shepherds, while the dogs themselves are the most graceful and eye-catching creatures of all. Now a French sporting magazine goes over the top for them, lavishing praise on their intelligence, fidelity and precision. Never before heard the origin of the name as given by the French. First the article tells us that the border collie takes the first part of its name from the frontier between England and Scotland. On these high plateaux of tempestuous winds or drenching mist, enormous flocks of black-headed sheep lived in freedom. These were called "coalies" from the word coal. "Coally, colly collie, colley . . . and so, too, were named the various sheepdogs that were used to guard them."

It suited them well, for all of them had blackened coats. Other colours are permitted, but the black-and-white coats are the norm. The coat is moderately long and not heavily textured – a tail like a fox. But above all, the writer says, the dog is noticeable for "the strong eye", controlling the movements of the sheep from a distance by the intensity of the look he directs at them, as if to paralyse them or to hypnotise them. On the way to today, the collie has absorbed, we are told, certain qualities from crossing with Gordon setters. His slow crawling approach has something of the game-dog's style. He has, moreover, a sense of smell that leads him to straying sheep.

"Right, left, forward, push on, back, stop." What you hear on television seems more cryptic and, the writer notes, that the master often doesn't have to say anything – just a gesture, a look, and the dog bounds off. (And there are some odd secret-language indications, you would swear.) Even on his own, a kilometre or two away, the dog, it is said, takes his own initiative and brings the sheep to his master's feet. Australia, New Zealand, South America, all sheep countries have adopted the border collie.

The writer asserts that, to get a pedigree, a dog has to go through his paces with a flock of sheep, under scrutiny. The writer, Dominique Simon, advises people who haven't sheep not to keep a border collie; he likes children but he needs to work to channel his energies.   Y

AUTUMN

AUTUMN CAME: OFFICIAL · 30 August 1990

 Just for the record: autumn came in about a fortnight ago and, in spite of the on-again, off-again good weather, has consolidated its hold. The birch were the first trees to start closing down, sped on their way by the drought, of course. Other, less volatile trees like oak and hornbeam and ash will take their time; but much depends on the site. No one who has been asked can remember a year of such fruit cropping. Apples are abundant, both cultivated and wild. Hedges are laden with haws, red already. Elders drip with purple berries. The blackberries are going to give the best of seasons. Not much sign of sloes in certain areas. And, most disappointing of all, hardly a mushroom in the experience of neighbours and friends. Were there parts where a modicum of rain brought them up? The beech mast has been widely recognised as a record. But the oaks are even better. Now swelling towards fuller than full size, acorns exist on some trees sufficient to plant an entire forest.

Once again, September chore for the very young – collect acorns and ask your parents and/or teachers for a little plot to plant then in. And for everyone who has even an acre or two, the Gulf crisis should remind us, not for the first time, that wood can keep you warm. And wood grows fast in Ireland, especially ash and some less worthy poplars. And even if you don't survive the two decades or less which would bring these trees to sufficient maturity to keep you in fuel, your children will bless your memory in a cold world.   Y

MAKE YOUR OWN ELECTRICITY · 4 September 1998

The willow is not just for making cricket bats or for basketry work, but can be the source of electric power, and is being so used on this island. John Gilliland, having land surplus to food production, looked to the willow as the raw material from which he is able not only to be self-sufficient in heat and light, but can also sell electricity to the official grid.

Anyway John Gilliland, according to the official Northern Ireland magazine *Omnibus*, tells the readers that he operates on a three-year rotation, for willows regenerate themselves every three years. "We plant a third each year and harvest a third each year." This gives him a continuity of supply for his power plant. His farm, the magazine states, "is the first in the UK to use willow as a power source". He favours a project on this scale because it allows profit to be retained at farm level and ensures employment. For, mind you, he is talking in significant figures. Over the phone he explained that his willows cover 110 acres, so his third each year is about 35 acres. A lot. In all, his Brook Hall Estate is 650 acres. A hard-working man. His land is just north of Derry on the Culmore Road.

The willows are harvested in winter and chip is made from them. "These are then dried, using a grain floor drier and fed into a plant called a gassifier. The process is similar to making charcoal and produces a gas which, after the dust has been extracted, is fed directly into the air intake of a diesel engine. Using 10 per cent diesel and 90 per cent wood gas, the engine drives a generator from which we make our electricity, with the heat from the engine and the exhaust used to dry the woodchip, the grain and heating houses on the estate."

The article says that already two manufacturers in the district are considering using willow grown locally in the same manner. John Gilliland has also had people coming from every continent to see the project in operation. Anyone operating such a scheme this side of the border?   Y

"FIVE SPRIGS OF PARSLEY"   22 September 1998

You sometimes hear it said that the ubiquitous supermarket and the increased mobility of the rural community have between them almost done away with the kitchen garden, even among farmers. But as those great autumn festivals known as Agricultural Shows – the modern replacement for the gatherings of long ago so well recorded and recalled for us by Máire Mac Neill in her great book *The Festival of Lughnasa* – demonstrate, the kitchen garden lives on, and even the farmyard keeping of fowl, though that may be rare enough. For, although the biggest draw at such shows is always among the champion horses and cattle and sheep – indeed they are the main reasons for having such an event – you will find in those newspapers which report them in detail (good for them), that prizes are still given for "five stems of parsley" or "best two cucumbers" or for "five shallots".

You might argue that when the honours are given to "five tubers of Golden Wonders" or "five tubers of Roosters" or of British Queens, that these came from a huge acreage of these potatoes, but five sprigs of parsley surely can only come from a spot not far from the kitchen door. And there are clearly defined classes of Home Industries, notably in the baking of bread and cakes: potato cakes, wheaten cakes, sponge cakes, boxty cake, apple tart, shortbread and much more. Jams, too, of course, gooseberry, blackcurrant, rhubarb, apple jelly and so on, then chutney, bottled fruit and homemade pickle.

Wines, too, white and red. Would the white be elderberry flower and the red from the fruit of the same? We are reading all this in the two-page coverage in the *Anglo Celt* of Cavan (3 September) and the page in its contemporary and neighbour the *Meath Chronicle* of 5 September, of the Virginia Show, one of them remarking that "the Show seemed almost threatened by its own success, with packed car parks on all approaches". And there's also craftwork and fruit and flowers and dogs, and, because all the community gets on stage, children's classes including – bravo in this mechanical and electronic age – handwriting. Many, many more classifications while, as noted above, the main *raisons d'être* of an Agricultural Show – horses, showjumping, cattle, sheep, etc. – take pride of place. But so much has been made, even here, of the apparent decline of the kitchen garden and farmyard poultry, it's fair to show how much contrary evidence there is.   Y

FLATTEN THAT GRASS   19 September 1986

What is behind this urge to tonsure and flatten all grasses, to have a garden which, flower and vegetable beds apart, must be like the surface of a billiard table? The lawn around the house, it is conceded, should be trim and flat and green. (Though a spread of hay with wild flowers among it is equally acceptable.) But why must the reaches beyond the lawn, where meadowsweet rivals the best bedding plants, be scoured and scourged? Why must the flaggers, whose waving spears are comely and graceful, be slashed, and the ordinary common reed, the phragmites, which in autumn turns such a lovely cinnamon colour, be regarded as a weed? Even some of the gross umbelliferae, which draw the seed-loving birds, are spectacular beyond anything from a packet sowing. But there is an urge in man – and woman – to conform. The trees look better, it is said, rising from cropped green rather than from a natural surround of free-growing grasses and freebooting plants.

The idea helps to sell sit-up mowers and weedeaters and slashers and chemical killer-stuff and other weapons of warfare. Not everyone is convinced.   Y

MOST FASCINATING SEASON   9 October 1998

 There are over 60,000 townlands in Ireland and, honest to God, you would swear there was a different climate in every one. Just go by the trees and bushes, for a start. One magnificent old oak in the south of Dublin produced this year the greatest bloom of male flowers seen in two-score years. Came the frost. Complete blitz and they were all reduced to dust, practically. So now we see that a tree which in good years can produce two barrelfuls or binfuls of selected acorns has not one. It does have a great crop of parasite marble gall with its comfortably tucked-up white grub. Not 200 yards away, on another old oak, the result seems to be similar. Yet in an hour's drive, a planting of young oaks is brassily flouting its first good crop.

And in that same plot, only the horse chestnut shows signs of autumn. The red American oaks are green as ever. No brilliant scarlet leaves. You plant that odd bush, liquidambar, for colour. Two of them, 100 yards apart, are still green, one showing only a couple of purple leaves.

Best joke of all: the mulberry, its few measly berries long taken by the birds, is now putting out the equivalent of the Lammas spurt, much seen in oaks. The huge, glossy, dark leaves of this tree are now set off by two-foot shoots of exquisitely light green leaves. Berries: the elderberries were good, now often gobbled up by the birds and taken for jam by humans. Hardly any black-berries. Everywhere haws, the bushes leaning down under the weight.

Rowans quite productive: the old-time equivalent of chewing gum and likewise spat out after mastication. And the Meath grass keeps on growing (reservation: in this townland anyway). Fungi of odd appearance come up in a cluster of willow trees. Do not let even the dog near it. Lawyers' Caps in the drive. Grey squirrels at the bird-hangers have now a rat as rival. Get out the airgun. But no mice in the house, while you have bought a box of 20 traps. Hazelnuts are well gnawed under every clump.

Shelter, east or west-facing, mixed quality of soil, all play their part, but you can say without fear of contra-diction that every autumn is different, every tree and shrub is working its own way. This is the most fascinat-ing of all seasons. (The arbutus is still doing fine.)   Y

THE HUMAN BAROMETER   31 August 1989

Sometimes the human body seems to be little more than a barometer. Humiliating, this subservience to weather, as if we were like the proverbial hank of seaweed which some people nail up as a guide to the weather. Hayfever is not yet over for everyone; for some, you don't need all that much pollen; many growing things give off the spores or whatever it is that sets nose and throat going. If you are at all creaky at the joints, the sudden changes of temperature make you groan. Even a well-healed broken bone may give you a jab when frosts come. Many people suffer from bad headaches in the run-up to a thunderstorm – even sensing it for hours beforehand. Heavily overcast skies alone may bring on a buzz in the head. Wind, of course, immobilises some asthmatics and others, affected in the chest. No wonder that on German television they have a section devoted to bio-weather, i.e. how today's weather will affect the variously afflicted or variously sensitive. Man (all right, mankind) has been called "the thinking reed", and "that two-legged unfeathered thing", and so on. But the plaything of the weather is today's analogy.   Y

A HORSE PERSONALITY   13 August 1986

 In a quiet back street of a small town in southwest France there is a notice in an aperture about six feet above the street level. It says in beautiful, hand-printed letters (for the benefit of the binman no doubt): "Monsieur, this bread is not for the rubbish bin, it is for the horse." And people of goodwill do leave their unused bread hanging in bags from the iron bars of the opening. On either side of the stable door an artist has portrayed in colour a horse's head. Perhaps the predecessor or predecessors of the useful and much noted animal inside. They still have working horses in that part of the country and due respect is paid, as in this case.   Y

MUSHROOMS, SNAILS AND PINE NUTS
28 September 1998

This is a seaside town, a holiday town, though not entirely, which was built several decades ago into what had been a forested and often marshy flat space near the foothills of the Pyrenees. Of all the various species of trees with which the planners replanted the new avenues and open spaces, none is more appreciated than the stone pine (*Pinus pinea*), which not only looks handsome and shapely, even when well grown, but is a source of nourishment to more than a few inhabitants and visitors. You often see people in pairs, filling their plastic bags with the pine nuts which cover the gravel or tarmacadam on the streets under the trees.

These nuts, about three-quarters of an inch long, fall at this time of the year as the large, orange-sized cones open and scatter their scores and scores of nuts. It is not difficult to open them with a rap of a stone or some heavy object and inside you find the softish, bland nut which in Ireland we buy in packets in grocery shops for salads or for decorating cakes or confectionery. Or just to nibble when roasted. In French, they are known as *pignons.* Hard work to get enough, but the French are a persistent people with a taste for what is good.

And when it rains and the snails come out, the culti-vated, grassy and bushy strip of land along the sea is swarming with gourmets, bearing plastic bags and bas-kets to collect not only the snails, but also any mush-rooms which may have come up. A favourite and famous dish here is called a *cargolade* – snails roasted, prefer-ably over a fire of vine twigs and branches.   Y

MUSHROOMS GALORE   2 October 1988

And more from our travelling gourmet in France, who is now well up in the lore of mushrooms – mycology. The heavy rain after an Indian summer, he writes, may discourage many, but not the enthusiastic mushroom hunter. Armed with a penknife, a box with several compartments, and a cam-era, he or she dons wellington boots and heads for the woods. Also useful are a map and compass, a magnify-ing glass and a mushroom guide. He recently acquired *Le Guide des Champignons: Reconnaître, Ramasser, Cuisinier*, a comprehensive guide to recognition, gather-ing and cooking of the same.

The first piece of advice is to pick only young speci-mens, leaving old, wormy, water-engorged or frost-damaged fungi to spread their spores in peace. Then, before picking, observe the situation of the fungus so as to learn which conditions favour its growth. If you recog-nise the fungus as safe, cut it neatly at the base; otherwise remove the whole foot, which makes its identification eas-ier. Once picked, brush off any soil or leaves and place gen-tly in a basket, taking care to separate different species. Because fungi are so delicate, it is advisable to handle them as little as possible, and to eat them without delay. Failing that, the best place to keep them is the vegetable compartment of the fridge – feet in the air.

But who owns them? In France, home of many enthusiastic mycologists, Article 547 of the Civil Code decrees that mushrooms belong to the landowner; in national parks, collection is sanctioned, but for familial rather than commercial consumption, and harvests can legally be limited to two or three kilos per person. What regulations exist here?

"God be with the days," said one of his relatives, "when we went out of an August evening, each armed with a white enamel bucket, through the fields of neighbours in Islandmagee, County Antrim, and often filled them. You could see the beggars grow. First time around the field there would be little buttons lurking in groups; an hour later they would be noticeably bigger and before darkness had completely fallen, you had your share of nice, flat-topped items, just right for the egg, bacon, potato-cake and sausage cooked breakfast. Just the one variety of course, your ordinary field mushroom. And then, I suppose, came the new chemical farming." You don't have to believe him, but it wasn't too far off the truth.   Y

SLOE GIN   9 September 1995

Michael Viney was writing recently about some of the possible effects of global warming as seen in his garden. He mentioned that his oaks are flourishing as never before – and oaks can have a bad time on the western seaboard. Here on the east side, in just one case (don't build a thesis on it), the prunus has taken a great leap forward. In the first place, a huge shrub under which there is a bench for sitting peacefully in shade, very much seemed to be the chief function of the tree, secondary to giving in early spring a lovely mound of white flowers. Occasionally a fruit or two would be spotted, and the children were lucky to get maybe a dozen after poking with fishing nets on the end of poles. The fruit were edible and welcome, but far too sparse to be concerned about. This year, to everyone's surprise, the tree is loaded with them. And not merely out in the sunlight, but in the shady interior. Cherry plums, they are called, fruit of the *Prunus cerasifera*. Bigger, in fact, than any cherry, and just sweet enough to be different. Don't let them get too ripe. They lose their tang.

But there's another development which is more remarkable. The blackthorn, that is one particular black-thorn, which stands in a good, sunny sheltered position, is now – early August – already bearing sloes which are the size of damsons. Honest. Never seen before by this pair of eyes. Moreover, they will be coming on fast, you think, because they are already purpling up. There is, of course, only one use for sloes. Even Jane Grigson in her *Fruit Book* in Penguin acknowledges that the fate for the sloe is to go into gin. Two thirds gin, one third sugar, say some. Less sugar for a liqueur with bite, say others.

You all have your own recipe. But do you have fine, fat, juicy sloes? This may be a purely local phenomenon. Ireland, remember, has a hundred and fifty climates.   Y

A LIQUEUR FROM ACORNS   5 October 1990

"Why are you picking up all those acorns?"

"Because I'm doing your job for you. All you people keep on telling us that this is a bumper year for apples or blackberries or whatever, and I'm going to translate this oak crop into figures. For once I want to know what is the meaning of 'bumper' down to the last hundred or so anyway."

"So you're counting every one, every day?"

"Not quite. I'll miss a lot through birds getting up earlier than I do, and through cars and feet mangling more. And then, the mice get a lot at night. I may miss the odd day altogether, but by and large, I'll have a hard figure for you towards the end of this month."

"How many are there in that bucket?"

"There were thirteen hundred when I stopped for lunch. In the end, of course, I'd like to know from you and your like what damned good acorns are. You can't eat them . . ." He went on gathering.

You can eat them, if stuck. There are records of people eating them in the same way that they eat sweet chest-nuts. They can be roasted as a coffee substitute. This was widely done in Europe during the last war. And one writer of 1849 claimed that when sprouted acorns are treated like malt, "they afford a liquor from which a strong spirit may be distilled". He didn't tell us how, but they probably know down in the west. Didn't Charlie suggest legitimising poitín? There's another idea for him. Oak (sessile) is, after all, our national tree now.   Y

FRUIT OF THE VINE   10 October 1997

We seem to be growing very wine-conscious, though not every one of us can understand all the verbiage that is thrown around about it. There are a few on British television who enjoy attributing flavours to wines which at times soar into surrealism. Or just taking the Mickey out of us. Aromas or flavours from wine could be as far out as Christmas pudding or boot polish. But the Michelin guide to an area of south-west France reassures us: you don't have to be an expert to enjoy wine-tasting, it says. You just need a little curiosity, a lot of passion, and a few hours' practice.

You begin by examining the colour and limpidity of the wine in your glass. It differs with each one. Then you look at the surface to make sure that nothing alien, such as a bit broken off from the cork, is there. Now to the aroma, the fragrance or the smell. Those which are evoked by wine are classified in eleven families, Michelin tells us. There is the animal family (musk, game, fur); the wood family (often arising from contact with new wood); the spice family; the balsamic family (pine, resin, turpentine, incense, vanilla, juniper oil); the chemical family (alcohol, chlorine, sulphur, iodine); the fruit family; the vegetation family; then a very broad one which includes smoke, roasted almonds, baked bread, burning wood, burnt stone, flint, caramel, coffee, cocoa, leather; then there is what is called the ethereal family and fermentation odours (candle, dairy produce, leaven, cider). A wine of some age gives off more exotic and spicy aromas. A wine which has 'nose' is rich in aroma.

You begin the testing, they say, by inhaling, but without shaking the glass, then roll the glass and the aromas are released. There are three stages of the tasting. First is the impact in the mouth, lasting a few seconds, while the wine contacts the tongue. Then, rolling it around in the mouth you can appreciate at more length all the nuances it has. You may then swallow a little of it and spit out the rest.

Well, thanks to the Michelin guide people. This is, as translated with a few blips, from the French. The English language edition doesn't carry it.   Y

BLACKBERRY HUNT   12 October 1987

The hedgerow hunt for free fruit is on and the first weekend of October saw a lot of city children, with an assortment of containers, biking it up the Dublin mountains in the search for blackberries. Southside children are envied because they have 'the mountains' to pick, but the reality is that children on the northside have a far better territory for blackberries and sloes than those south of the Liffey. The hedges of north County Dublin are far more productive and are generally sheltered while the few places where the blackberry brambles establish themselves on the southside lack shelter so that you get a hard, stunted and very 'dry' blackberry.

The higher up the hills or mountain, the drier and harder the fruit: the blackberry is the one fruit which needs a lot of water to swell it out. The elderberry fruit similarly fruits better in lower ground or on hedges with good ditchwater.   H

GLOBAL WARMING OR JOSEPH'S CYCLE?
18 October 1995

Is this global warming in earnest, or could it just be a one-off? Or a cyclical thing, like the seven years of plenty and the seven years of famine which Joseph predicted from the Pharaoh's dream? Anyway, so far it has been great. Latest unexpected bounty is of an abundance of well-ripened, full-skinned sweet chestnuts. You know, the kind you see being roasted over braziers in the streets of Paris. The kind that go to make that most costly and delicious sweet – *marrons glacés*. Anyway, there they were, and who knew how to use them beyond the obvious, and very welcome, roasting? Mrs Beeton gives a recipe for chestnut soup, involving three-quarters of a pound of peeled chestnuts in the stock until they can be mashed up, then they are put through a sieve. Add stock and seasoning, bring to the boil, add cream and you are there.

This chestnut, she says, is the least oily and most farinaceous of all nuts "and therefore the easiest of digestion". She doesn't tell us how to make *marrons glacés*. And there are all sorts of fruitfulness in this the first of our possible seven Josephean years. (If that's the adjective.) The fields and woods seems to be alive, never mind the chemicals sprays, with fungi. One young man gathered four or five pounds of field mushrooms very quickly in Meath, and didn't even touch a huge expanse of Shaggy Ink-caps or Lawyer's Wigs, those torpedo or phallic-shaped scaly jobs, which after a day or two seem to collapse into a black liquid mess. There are several varieties. A mushroom manual notes "edible with caution" of another coprinus, *Coprinus atramentarius*. Which means that if you take alcohol with it you get palpitations, chills and other symptoms "which, however, soon disappear without consequence".

And, of course, you have already had your fill of blackberries, crab apples, sloes, to say nothing of other jam and jelly-making berries like the elder and the rowan. The latter, half apple, half rowan, it is said, making an excellent accompaniment to game and lamb.   Y

WE ARE EXPORTING TREES   11 October 1990

 You may not be aware of it, but among our exports are trees. John Healy, in his magazine *Environment Ireland*, says that Ireland has always done a brisk business in exporting conifers and others. This year apparently, there has been a big demand from Germany for young oaks, as the Germans lost many old oaks in the recent gales. That might seem a bit like exporting coal to Newcastle, but the source of the statement is Gerry de Brit, nurseries manager for Coillte, the State company. And the Coillte nurseries have quite a stock of young plants ready for sale – 40 million no less. And, of course, there are companies in the private sector who are in a big way of business. They would need to be, for, according to Healy, there is a big domestic demand for the same trees because of the generous grants for planting from the EC.

Those oaks now. They may only be a small proportion of the Coillte 40 million trees, but suppose there were one million. Just try to envisage the one million acorns from which these spring. Quite a pile it must be. And how to keep them stored before planting has worried a correspondent from Virginia, County Cavan. He has tried and found they went bad. The official answer in *The Collins Guide to Tree Planting and Cultivation* by H L Edlin says, of acorns, "store . . . in a cool and slightly moist spot, protected from mice, until the spring". If you can find one. Some people are said to store them in the fridge – not the freezer. Others keep them in cool outhouses layered in sand. Again, beware of mice. All these work. If you plant them in the ground directly at this season, mice will certainly get them. Healy's mag bursts with optimism about our forestry future. He has a good, battling piece, too, about fish farms.   Y

HARD AND SOFT   5 October 1988

The argument about hardwoods and softwoods will go on forever in this island. For commercial purposes, conifers are absolutely necessary, we are told. Hardwoods are slower to grow and harder to market. But a correspondent writes, somewhat crossly, to advocate more propaganda for the hardwoods. She points to the fact that an advertisement has appeared in this newspaper for wild cherry trunks of more than 45 centimetres in diameter. Laburnum, she claims, is "a superb, fastgrowing hardwood". Fine. May the gospel spread. But it is worth saying that if you do have good hardwood available, you still need a purchaser. Thus, walnut, we so often read, is most valuable for precious furniture. But a neighbour who is thinking of taking down a splendid specimen for safety reasons has been very disappointed at the price offered. It would do little more than cover the cost of felling.   Y

A MONTH OF TREES 6 October 1997

 We'll be having trees drummed into us all month. Even tonight at, mark you, the James Joyce Centre in North Great George's Street, Dublin, Professor Risteard Mulcahy will be talking as part of Crann's Samhain Festival of Trees.

Looking out the window, the old oak has never had so many acorns, nor so many big ones. They are falling, and not all bearing good news. Writers on trees tell us often that the oak is remarkable in acting as host to something between two and three hundred creatures. This year some of the baddies are thriving. For a remarkable number of the early-falling acorns bear a neat circular hole. Inside, as you cut it with a knife, you find a short passage and at the end a brown mass of what must be eggs. Not all the guests are welcome.

And still the leaves are deep green. A man from the west just arrived says they, too, have massive amounts of acorns, but got no apples this year. The brightest thing in the trees that are still in pots, are the American oaks, sometimes called red, but in this case firmly described by an expert as burgundy in colour. There will be Tree Day after Tree Day. Crann, in a little pamphlet, lists a score and a half of occasions but there will be more.

Some people plant trees as a business, just as other people raise cattle or sell motorcars or pull out your teeth. But trees have a dimension or two of their own. Personalities if you look, sometimes. In cities, we know, they help purify the air. Around houses in the country, they give shelter. For farmers, they are now, with good subsidies available, a part, maybe not big, of their income. But trees are also for looking at. Trees are things of beauty, to wonder at. We had a splendid book from Thomas Pakenham of trees of distinction, age and beauty. Mind you, for age, it would be hard to compete with some of the claims made for trees in France. There is said to be a yew at Calvados which is sixteen centuries old, or an olive tree at Roquebrune in the Alpes Maritimes which might have been planted by the Romans at the beginning of the Christian era.

There are trees associated with great deeds or holy men. But there are also the trees that you, personally like. Maybe climbed in when you were a child. Not necessarily beautiful, but as Robert Bourdu, a writer on trees has it, a "witness" tree, a tree that stands for some event or mark in your life. Or just a lovely thing.   Y

MUST TREES SUFFER FOR AUTUMN BEAUTY?
16 October 1997

Waiting, waiting, waiting for the full autumn colours to get going. We need a bit of consolation. Seems incredible – not one of the many big American oaks has tinted up, and surely, at this time, in other years, they have been in full blaze by now. That's what you get them for. But then you read in an English newspaper that trees must suffer to produce great autumn colours. So says Professor Peter Davies, a British scientist working at Cornell University in New York State. "The more the tree is under physiological stress, the more colour will be developed," he says. "Thus, a dry summer, leading to drought stress, will probably give more colour in the autumn than a moist rainy one." In the forests around New York State, the leaves are now deep, deep yellows, bright oranges, absolute scarlets, deep purples and mauves. British trees look "a bit miserable by comparison".

Back in Ireland: normally those American oaks head the process, but now other trees and shrubs are leading them. The liquidambar is beginning to show purple. The Japanese maple has been going through its lovely routine of yellows and peach colour and is now shedding. Young beech show a bit of movement, but birch look a bit tatty here and there, but our own pedunculate oaks stay massively grave in deep, deep green. Shiny, too.

But one plant announces the season in its usual multi-coloured way. The cornus hedge is going through its unique range of colours. The lovely big leaves – and there are a lot of them, for the hedge stands about ten feet high and is nearly as broad – make their usual start with a mild lemony hue and then go through a symphony of colours ranging from the obvious red to an odd charcoal grey, or is it purple? Streaked, then covering the whole leaf. You walk along the drive and at every yard seem to find other variations. For your own satisfaction and to convince others, you try pressing the leaves between book pages. A few months later you find only a ghost of the leaf as it was. All muted now.

But one very young tree has been forgotten. The tulip tree with its curiously flat-ended leaves has taken on a look of toast, lightly done. But what, says someone, of the first-year American oaks mentioned here a few days ago as being of a burgundy hue. They were in pots. And their brothers and sisters, so to speak, planted directly into the earth are still green. Trees are sent to make us think.   Y

HEDGES: OUR SUBSTITUTE FOR WOODLANDS
21 October 1995

 Hedges. The most striking seen in a long time was in a garden on a roadside, protected by a simple wire mesh fence – and it might have needed some protection, for it was a trimmed, squared-off hedge of arbutus, covered in the rich red and yellow "strawberries". What a temptation to passing children. But this was in a country area of France, not too many people around. You see fine bushes, trees even, of *Arbutus unedo* in Ireland: there may indeed be a lot of garden hedges just as described. Lucky people, green-fingered people. Over much of Ireland, a hedge is something to keep animals in or out. It is a sturdy, utilitarian thing. You could almost say that it is the poor man's woodland. For, added up, the species include about sixty Irish trees, shrubs and woody climbers. So writes Declan Doogue in a book published in 1987, a very handsome volume with excellent contributors. It is called *The Book of the Irish Countryside*.

Hawthorn is, of course, the basis of hedgerow planting over much of the country. Perhaps with some blackthorn, further to discourage break-outs and break-ins. To this may be added brambles, woodbine, ivy (sometimes), and, for decoration, ferns, mosses and woodland flowers. In the eastern parts, and beyond, ash makes up much of its defences. Sometimes allowed to grow into trees of considerable height, more often kept to reachable and cuttable proportion. Wild cherry happens, too. And, according to the area, holly and hazel. In the west you get miles and miles of fuchsia, beautiful, prolific and sheltering, but hardly impenetrable. While Doogue reckons that at least sixty trees, shrubs and woody climbers have now been found in our hedgerows, including some of considerable rarity, nevertheless he warns, you cannot apply the "one species per century" to date the hedgerows, as some in England claim they can. And he gives his reasons.

For internal garden beauty in autumn, try a hedge of the right dogwood. Red American oaks cannot compete for colour. The book was a combined effort of Blackstaff Press Belfast, TownHouse and CountryHouse in Dublin, and was supported by the Kerry Group plc. Price about £15.   Y

QUINCE TIME   21 October 1988

Quinces may disappoint you at first encounter. For, while they bring a lovely, subtle smell into the house (you'd like to say fragrance, but that word has taken a beating recently) and retain a shining yellow skin, they are hard as wood until quite ripe. This year again a friend donated a basket of them. For the first time a couple of the bigger ones were roasted, as with apples, having been cored (with some difficulty – and the hole filled with sugar and raisins). Very good and distinctive. Cook books recommend that you make of them compotes, for sweet and savoury purposes; that you use slices with cooking meats, or make quince gin, as well as the usual employment in apple and other tarts.

If they had no culinary use at all, they are still worth their weight for the scent and the handsome appearance.   Y

RIPENING BERRIES   29 October 1986

 The blackberry and elderberry crops have been spotty this year and late to boot. Home winemakers will have to fall back on the commercial packages of elderberry. In some places the elderberry is still ripening but the berries are not as full and as luscious (to look at, that is) as in other

years. The amateur winemaker is resourceful and between blending and substituting can get out of most tight situations in a poor cropping year.

Those who make rosehip syrup for young children – a dwindling number, we fear – will have good pickings in another week or two. Late like everything else, the October sun did a good job of ripening the main crop but there is a fair amount of green hips still showing. The crop needs a week of night frosts to really make them ready for processing.   H

DODDER DAMAGE   16 October 1986

The trouble with maintaining a river park like the Dodder is that it is linear. And when a disaster like the Dodder flood hits, the damage can be enormous. The other day a father watched his son build sandcastles on the banks of the river near the North's Mills, so great was the displacement of silt and gravel.

This page has had some comments from anglers about the clean-up being done and the way overhanging trees have been hacked. The comment is fair. Equally, however, praise should be given to the Parks Department for the way in which the men have tried to preserve trees, especially weeping willows, which were practically submerged by the floods. Some broke and have been replaced by new trees. Others have been restaked. The hundreds of tonnes of gravel and silt have been bulldozed slowly from the park paths and spread on the football field, which was itself flooded at Orwell. It will be a bigger job to restore the footpaths where the floods lifted the tarmac and washed away some of the banks.   H

THE BIG OLD TREE   18 November 1998

 The last branch of the ancient willow by the river is down. It had been hanging on for some months, a crack near its base of about an inch wide. But it was in a place where none but the owners would walk, and they told the woodman to leave it to nature to do the felling. It would bring down, in falling, a couple of ashes in the plantation, but it would be dangerous to try to meddle with it.

Now only the stump, about eight feet high, stands; but life goes on, for through the bark of the same trunk two willow shoots, one about an inch-and-a-half thick and all of six feet high, are creeping along the old wreck, and eventually they may take over, feeding on the crumbling interior.

When the tree lost its crown, no one remembers, but for years only two huge branches spread along the field edge. The first of them to fall, a couple of years ago, all of three feet in diameter, gave one of the family the idea that slicing it in rings of about six inches thick would make rustic table-tops. One young man brought home two and made an artistic feature with them in his conservatory. Much admired. This latest branch is less thick but uses will be found for it. It was measured at 20 paces, generously thought to be 60 feet. Away back, 30 and more years ago, two little sisters from a nearby farm had their secret place in the platform where the branches spread out. From home, they could not be seen, though only a few score yards away. In later days ducks would sometimes nest there. A century-and-a-half ago, one expert reckons, a local landlord planted willows along much of this little river. Some are still awaiting the next storm, their roots exposed by the rushing waters of winter. H L Edlin tells us in his *Collins Guide to Tree Planting and Cultivation* that *Salix alba* forms a large tree with a rather untidy, wide-spreading crown. It rarely grows erect (this did, more or less) "and it tends to fork low down". This one did. Then he gives us *Salix fragilis*, of which he remarks: "Not a desirable tree for planting save in the rare instances when a patch of damp rough ground must be filled with something that is acceptable to the eye and is virtually indestructible." Well, it is still standing and it stands on what, before the Boyne drainage, was a fine damp spot. It has lovely chestnut-red bark. Still standing, remember.   Y

NEIGHBOUR   30 September 1986

The man everyone seems to be talking about – there he was, easing a dozen or so milking cows along the back road. Age about sixty; from the weather-beaten complexion and the gait, a man who had worked hard in hard conditions. "It's the worst yet," he said, "things have never been as bad." And he would remember the economic war of his father's time. Yes, he was the man everyone is urging or ordering to get out of dairying.

Right. So what's he to do?

Oh, er horticulture; we need more fresh vegetables.

Yes, but the big buyers and distributors need massive supplies. They are not interested in the small men's vegetables.

Well, couldn't he go into trees?

Only one question. What would *you* say if people kept ordering you to stop doing what you do and try something quite different. The problem is one of the big social headaches of this country and this century, and that neighbour on the road deserves more constructive suggestions and less barracking.   Y

A MOAN
23 October 1995

"Haven't seen anyone playing conkers for years and years," he suddenly came out. "All that stuff has gone with television. Do you remember how champions used to have their special recipes for making the chestnut hard and durable. Putting it into the oven with lard on it. First steeping it in vinegar. That used to take up our early months of the autumn term at school. There was a time for everything, a sort of rhythm of boys' and girls' games. When did marbles come in for boys? Spring, was it? Hopscotch was mostly for girls, but lads did it sometimes. Skipping was a girls' thing until athletes discovered that it was a useful part of training for many sports. And spring was for kites. March. Though, with our climate, you could find wind at any time of the year. But these childhood and youth activities had their own rules and rhythms. Spring was when you collected frogspawn to put into a big glass bowl and watch the tadpoles growing. Sometimes in the schoolroom itself, in what used to be called nature study. It would surely be incorrect, to say the least, to do it today. And as for the old practice of bird-nesting, that is not just reprehensible but illegal.

And, of course, where there were good pavements, great ingenuity was exercised in making four-wheeler miniature cars out of planks or halves of packing-cases to run down sloping pavements and alarm the adults. The wheels came from old prams. Making huts out of sheets of whatever, or wigwams out of any kind of cloth was a great occupation.

And there was a season for certain sweets – in the autumn and into the winter, toffee apples. Poor scrawny fruit impaled on unhygenic sticks from, again, the remains of old boxes. No, children today don't have a real adventurous childhood. They play organised sport or watch TV all the time. They don't have half the enjoyment we had."

He had had his say.   Y

DO WE NEED NEWGRANGE MARK 2?
22 September 1990

Will tourists one day run amok on a grand scale and bring us to our senses? You see them arrive in half a dozen buses at an extensive tourist facility. They swarm in their hundreds around the gardens and arboretum. They then pour out into the café and shop area. There is standing room only for many. The souvenirs, the postcards, are bought in quantities: empty tins of soft drinks roll around under the café tables. They depart, and, if as many came in again immediately, there wouldn't be much to eat or drink or buy. Some day, somewhere will there be a revolution when a visiting horde to some city or province finds that there are not enough golf courses, or old stone memorials or castles or museums or eating and drinking and sleeping facilities and that all their urges to spend and enjoy are frustrated? Will they fall on the offending place and destroy it? It's not entirely fanciful. And the lesson is that tourist venues should never oversell themselves. A few score or even few hundred disgruntled private visitors can be relied on to do little more than grumble, but the organised planeloads and busloads of today are another matter. We ought to know, because nearly all of us are tourists of this kind.

Historic sites such as Newgrange must be one of the chief worries of any tourist organisation. In France, the Lascaux cave with its wonderful animal paintings was long ago closed. Now they have constructed a Lascaux mark 2 nearby. And the paint on it is suffering too, from human breath and the effects of so much throughput. Have we thought of building a dummy Newgrange, exactly to scale? Or will the original survive at all as the years go by?   Y

INTRUDERS   11 September 1998

 What creature is this? "Worldwide distribution greater than any other mammal excepting man." It is the common house mouse – *Mus musculus*, according to *The Collins Field Guide to Mammals of Britain and Europe*, and the book was dipped into in the hope that it might be in the remit of the authors to tell us how to keep mice at bay or to discourage them, for we are now heading into the "Months of the Mouse". Are these invaders who somehow come in behind the drawers in the kitchen and chew through your plastic bags of pasta, or romp around an unoccupied bedroom, even distributing their dirt behind the pillows, are they house mice that have come back from their summer outings in the fields and ditches, or are they field or wood mice that live and breed in the area around, and just come in from the cold from autumn to spring? They hope, for not many of them survive the deadly lure of melted chocolate as bait on a trap, which they can't snatch away without bringing the executioner's chop down on themselves.

It would be preferable to keep them out in the first place – by deterring them with some odour (cat is not feasible in this case). Away back it was read somewhere that the green leaves of walnut trees were a sure repellent. Fortunately, a big tree was available, and drawers and corners and the space underneath bookcases and suchlike were stuffed with the greenery. To no avail. Maybe it even pleased them – raw material for the nest, though, on the rare occasions that you come across one in the boiler room, it is made from chewed-up newspaper.

For it is written in this book that *Mus musculus* – if that is what this intruder is – may, if food is sufficient, produce five to ten litters of four to eight young per year. This Collins book mentions 17 varieties of mouse world-wide; Fairley in his *An Irish Beast Book* tells of the term bean mouse given to the field mouse, for they have been known to carry off every single bean or pea planted in a garden near Belfast. Thompson, the Northern naturalist, summed up enigmatically: "Traps made of a single brick were successfully used for their destruction." Then there was the singing mouse. That is for another day.   Y

DO ENGLISH OTTERS SMELL SWEETER?
20 September 1995

The otter is certainly, as James Fairley states in his *An Irish Beast Book*, "the most elusive of Irish mammals". In spite of which, film-makers such as Éamon de Buitléar, Michael Viney and David Cabot have managed to give us delightful pictures of them gambolling on the sandy beaches of the west. But you can live on a river for half a lifetime, regularly find signs of their nightly presence, and yet get no more than an occasional glimpse of the animal. It is, however, a creature of habit, and you will find its marks in the same places year after year. They are paw marks in the mud or sand, but, more often spraints (their faeces) with which they seem to mark out their territory.

These spraints are usually about three inches or four long, dark in colour, black or greeny black, though a spraint which is regularly placed on a rock in the middle of the river rapidly becomes dried out so that it looks not unlike a long cigarette ash – except that you can see the tiny crayfish bones. They mostly have crayfish bones in this particular part. Now for the ticklish rather malodorous bit. James Fairley – and remember that he is a professional zoologist – notes: "The smell is absolutely diagnostic: a strange musty, fishy odour, which, once smelled, is never forgotten." Yes diagnostic, i.e. distinctive, but the otters on the eastern side of the country seem to differ in odour, or, at least the otters on this particular waterway. For two observers here argue as to whether the smell is of liquorice, or treacle, or cinnamon, though very strong and pungent. Maybe with a little fishy smell, though that, perhaps, has faded. You would need the nose and other equipment of the wine writer to do it justice.

And then the man who wrote the marvellous *Tarka the Otter* gives his contribution. In *A Clear Water Stream* (in south-west England) spraints "most curiously smelled sweet, with a scent not unlike violets". Exclaimer!   Y

WILD BOARS AND SONG THRUSHES
30 September 1995

 One predator the Irish farmer doesn't have to deal with – yet – is the wild boar. Now, in the south of France on the Mediterranean slopes of the Corbières range of mountains, the place "swarms with" these animals, according to a wine writer in a French magazine. And the boars particularly like a grape which goes to make a well-known "good red rustic wine" known as Fitou. The wine growers later have their revenge, when the shooting season opens, and they go after the boars with enthusiasm. Full revenge, indeed, for nothing goes better with roast or stewed boar – or hare or deer for that matter – than Fitou wine. This writer, by the way, tells us the "nose", as the experts say, is of "broom, red berries, burning-hot stones, wood, etc.". You'd like to know what the "etc." embraces. A dearer version of the wine has a nose of fine gameyness with suggestions of tobacco and spice, according to the writer.

The same magazine gave an overview of hunting prospects for the season just begun. Out of the seven separate hunting regions the wild boar was "very good", that is plentiful, in four. In the other three it was "good".

At this time of year the local newspapers and the specialist magazines resound with the booming of gunfire. But there are other methods than the gun. One magazine details the, "traditional" and legal, method of catching song thrushes (for eating) with a horse-hair snare. This is special to the Ardennes region. Song thrush in French is touching – *grive musicienne.*   Y

WILD BOAR   13 October 1988

The opening of the shooting season in France gets lavish coverage in the press, said the traveller. Opening dates vary, of course, according to region, but the last 13 departments came on stream on 2 October. Most of the game is familiar to us (and what the French consider game we do not always consider game – rabbit and pigeon). Otherwise there is pheasant, hare, duck, grey and red partridge, various four-footed fliers and, absolutely beyond our acquaintance, the wild boar.

Some animal, that wild boar! It may weigh as much as 120 kilos and runs like a fast tank. Some day, someone is bound to try to introduce or re-introduce the wild boar here. In England they are being farmed in fenced woodland by at least one entrepreneur. He has striven to breed them as close to the fully wild-blood European animal as possible. They forage on roots, nettles, beechmast, chestnuts, crab-apples and acorns, according to a note in the London *Independent*. They are raised, not for shooting, but for butchering. The meat, it says, is lean but succulent and "sweetly gamey". Smoked hams after the Westphalian manner are produced and the sausages are "superlative". Ignominious fate, that, for such a terror.   Y

BADGER BLAME   23 October 1986

If patriotism is the last refuge of a scoundrel then blaming the poor badger for the national failure to get on top of bovine TB is about as low. For all the billions we have spent on eradicating TB in cattle – and we started on that long before we started on wiping out ignorance by the later introduction of "free" education – it is still with us, the original agricultural gravy train.

Farmers blamed vets and vets blamed farmers and then both blamed the Department of Agriculture. Our membership of the EEC with a floor price under beef and milk now about to end, is changing things and the old recriminating dialogue as well. Now it is the badger which is copping it as the bogeyman. Cattle with the disease suffer it in areas where there are no known badgers. Badgers are not that plentiful in, say, the west of Ireland where TB has been worst. If the badger is to be cast as the villain of the piece, some would say the two-footed variety must carry a fair bit of the blame first.   H

NEXT FOR SLAUGHTER?   19 October 1995

TB can affect any animal, it is believed. Our Department of Agriculture, according to a report in this newspaper, plans to kill 4,000 badgers to study the impact on bovine TB levels. But there are other field animals which will have some contact with cattle in the pastures by leaving their droppings around which, in turn, may be nosed by browsing herds. And pass on infection? So does the Department, with its death squads, move on next to the hare, the rabbit, the squirrel, the fox, the mink, the otter, the pine marten? And, in certain areas, the deer? One shouldn't treat this subject with levity, the Department may say. But the scepticism which the badger-killing programme arouses comes from the fact that the TB-eradication scheme, or one TB eradication after another, seems to be a staple of Irish life.

Is it all the badger's fault? If so, why did we not hear of the devastation wreaked by this animal decades ago? And it would be well for any spokesman for this badger-extermination scheme to tell us the other reasons why we still have so much bovine TB. How much is due to care-lessness or bad farming practices? Are such killing schemes affirmed by the whole veterinary world? By university specialists? And above all, does the cow give TB to the badger more than the badger gives it to the cow? In the latest test where 2,000 badgers were "removed" in the words of the newspaper report, 7.5 per cent were found to have gross TB lesions. Compared with what in cattle?

Mrs Angela Tinney of the Badgerwatch Association claims that the badger is being made a scapegoat. What is needed, she says, is a new test for bovine TB. Most of us just don't know. There are an estimated 200,000 badgers in the Republic. How long will it take us to work through and kill them all? And what animal comes next for the slaughter?

And, yes, everyone in the country is aware of the vital part in our economy played by the cattle trade. All the more reason that everything about it should be open to scrutiny at every step.   Y

SLOW, SPINY, SURE   3 November 1998

The bonfire is going out of fashion – except in the North, that is, specifically on July 11th and on whatever day they burn Lundy in Derry, if they still do in these transition days. In suburban gardens down here, you hardly ever get that delicious smell of woodsmoke from burning leaves. Probably there is a law against it, though most gardeners have learned the value of turning their clippings or cuttings into compost. Anyway, the same seems not to hold in Britain; for a letter to *Field* asks its readers to make a careful last-minute check of their autumn bonfires for, to the hedgehog, piles of leaves are the very thing for their winter sleep. And every year, claims the letter, many of them meet a painful death by fire. Readers are asked to check before igniting the pile. "Hedgehogs are the gardener's friend," goes the letter, "please look after them."

Well, we know they eat slugs and snails and take it for granted that they are in no way destructive. There is a British Hedgehog Preservation Society in Shropshire. To many people the hedgehog is the flattened mass you see on roads, mostly motorways, and not so often alive and ambling around your garden at a rate which has been calculated as averaging three metres a minute and, as someone said "a top speed only a tortoise could appreciate". Others interpret this top speed as perhaps 30 to 40 metres per minute. Not bad.

In spite of their having some 6,000 to 7,000 prickles, there are predators who can overcome them and eat them – badgers, apparently, foxes, and pine martens. Mind you, they climb well and swim well. They have, according to the books – never come across it – a behaviour known as self-anointing. The team which gave us the tortoise comparison believes they do it – flicking gobs of foamy saliva over its own spines – when stimulated by a novel scent, and this is illustrated by a photograph of a hedgehog face to face with a toad (*Natural*

History Magazine, July/August, 1998. "Thirteen Ways of Looking at a Hedgehog" by Chris Reiter and Gina C Gould).

The animal is mostly nocturnal. Hence Thomas Hardy: "Some nocturnal blackness, mothy and warm/When the hedgehog travels furtively over the lawn."

And symbol of single-mindedness. Isaiah Berlin refers to Dante, Plato and Hegel as hedgehogs for their devotion to "one big thing".   Y

MICE MOVE 1,000 ACORNS IN A NIGHT
23 November 1998

Rats have the reputation of being cute and cunning. Not so mice. After all, you might think, they get the chop so easily by eating the bits of cheese you put in those primitive traps. Now rats: one brown villain is so agile that he can climb a tree, shinny head-first down a four-foot perpendicular wire from which a bird feeder is suspended and, when he has had his fill, or as much as he can be bothered to strive for, runs effortlessly up again. But a new respect for mice emerges as you read through a cutting sent by a friend. It is from an old *National Geographic Magazine* and concerns the habits of mice in woods on Long Island. In summer the mice, called white-footed, subsist mostly on insects, but as autumn comes on, they begin to store small caches of one to three acorns, called scatter hoards, against the coming cold weather.

An odd thing now. The article runs: "Never satisfied, they move the hoards around each night. The mice rely on smell to locate the acorns underground – seemingly unaware of where they last dug and thus constantly steal from one another. When Bob Unnasch [presumably one of the team] buried a thousand marked acorns, mice had moved every one by the next morning." If it wasn't written in a prestigious journal like the *National Geographic*, you would find that hard to believe. Is it that they are constantly shifting their larder for stability? Neither the mice nor the acorns looked very big, according to a photograph. Some acorns from big trees are small: it's the kind of oak they are. The article further tells us that more than eighty North American birds and mammals include fresh acorns in their diet. (Some humans used to, also, in hard times, ground and mixed with flour.)

The article goes on to tell us what we all know: many of our oak trees are probably the result of a small cache of acorns buried by, perhaps, a squirrel or a jay, and forgotten. Not so often do acorns which fall and begin to sprout under the carpet of autumn leaves, survive. On one unusual year, acorns fallen into a lawn which was more moss than grass, and seldom cut, suddenly in a wet early warmth, shoved their way through and presented the owners with about a hundred useful seedlings. Some are now trees thirty feet high.   Y

STING MONTH   8 October 1987

 October is stinging time where the unwary are concerned. As fruit crops ripen the wasps especially fall on soft or damaged pears or apples, and windfalls are a particular attraction to them. The unsuspecting can pick up a fruit and find, too late, that the wasps in possession do not like the human intruder and will rush to attack him or her. The wasp can sting several times, unlike the wild bee who gets only one chance, the bee-sting having a barb which prevents him withdrawing the sting.   H

FIFTY VERY LONG TAILS   20 October 1995

Our bird-feeding correspondent rang up in a high state of excitement to announce that she had just seen a huge flock of long-tailed tits descend on her array of feeding devices – the biggest flock ever.

"They kept hopping from one branch to another, but I'm sure I counted up to fifty." Well, she obviously had had a big visitation and it wasn't easy to count, what with all the dashing to and fro of the birds. But fifty? Then you turn to David Cabot's recent *Irish Birds* and read: "In the autumn family parties come together to form roaming bands of up to 50 birds which work the woods and hedgerows for insect food." And, in this case, for the soft target of monkey-nuts.

It is a tiny bird, black, white and pinkish, with a thin tail which is long to the point of caricature. When you learn that the bird builds a nest which is bottle-shaped or egg-shaped, with a hole near the top, you wonder how the tail fits in. One bird book tells us that when brooding, the parent holds the tail erect over its back; and the top of the head and the end of the tail effectively block the entrance.

If you've ever seen one of its nests, you've seen a miracle of craftsmanship. Craftsbirdship. For it is light in weight and soft to the touch, and consists of moss, cobwebs, lichens and is lined, it is claimed, with between one and two thousand small, soft feathers. Anyway, if you see the flocks around now, mark, above all, those ridiculous tails. For some reason – they make you laugh. One of God's more humorous touches. Both Cabot and Christopher Moriarty (Mercier, *A Guide to Irish Birds*) give the Irish as *Meanntán fada*. The English have literally dozens of pet names for it, as given by Francesca Greenoak in the Penguin *All the Birds of the Air*.

For example, from the shape of its nest, Jack-in-the-Bottle; Bottle Tom; Feather Poke; Oven Builder and about twenty more. These characters ought to be, and maybe are, in Shakespeare.   Y

SIX DEAD AFTER DRINKING BINGE – STARLINGS
27 October 1995

 Half a dozen dead birds were scattered over the Place de la Synagogue in Geneva, records a local paper. Lying on their back, beaks gaping. They showed no signs of wounding or injury and one and all were fine and plump. What had happened to them? This Place, with its eight big plane trees, is one of their favourite roosting places. Hundreds gather each night. Patrick Jacot, director of the Ornithological Rehabilitation Center, said that he knew of this kind of death well, having already come across the same situation. They were dead, he said, from a binge, a drinking binge. Alcohol. You may ask how that could be. Patrick Jacot explained. The specially fine weather did wonders for the grapes, which had a very high sugar content. Very ripe grapes then fall, singly or otherwise, and quickly ferment. Hence the intoxication and death of the birds. For they seek their food far from their roosting places. Maybe, he says, within a radius of 40 kilometres, and thus can do a round of the greatest vineyards in turn. The wonderful aerial ballets which they have been carrying out, probably won't last much longer. For they are on their way, at this season, to the warmer winter climates of the Midi or Spain or North Africa. All this in the *Tribune de Genève*.

And our bird expert reports that the aerobatics of the starlings give rise to spectacular feats by falcons, especially by a "superb peregrine" which flies along at tree-top height, seizes his prey and takes it off to the aerials over the big post office on the Rue Mont Blanc, in mid city, and enjoys his starling dinner in peace. From time to time another falcon, a hobby, tries to cut in on his prey, but in vain.

The article says that the starling is one of the most intelligent of birds. A historian, persecuted by Napoleon III, taught his starling to cry: "Down with the Emperor". And what about Laurence Sterne?   Y

ON ONE LEG   15 October 1986

Are seagulls more prone than other birds to losing a leg? In a flock of about two dozen birds on Keel beach the other evening no fewer than seven were one-legged birds. There was no question of mistaking them as standing on one foot because when they came to lift-off they had to hop to get airborne, when it was very clear that they were a leg short. Blackbirds in Achill for the last few years have also appeared with one foot missing.

One wonders whether it is a malformation – a mutation – due to chemicals or a genetic effect from some form of pollution. Mercury pollution, for instance, can produce such an effect on both birds and animals, as well as in humans.   H

TEN YARDS OF WONDER   7 September 1989

 Young people today enjoy holidays in the sun, where they need never worry about the sea because the hotel or summer camp has a swimming pool: sometimes two or three. But it's hard to beat the real thing. Only a few days before the holidays ended, two young boys were surveyed as, under the eye of someone who may have been their grandmother, they quartered a small patch of Irish beach, oblivious of the twitcher standing nearby.

First they came on a small, dead green crab; then what might have been part of a starfish. They examined closely a thin piece of a bird skeleton, hardly more substantial than a scrap of white paper. There was a slab of cork, probably from one of the nets bobbing just off shore; a small bottle, no message inside. They compared the colours of the stones at the top of the tideline. Red. Could it be a piece of brick, smoothed down by the action of the shingle? There were black pebbles and white pebbles, the colours of the cliff on the other side of the road; there were flints, for it was the Antrim coast. Could this piece be a primitive scraper such as their teacher had told them about? And they drew patterns on the sand with it. There were two kinds of seaweed, and under one patch a small splashing fish. They dug a hole in the sand for it and filled it with water. Their noses were seldom more than a few inches from the level of the sand. Only thing was, they would hardly have swum. It was deadly cold.   Y

POISON IN SEA SHALLOWS   8 August 1998

Never mind the dangers lurking in the depths of the sea – here's one from the shallows which gave a fright and a wound to a young bather and his family. It was on a beach near Murvey, outside Roundstone. The boy was wading through the shallows to the deeper water when he felt a sharp prick or sting. He saw nothing of his assailant. Now, if near rocks in those parts, you just might stand on the sharp prickles of a sea urchin, which go deep into your foot. Or maybe jellyfish sting at times. But he saw nothing and felt only the sharp sting.

Soon afterwards his big toe began to swell, and then his whole foot. To enormous size. There was no possibility of him putting a shoe on that foot. Fortunately, his father was at hand and in no time he was brought to a doctor. There he was given some antihistamine, a painkiller and a small ice-bag. He was told that he had been pricked by the spines on the back of a weever fish. And the doctor concerned sees a lot of the results in the holiday season. By next morning the swelling had gone down, but it was a day or so before all the evidence had disappeared.

The boy was fortunate in that his father was so alert, for in a book on sea fishes, published by Frederick Warne of London and New York, the particular weever fish concerned is described as "capable of inflicting a poisonous wound, a wound sufficiently venomous to cause great pain and, in certain circumstances, real illness to human beings, old and young alike". The more common (and also the more venomous) species is the one our young friend came across. It is the lesser weever, *Trachinus vipera*, which stays around the coasts, especially where, as the book states, "the shallow sandy seabed is conducive to the breeding of shrimps". The weever fish lies half-buried in the sand and snaps at any shrimps that pass by. So, if you're paddling in shallow, sandy water, even on your way to the depths, it's wise to kick the sand before you, to scare them off.

The poison is contained in a sack at the base of the first dorsal fin; these fins are grooved, and so the poison shoots up when the spines are stood on. The fish itself is about seven inches long, a dangerous, ugly-looking thing.   Y

OLD AGE KILLS TROUT   9 August 1986

 From Calais to Amiens and the Somme there seems to be an abundance of water: rivers, streams, marshes, duck-ponds, and the odd stretch that might be termed a lake. On a recent Sunday, practically everywhere there was water there was a car, a man, and the man had in all cases, a rod. Some had an umbrella to keep the sun away.

The concentration of Frenchmen – and sometimes Frenchwomen – where fish are to be found is remarkable to the Irish angler. Last Sunday, for example, on a medium-sized midland lake, you had nearly to go looking for the rods.

All of which makes sense of the theory, propounded by a fisheries expert, that there are not enough anglers in Ireland and that as a consequence far too many trout die of old age. Imagine, tens of thousands every year covering the bottom of your lake with their bones.   Y

SHARKS!   4 August 1986

The salmon men of Achill, dogged with losses caused by seals, ran into another and more damaging problem this season. A heavy run of blue and porbeagle sharks fouled their nets and did "tremendous damage". The porbeagle ran to 200 pounds and better with the blues making 150 pounds. Unfortunately for the sea anglers who frequent Clew Bay, one of Europe's richest fishing grounds for anglers, both species are out of reach of the boats which are restricted to an eight-hour competitive fishing day. The run is some twenty miles off-shore. A number of big sharks identified as makos were also taken: this species is not common in these waters. Clew Bay holds the national record for both blue shark and porbeagle shark. One boat claims that a whale got so entangled in the salmon nets it towed the trawler for six nautical miles, surfacing regularly to blow before the net finally broke. The main run of the porbeagle remain under the 100-pound mark but do irreparable damage to salmon nets.

There is a regular continental market for porbeagle steaks but the salmon men considered the smaller fish were not marketable. A greater familiarity with the French and Spanish fish markets where 30- or 40-pound tope and porbeagle are exhibited and sold in steaks cut to individual demand might have encouraged them to bring the sharks in to the co-op.   H

SMOKED EEL FOR PREFERENCE   20 August 1990

 A Paris gourmet says that he prefers Irish smoked eel to Irish smoked salmon – and he likes the salmon a lot. Not many of us would agree, but this is a man who has eaten in all the best restaurants in most of the best countries. He may be seeing more of this favourite smokie in the future, for an expert on the eel, Dr Christopher Moriarty, tells us that eels are now more abundant on the Shannon system than on Lough Neagh, which is saying a lot. Lough Neagh has always been the big eel exporter. The Shannon now produces 100 tonnes of the fish, while Lough Neagh has 700 tonnes. The current population of eels in Shannon, it has now been found, is at least double the population in the northern Lough and may even be four times its numbers. So Shannon has to exploit that resource. Dr Moriarty estimates that the produce could amount to 1,000 tonnes. Eels you eat, by the way, are between ten and 20 years old; several times the age of your average salmon on the plate. All this in John Healy's magazine *Environment Ireland*, July–August issue, and much more on trees, on shooting, on coastal rights, not forgetting, as you might imagine, a fair dash of politics.

Footnote to all those folk stories about eels. Mrs Beeton quotes one Sir John Hawkins in a comment on Izaak Walton's famous tome on angling. Hawkins drained a canal from which he had missed some young ducks. Huge eels wriggled in the mud, and when opened "there were found in their stomachs the undigested heads of the quacking tribe which had become their victims".   Y

COCKLES AND MUSSELS AND RAZORFISH
5 September 1998

Razorfish, or razor clams as some call them, are, according to a "top chef" quoted in a recent *Country Life*, "positively the smartest shellfish around this summer". They are best grilled, he thought. This followed the huge impression made on the English press when a lot of people were cut when walking barefoot on a Devon beach. "Razorfish Slash 800 on Beach" ran one headline. The London *Times* explained that the razorfish (so called because the shell, about eight inches long and an inch across, resembles an old cut-throat used in shaving) normally burrow in sand that is too far out for paddlers, but that unusually low spring tides meant that holidaymakers could go much farther out and thus stumbled on the shells.

The razors used to be taken mostly for bait, according to a local fisherman, and the method was that used here – putting a little salt in the breathing hole they left when the tide was out. Up came the unfortunate. To fish for them on a commercial scale you would need to dredge, which would not be good for other marine life. Or for birds. Interesting that chef's remark, for it seems that up to then they were neglected widely at home but sold abroad – to Spain where they are used in paella. The Japanese, also, like them. What fish do they not like?

A supplier to the London fish market is quoted as saying that the trouble with them is that they are "sporadically seasonal". That may be why Destry's of Clifden, County Galway, who, a month or two ago, had the razors on the menu, told an enquirer last weekend that they hadn't had them for some time. Not only are they said in London to be sporadically seasonal, but they are also inconsistent in texture and flavour, according to this London supplier. But the idea is alive and running. Mark Hix, executive chef at the London Ivy and Caprice restaurant, told *The Times* he had been experimenting with them for years.

They need, according to him, to be cooked for a minimum amount of time. Take them out of the shells, cut the toughest bits away, put them back in the shells and macerate them with some herbs and breadcrumbs. He believes that, in spite of drawbacks, they have a future in restaurants. No mention of any of the aphrodisiac attributes claimed for the oyster.   Y

YOU THINK WE HAVE POLLUTION? 17 September 1998

 We have our own problems of pollution, much of it attributed to an overdose of fertiliser being washed into rivers and lakes, sometimes to slurry – often to slurry, perhaps. But we are not alone. There is an amazing statistic on the subject in a French fishing and hunting magazine. "Heavy Pollution of Rivers in Brittany", the heading is something of an understatement. The article runs as follows: It is in summer and particularly in the month of August, when the rivers are at their lowest, that pollution coming from animal rearing makes itself most felt in the rivers of Brittany. In about 7 per cent of the national territory, there are concentrated 3 million cattle, but more significantly 15 million pigs and more than 100 million fowl from which the waste (to put it politely, and because the word used in French, *déjections*, isn't in the dictionary to hand) represents every day 200,000 cubic metres, which according to the article, is the equivalent of that from a population of 40 million humans. (Can they be right? France's population all told is about 60 million.)

Anyway, the short article goes on to say that profiting from the Mad Cow Disease scare and an infatuation on the part of consumers with pigmeat and poultry, the industrial farmers of Brittany have in the past few years gone more and more for concentration of effort, to the detriment of the quality of the product and at the same time the quality of the environment. Fishermen and farmers are often in dispute about water quality, but these figures, if 100 per cent accurate, make our own waters seem as pure as a crystal well. Short, because there's nothing more to say. We will await the next issue of the magazine concerned.

The *Meath Chronicle* tells its readers that a pollution early-warning system is to be introduced for the Boyne and Liffey systems. And the monitoring/management will be developed along with substantial investment in sewage treatment infrastructure in the catchments concerned. There will be more about this. And did someone say: "About time"?   Y

WHEN DO SALMON EAT?   18 September 1995

The odd query remains about the salmon story. We know that when it migrates from its natal river, it goes out into the Atlantic, maybe far north, and in due course comes back to its own river. Unerringly. By smell? Maybe that is proven. And one thing that most seem to accept, is that when the fish reaches its own river, it does not, from the very day of entry, eat. Why then does it snap at an artificial fly? At a metal lure? Or even at a fake prawn? Just from irritation some reckon. Or for sport. And it may be that, in fact, some errant salmon do take an odd nibble of real nourishment, or more than a nibble. Are we sure of all that? And there is a rider to it. In years when salmon have to wait an inordinate length of time, perhaps months before they can ascend the river and fulfil their natural function of reproduction, do they never, growing weaker, take to eating again? A friend recently caught a salmon at the mouth of a river in the west. It was in a dreadful condition, he said, thin, slatty, even, as if it had spawned. He put it back, of course. But would not the mind-set which drives the fish to overcome all difficulties in order to reach the spawning grounds and ensure the continuity of the species, would not that same mind-set encourage it to keep in condition to do so, by eating?

Has an angler found that this regimen of not eating has been seriously broken? As this is written, friends are still waiting for the floods that will make the rivers viable and release this pent-up energy, waiting in the sea around. And they wonder if those fish that get up the river will be in condition to breed successfully.

Flash from Ballycroy area of Mayo. "Hooked one salmon and lost him. But on yesterday and today we gathered fifteen pounds of mushrooms each day, including chanterelles. Will have to make chutney. There go the pips. Cheerio."   Y

A NOVEL FISH FARM   25 September 1997

 Fish farms are not always those circular or rectangular floating rafts which we see out in the bays and river mouths of Ireland. We also have inland fish farms. An Irish woman who spent a few days on the west coast of France recently writes that she wandered around fish farms on the delta of the Leyre river at Arcachon (southwest of Bordeaux) on the Atlantic coast, farms which had been there since the beginning of this century. "Those I saw melted perfectly into the environment; edged by trees and shrubs – rather murky waters – and visited by herons, egrets and other water birds."

But, she says, they are still in business, though not on the scale of earlier days. It all came about this way. Originally this territory was a salt marsh and at high tide, the fry of various fish would pour in. If they could survive in such water, it seemed to some enterprising people that provision should be made for their retention and their cultivation. All you had to do was go to arrange the territory and its waters so that the fish which came in were kept in by dams or dykes with sluice-gates to control flow of water and movement of fish.

Not all fish could flourish in such conditions, often with great fluctuations of temperature and availability of oxygen. The eel could survive, mullet, too. Also a fish called *bar* in French and, according to a document issued by the EU, meaning in English bass. Hmm. All this caused alarm among the coastal fishermen who saw their employment endangered. In fact, it is stated over-fishing was simply the cause of any apparent drop-off.

Meanwhile, the farm or captive fish became mature, according to the species, in from three to nine years. Some of these ponds or lakes must have been extensive, for they used big nets to take them in. At times eels were harpooned. There seemed to be no question of artificial feeding. Sometimes the vegetation went wild and had to be raked or otherwise cleared out. From the 1950s on, costs went up and in some cases nature is taking over. But there is still production on a smaller scale, and, of course, this makes it all more attractive for visitors. In fact, the delta of the Leyre is now likely to become a tourist draw as it never was before. And fish production goes on. And, as far as can be gathered, no artificial feeding is needed.   Y

"A FEW OULD PIGS, A FEW OULD TROUT"
12 October 1989

"All that fuss about a few ould trout," the pigman says. "Sure I give employment and feed the people. What do those anglers do for anyone?" But, of course, it's not about a few ould trout. It's more about a few ould human beings and very young human beings. For the spew from the pigs can penetrate from the river into which it is injected, often cautiously and calculatedly via ditches and rivulets down into the water table; and so to pollute wells and, farther downstream maybe, reservoirs. Don't talk to him about good citizenship or patriotism. Try to educate his successors. He is a type, you would hope, that is becoming obsolete.

A friend was asked to give a talk to a country school about the local rivers and fields and the ecology gener- ally. A good idea. But should not care for the environ- ment, or creation, or whatever you call it, come in at the child from various angles and at regular intervals? Should it not be a part of the teaching of geography, of history, of the learning of the Irish language, the English language? So you want to start with the training of teachers? Yes.   Y

PRODUCING MONSTERS
24 October 1997

 What is a transgenic salmon, for God's sake? It is a "genetically modified fish implanted with genes from other fish to increase growth rates". Obvious, you may say. And we have heard of growth-promoters in cattle, haven't we? And in America these genetically engineered processes have produced smolts – the young salmon that go down to the sea about a year after hatching in the river, some- times two years – in three months and adult salmon in 12 to 18 months. "A time-saving of 600 to 700 per cent." The fish, writes Michael Wigan in the English *Field* for November, "must grow almost as you watch them". With some understatement he adds that "this is possibly disturbing for the consumer".

A land-based hatchery in Scotland has experimented with this technology under government licence. Tough containment measures, we are told, were in place "because of the unquantifiable dangers of any escape". He refers to a report, *Leaping in the Dark*, which "tracks with determination the route by which, weaving through the imperfect net of controls, transgenic production commercially could become a reality, if not in Scotland then in a competing reproducer state. There are no controls for example to prevent transgenic ova being exported outside the US." Open sea farming, he decides, is a better idea.

All this arises after salmon farming in Scotland has begun on east-coast rivers, having, in the eyes of many, devastated the river angling of the west coast where salmon farms are found at almost every river outlet. The writer instances the short, broad River Shiel, which used to give 300 sea trout and 150 salmon from each bank. Now it is virtually fishless. And, more ominous, electrofishing in the upper reaches yields nothing. There is no next generation of migratory fish.

The big point for the British government is that salmon farming yields 1,110 jobs. And, of course, it is argued that salmon angling is practised by privileged people, while salmon farming gives real jobs. All the lines to which we have grown accustomed in light of our own decline. All the unwillingness to look squarely at the evidence of mordant sea-lice chewing the heads off the young smolts. Some people don't or won't see what their eyes take in. Open sea farming, according to the writer in *Field*, gives the best of both worlds. Thought: is it possible that the disappearing sea trout and the arrival of the salmon farms is a matter of pure coincidence? Some appear to believe it. Not anglers.   Y

LIVELY TROUT   20 October 1986

Despite the enormous damage done to the Dodder riverbanks and the bed of the river itself, trout life does not seem to be troubled.

On a quiet mid-October evening just under the water-fall below Orwell Bridge – and with a pair of ducks working overhead – five trout fed steadily on nymphs, just bubbling the water as they sucked the young flies-to-be split seconds before they burst through the membrane to escape into the evening air.

On the stretch from there to North's the run of the Dodder has changed enormously and there are now several fine-looking stretches with ready-made spawning redds set up for the spawning fish. The sea trout will come up later and may use them.   H

BAY MACKEREL   24 October 1986

 How the year fares for anglers on lake and river is always well documented in our papers which report good catches and good fishing conditions. Dublin Bay is the angling haunt of thousands of anglers between the pier fishermen, the shore and beach casters as well as the estuary boatmen who also fish the bay itself. The year 1986 will go into the books as the poorest one for mackerel. Our yawl is out each Saturday and the skipper reports it was a bad year all round, lightened only by the discovery of a good drop for plaice on the way to the Kish. The mackerel were always "promisers"; you picked up one or two and reckoned they were the outriders of the shoals. It was a year of straggling outriders and the shoals never showed.

On the other hand one friend reported the taking of a magnificent 26-pound cod off Dalkey, almost on the shoreline: it fell to a local boat angler. It was a year with a bigger proportion of on-shore east winds than one usually gets on the Bay. The Greystones ridge, on the other hand, fished very well for most of the season.   H

WOOD MAGIC   28 November 1986

 There are plenty of people going around at this time of year selling logs. Many of the logs will be green and sappy. If you work a year or so ahead, you can store them until they dry out. If not, the only safe buy is ash. If it's ash, you can throw it on the fire or into the stove from day one. John Stewart Collis, author of that splendid book *The Worm Forgives the Plough*, had a cult feeling for the ash, not only for its beauty and grace but for its practical, burning qualities.

"One of the reasons why I am especially attracted by ash is because it has so much fire in it. That may not be the proper way to put it; but it certainly seems as if flame resides inside the wood. When we have put fire to wood, what do we see? We do not see the fire devouring the wood as it goes along: we see the wood becoming fire, 'bursting into flames' as we say . . . Of all the receptacles of fire in the world, wood is the most famous and our debt to it without measure. It is easy to understand how the ancient Aryans regarded trees as the storerooms of heat and that the sun itself was periodically recruited from the fire which resided in the sacred oak. And of all trees, ash becomes fire best."   Y

WOOD FIRES   5 December 2000

If you're thinking sentimentally of burning logs – as distinct from a big yule-log at Christmas time – and haven't done anything about it, you're probably too late. People come around, particularly in the suburbs of Dublin, offering cut logs about this time, but they're likely not to have been seasoned. And in spite of wise words in the old rhymes, there is no wood that can be burned successfully just after it is cut.

In an often-quoted rhyme, the last four lines read:
"But ash logs, all smooth and grey
Burn them green or old,
Buy up all that come your way,
They're worth their weight in gold."

That's a good selling line but you might be disappointed if the ash has just been cut. No doubt you can blow flames from them after much use of firelighters and the bellows. (You'll always have slaves among the children who will cheerfully fight to get their turn at the bellows. They see it as a great game.) Of course, you can always throw on some turf briquettes.

A man known to this corner planted several hundred ash trees on his land about 20 or more years ago when one of the several oil crises were on us. He knew he wouldn't get a very quick return, but there was the combination of quick-growing qualities of the tree and the reputation it has for early, easy burning. He hasn't had to use it yet, for although he has central heating, he also keeps an open fire going.

He never had to buy in logs for, soon after he moved into the few acres, he had to have a big tree near the roadside taken down. It wasn't one of the recommended firing varieties – a very old sycamore – but it had many half-dead branches and, anyway, along with some turf, did very well for the household for a year or two.

Then as other parts were trimmed or cleared, somehow there was always enough burnable stuff of one sort or the other, and old enough to stand in well for the better kinds which, we are regularly told, includes beech (yes, when kept at least for a year). Poplars that had to be taken down aren't mentioned in the rhyming advice, but two that had to be felled came into use a year or so after. Not the best, but good enough. The ash that was planted at the time of the oil crisis has been left to grow and bits here and there from other trees get you by. Hawthorn is great but too precious in the hedges to waste. Only an odd casualty of storm is used for burning.   Y

RING HISTORY   10 December 1985

 The ring is nature's greatest recording apparatus. Twenty years from now forestry men looking at a cross-section of a newly felled tree will point to a wide ring beside two very narrow ones to prove that 1985 was a wet year which was great for growth and followed two years with "dry" summers.

Similarly a biologist can take a scale from a fish and

"read off" the feeding conditions which the fish enjoyed in any given year of its life. In a good year of rich feeding the ring will be wide as on a tree cross-section. If the food supply is poor the ring contracts. The basic information "imprinted" on a fish scale allows fishery management staff to profile changes in food in selected waters and to adjust fish numbers accordingly.   H

THANK GOD FOR CENTRAL HEATING
15 December 1998

Not so many people go in now for log fires, either in open fireplaces or in stoves. One wise user of logs says that he orders beech in autumn for use 12 months hence. For, no matter how eloquent the seller is, in general the bluer the wood, the better is the fire. There are those who say that they have read somewhere (perhaps here) that ash can be used almost when cut. The answer to that is yes and no, mostly no. There is an old rhyming formula for all this:

"Oak logs will warm you well
If they're old and dry.
Larch logs of pinewood smell
but the sparks will fly.
Beech logs for Christmas time,
Yew logs heat well.
Scotch logs it is a crime
For anyone to sell.
Birch logs will burn too fast,
Chestnut scarce at all.
Hawthorn logs are good to last
If you cut them in the fall."

Of course, not everyone can be so choosy. The vendors of logs are not often the growers. But the rhyme goes on to more pleasant examples.

"Pear logs and apple logs
They will scent your room.
Cherry logs across the dogs
Smell like flowers in bloom."

And then it finishes with praise of ash logs which, in experience, is somewhat exaggerated:

"But ASH logs, all smooth and grey,

Burn them green or old,
Buy up all that come your way,
They're worth their weight in gold."
 The book from which this was taken says "author not known – largely traditional verse". But it is also claimed that it was written during the 1926 coal strike in Britain.   Y

CANNY CHRISTMAS   16 December 1987

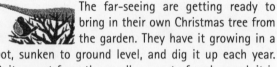

The far-seeing are getting ready to bring in their own Christmas tree from the garden. They have it growing in a pot, sunken to ground level, and dig it up each year. Quite apart from the small amount of cash saved, it is the convenience of not having to go farther than 10 yards for it. You can have it any size you want, of course. But if you don't need a giant, buy a pot-grown spruce. After Twelfth Day, simply sink the pot in your garden and, later in the year, give it a feed of spring fertiliser.
 The best type of pot to use is, of course, a clay pot. There are hefty peat-based containers which will last two or three years, but the clay pot has the advantage that it will constrain the roots and keep the height and spread of your tree within reasonable bounds. From experience, it is well, after about four or five years, to have a second tree coming on. The pot tree has two advantages over the topped tree. Firstly, it doesn't shed its needles as the others do, and is therefore safer. Second, you don't have all that business of screwing the stem into its base and seeing it topple a few days later when you load it with stuff. There's still time.   Y

GREEN THUMBS CHRISTMAS   11 December 1987

If your friends or relations are gardeners or tree buffs, you have no trouble at all in choosing things to give them for Christmas. Every one of the above needs gardening gloves. They wear them out, they get lost among the nettles. No one can have too many. There are even cheaper gifts. Pots of various sizes; plastic or clay, the latter making something of a comeback now. Tree ties of plastic or canvas. A small bale of peat moss. There are dozens of gadgets hanging in every garden centre and hardware shop. Plastic labels are useful: and the indelible pen to write on them. Even if he or she has a trowel, another will not be superfluous. For indoors, there are always dinky watering cans.

Don't buy trees or shrubs for the expert unless he or she is with you or briefs you in detail. The gardener who is hearty rather than skilful and scientific would welcome a tin of Band Aids against the scratches and thorn pricks. Add in a bottle of Dettol. And, where appropriate, a naggin of brandy eases stiff joints and speeds the work.   Y

FELLING PET TREES   14 December 1996

 Everyone is on about trees, even if it's only Christmas trees, and that's a different thing. But just now is also the ideal time for cutting down trees, trees you've planted yourself, sweated over, worried about. Were they in the right place? Did the soil suit these particular species? And, in the case of the very small saplings, did they need shelter? Now, less than two decades afterwards, it's a question of trying to cut for yourself a few gaps, so that you see out and feel yourself part of the neighbourhood. Broad gaps, in some cases, where you might see more than one cow at a time; where you might even glimpse, at night, a neighbourhood friendly light.

Then the trees that are simply too tight together to flourish as their nature dictates. Daft, for example to put so many pedunculate oaks in one biggish plot? Not really. You never know how a tree will thrive. Its roots might hit an obstacle, or find a poor stretch of soil, and thus not prosper. So you overplant. And eventually, where you had put twenty such oaks, your successors may cut them back to four or two. For you don't just plant and leave. We are talking here of planting for pleasure or landscaping, not of commercial foresting.

You don't have much compunction in thinning willows; they thrive like weeds. Ash makes such good firewood that, again, while admiring them as trees, you equally have them in mind as firewood. Even oak, most reluctantly culled, serves the same purpose after a few years maturing. And it's a big question to take out a Douglas fir, which has grown to an enormous height. The special pleasure here lies not only in its huge shelter-factor, but in those lovely, dangling, hairy or pointed cones. But there are more, if this one comes down. Birch, being slim, will be retained in most cases. A real heartbreak is to have to dig out a red American oak. With our climate, you do not find every year that brilliant scarlet which the leaves at times seem to put on overnight; but even in lesser shades of red, they make an autumn in themselves.

As to the *Pinus pinea*, the umbrella or stone pine, they were so doubtful a crop, being brought back as seed in a pocket from various countries, that they were particularly overplanted, being, of all, the most problematic of the species. Now huge and producing huge orange-size cones, they are crowding, and where twenty were, six should be.

Remember the oak-leaf count the other day? – 120,000 were raked up from the lawn. Still more lying, and more not yet fallen. The count may make the half-million, or more.   Y

THE APPLE FELL ON ISAAC'S HEAD 10 December 1998

The tree from which the famous apple fell onto Isaac Newton's head in 1666, inspiring his theory of gravity, is still there – though it was reputed to have been cut down after damage in a storm in 1820. But, according to an item in last week's *Country Life*, Dr Richard Keesing of York University is having DNA tests to prove that the tree now there in the garden of Newton's birthplace is the original. It may have fallen but it still lives on. True, new trees were grown from cuttings, but when Dr Keesing was given family papers from Woolsthorpe Manor, near Grantham, Newton's birthplace, he found a sketch of the original, by which he could track down its actual site. He literally stumbled over its fallen trunk, from which shoots had sprung years ago. The sketch he was looking at was, apparently, the image of the tree as it stands today – bent and curling but vigorous and well leafed. The report says that the 8,000 visitors who go annually to Woolsthorpe will know, given the DNA tests prove correct, that they are seeing the tree grown from the one that dropped an apple on Newton. The variety, by the way, is Flower of Kent.

Other trees have been known to rally and come on again after falling, when some roots remain in the ground, attached even minimally to the soil. This happens with mulberry trees, and the outstanding case to have come before these eyes is the specimen in the grounds of Breaffy House Hotel, Castlebar. There was a time when it was just a fallen tree – now it thrives, glistening leaves and authentic fruit, as something like a maze. Elbows of the fallen branches seem also to have dug themselves into the soil and rooted healthily. It's worth going out of your way in the west to see it. Willows, too, have good powers of survival. One veteran mentioned here before has, one by one, lost all its mighty branches, but from the bark of its stump new sprouts have been moving and will soon be fairly substantial. Not far away, another willow fell, some 40 years ago; its original trunk sinks lower and lower in softish ground, but the new, long shoots, now fine heavy branches, make a fine grove in spring.

John Stewart Collis, in his autobiography, tells of a yew tree of great age, the branches of which drooped to the ground and took root. All grew to be trees themselves, which similarly imitated the original pattern, for their branches drooped, rooted and sent up another generation of trees, making in all a small forest.   Y

POET'S TREES   12 December 1989

 Trees, trees, it's always trees. Did you see the bit about the exiled Russian poet Irina Ratushinskaya and her husband Igor, who have now made their home in London. They bought a small house – she is surprised that she can buy it from writing books – but they hadn't much to put into it, slept on mattresses on the floor at first. She doesn't tell us more about house furnishing but is emphatic about the garden. They are determined to have a walnut tree, because her husband's family always planted them and she believes (rightly) they will do well in the climate of these islands. They will, if they're the right variety. Then she wants, in the front garden, a blue pine, because Igor's family for 200 years have planted them back in Russia. Hugh Johnson's *International Book of Trees* doesn't list a blue pine, but it might be a Korean pine which has blue-green needles.

How many people plan their trees or their garden generally before they get down to the furniture and the fridge and the washing machine? In fact, quite a lot of people do. Trees are more than merely practical. A character of Walter Scott's says: "When ye hae nothing else to dae, ye may be aye sticking in a tree. It will be growing when ye're sleeping."   Y

HARDY'S SINGING SHRUBS AND TREES
18 December 2000

In all the recent winds and gales, could you detect the individual sounds it drew from various trees and bushes? Thomas Hardy, the great novelist and poet, who had more acute hearing than most of us, always listened to this music and wrote of it. Thus, of the wind on a hill: "Tonight these trees sheltered the southern slopes from the keenest blasts, which smote the wood and floundered through it with a sound as of grumbling, or gushed over its crowning boughs in a weakened moaning . . . the instinctive act of humankind was to listen and learn how the trees on the right and the trees on the left wailed or chanted to each other in the regular antiphonies of a cathedral choir, how hedges and other shapes leeward then caught the note, lowering it to the tenderest sob; and how the hurrying gust then ploughed into the south, to be heard no more." That's in *Far From the Madding Crowd*.

Elsewhere he writes of gusts of wind resolving into three: treble, tenor and bass notes were to be found therein. "The general ricochet of the whole over pits and prominences had the gravest pitch of the chime. Next there could be heard the baritone buzz of a holly tree . . . Throughout the blowing of these plaintive November winds that note bore a great resemblance to the ruins of human song which remain in the throat of fourscore and ten.

It was a worn whisper, dry and papery and it brushed so distinctly across the ear that, by the accustomed, the material minutiae in which it originated could be realised as by touch. It was the united products of infinitesimal vegetable causes, and these were neither stems, leaves, fruit blades, prickles, lichen nor moss." That's getting a bit beyond us. (It's from *The Return of the Native*.)

Some may recall a scene from Hardy's *The Woodlanders* where Giles Winterborne is planting, with the help of the girl Marty, young pines. She held the plants upright while he shovelled the earth in. "How they sigh directly we put them upright," she said, "though while they are lying down they don't sigh at all." He hadn't noticed.

She set one of the young trees upright in its hole and held up her finger: the soft musical breathing instantly set in which was not to cease night or day until the grown tree should be felled – probably long after the two planters had been felled themselves. "It seems to me," the girl continued, "as if they sigh because they are very sorry to begin life in earnest – just as we be."

Neighbours would remember him, Hardy wrote of himself: "He was a man who noticed such things", of many aspects of nature and life. Indeed.   Y

MISTLETOE RITES   23 December 1985

 The druid or priest, clad in white, climbed the oak tree bearing the golden sickle. He cut the sacred mistletoe from the oak; then two white bulls were slaughtered – and the feasting began. That's the story Pliny tells. So says the archaeologist Anne Ross in *Pagan Celtic Britain*. It's not explained how the amatory significance of the mistletoe crept in, but that seems to be all it is popularly associated with today.

It's said you can grow mistletoe from the seeds within the white berries. Keep them until February or March and then press them into crevices in your chosen tree – apple and oak are favourite. Or you can cut back a flap of bark and then fold it over the seeds. It has never worked in the experience of this column; but then that goes for many experiments of the kind.   Y

NO-GO MISTLETOE   20 January 1999

When the greenery and other decorations were being taken down on the traditional date recently, a friend admitted that, after about 10 years of sweat, he had given up trying to grow the parasite mistletoe. Why did he want to do it in the first place? For the hell of it, for pig-iron as some put it, and because, well, just because. He had read expert advice in half-a-dozen books and all made more or less the same points. Keep the sprigs with the berries (which contain the seed) in a paper bag in a cool place until May. Then you cut a flap of bark from the selected host-tree, squeeze the berry and its seed under the flap, where the stickiness of the berry is extra protection and holds the seed in the aperture, then close the flap of bark. Do this on the underside of the branch chosen and you are away with it.

Our friend has never seen even a shoot or leaf of the damned thing. One tip that is not realisable if you buy your mistletoe in shops is that it helps if your seed is planted into the same sort of tree from which your specimen came. As most of us buy it in shops, and as the greater part of that is imported from the continent, who is to know? Apple is a favourite host. Hawthorn, too, is recommended; mountain ash, and ash, birch, lime, pear.

Findings at the East Malling Research Station in England, writes Tony Venables in a recent *Country Life*, say that slits cut into year-old shoots on a tree give best results. In this case it was apple. Even if the seed takes, you may have little to show for a couple of years. Richard Mabey in his massive *Flora Britannica* writes about the aphrodisiac reputation of the parasite and tells us that "it is worth pondering that, at least until the 1960s, the inclusion of mistletoe in church decoration was frowned on in many parishes". And he goes on to say that early people, "especially the fearful medievals", saw mistletoe as entirely magical – a plant without roots or obvious sources of food, that grew away above the earth and stayed green-leafed when other plants were bare.

Further to the aphrodisiac/reproduction line, he notes, women who wished to conceive would tie a sprig round their waists or wrists. You wouldn't think the English needed to import from Normandy or Brittany, for Mabey tells us that there is a long tradition of mistletoe being grown on apple trees in England. At one time mistletoe was found on no less than 34 per cent of apple trees in Herefordshire orchards. But it was a long time ago. All authorities agree that, whatever Druidic connections may be made with the plant, the oak is one tree which seldom hosts mistletoe.   Y

NON-STOP   3 January 1986

 There is no non-growing time, even in the turn of the year. Frost has beaten and melted the long grasses down, the rain has washed away the surface soil here and there from the paths, so the tubers of the flaggers or wild iris can be kicked out of the ground with ease. They are all sprouting; some of the shoots three inches high – flourishing.

These same flaggers are said to die out within two years of drainage hitting the area. Far from it. They are healthier than ever, taller than ever (six feet in summer in places) and spreading from the former marshy bits into the politer bits. They look good – better than rushes and docks and thistles – and are recommended for filling out odd scruffy corners of fields which for some good reason you haven't planted with trees.   Y

SHARP NIGHTS   8 January 1986

A green Christmas, a full churchyard, the old people say. The colds and flus, the "noses" and the "chests" which marked the end of 1985, seemed to end with the two or three sharp nights of frost. Frost kills off the germs. Frosty weather is healthy weather. It does nothing for soft calendulas in the cold greenhouse. They had sprouted a good inch before Christmas and seemed sturdy in their pots on the top staging. The heat of one lighted bulb would have held back the withering frost which did for half of them. Still, there will be enough left to put in a warm spot in a garden in Achill.   H

FAST GROWER   17 January 1986

The eucalyptus tree, they say, likes to be within sight or sound of the sea, where they thrive. Rathmines may not qualify on either score but a seed pod gathered on Killiney hill yielded half a dozen shoots of which one now thrives. It is 12ft after four years in a sheltered garden, living up to its reputation as a fast grower. It is a bit "soft" and needs winter staking. The luxurious leaves are full of oil and, crackled in the palms, give off a rich bouquet. Young ones brought to Achill at the same time got smothered in weeds and went back. Now another batch are ready and this time they'll get a bed to themselves and we'll keep the grass down.   H

PLANTS LOVELY AND PLANTS UNLOVELY
17 January 1988

Never mind showing off your snowdrops or remarking on the ready-to-flower crocuses: what do you think about the first primrose of the year spotted just a week ago by a landscaper friend? Not in full bloom, but here it was in the ditch along the road from Navan to Athboy. He even named the townland. Then there is the other friend who chirps that the mimosa in his, admittedly sheltered, garden has just got its first few blossoms, lovely yellow balls of flowers which remind you of the Mediterranean and sun. It may be old news to people down south, say in Cork, but this is Dublin.

As to saffron crocuses, brought last year from Saffron Walden, old Nicholas Culpeper (1616–1674) speaks well of the condiment taken in moderate doses, but overdosing can be fatal. "Some have fallen into an immoderate convulsive laughter, which ended in death." Still on the positive side, however, are chives in a pot outside the back door, which already have been throwing up lovely, light-green healthy shoots, and are, of course being used. Normally this resurgence comes later. The pot stands under a bright halogen light, which may give it heat as well as light all night.

Now for the unlovely plants, the first and most bothersome being cleevers, cleavers or goosegrass, whatever you like to call it. It is everywhere, already, in some cases four to six inches high. How do you deal with it? Spray? No, there is no spraying here except of roses, effective though that could be with cleevers. Massive doses over a wide area would be needed – and near the river. No. It is just preparing to climb up every bit of sheepwire around the borders, to pounce on young trees (later in the season) and, if not checked, to weigh them down to the ground. So you get at it with the weed-eater, but find that the slower working-over with the four-pronged graip is more effective. A long job. And you still see the remains of last year's phenomenal growth, in yellow curtains of the dried weed along the wire.

Finally, among the baddies, what does one do with bindweed or convolvulus? Especially when one half of the family claims that the flower is the loveliest of all, large and white, covering at times perhaps a quarter-acre. In small areas, like herb-beds, you hoke out the roots; in an expanse of untamed boggy land, you just let it rip. Beauty is in the eye of the beholder.   Y

HOW QUICK IS QUICK?   5 January 1989

But I want quick-growing trees, says the man with the garden centre Christmas token. How quick is quick? Even relatively experienced growers need to be reminded that speed depends not only on the species of tree but on the soil in which it is planted, the location, the health of the individual tree and the care with which it is dug in.

There are other factors, too. Growth can vary so much. Ordinary birch, *Betula pendula*, planted in a friendly corner, which was damp but not boggy, which had received alluvial soils from frequent flooding, which sloped gently and was sheltered from the worst of the winds, which was splendidly open to sun for long hours, went from three feet to twelve feet in two-and-a-half years. And oh, yes, they were very carefully planted by expert hands. It is no surprise that Lombardy poplars set out along a river bank are nearing thirty feet in seven years. They were put in at about six feet. And, once more, oaks which pushed up their first leaves in 1977 under the

201

mother oak, were taken up with a trowel, left in pots for two years, and now, long established in favourable soil, are mostly around eighteen to twenty feet. That's how quick quick can be. Doesn't always work out, though.   Y

TREES AND FANCY   27 January 1989

Nowadays we are very matter-of-fact about trees. So many to the acre, yielding so many cubic tons of timber; so much subsidy from the EC. John Mackey, the great guru of afforestation in this new State, knew all the technology; he also saw the poetry in trees. In his book, *Trodden Gold* (Talbot Press, 1928), he quotes, among others, these three:

Walt Whitman: "Why are there trees I never walk under but large melodious thoughts descend upon me? I think they hang there winter and summer and always drop fruit as I pass."

Charles Kingsley: "In the presence of the wonder of trees, one becomes painfully sensitive of the poverty of words, of the futility of all word-painting."

Oliver Wendell Holmes was more fanciful than judicial in this: "I shall speak of trees as we see them, love them, adore them, in the woods and fields where they live, holding their green sun-shades above their heads, talking with their hundred thousand whispering tongues, looking down upon us, with that meekness that belongs to huge organisms; which one sees in the brown eyes of oxen, but most in these vast beings standing like great children while Nature dresses and undresses them."   Y

AMONG THE LAURELS   27 January 1988

Laurels have been given a bad name. Perhaps especially by writers of detective stories – of the old-fashioned kind. There, laurels were always described as damp or dark or dank. They were usually dripping, too. Sometimes they were sinister. Shadowy figures lurked there or even skulked. Dreadful things happened among the laurels. Bodies were often found under their funereal foliage. In fact, laurels are a fine, fast-growing bush and just now buds of their beautifully perfumed flowers are appearing. Later there will be dark berries which are not to be eaten, except by birds. But for filling a gap in a hedge or for making a hedge or screen, laurel is one of the fastest growing and best covers.

Small boys for generations have used crushed laurel leaves in a jampot to kill insects they plan to mount as specimens. There is a small charge of prussic acid in the leaves. This is the cherry laurel or *Prunus laurocerasus*. Then there is what the average person calls a bay tree – *Laurus nobilis* – but which the books call true laurel. The leaves of this shrub or tree are, unlike the cherry laurel, not tainted by prussic acid. In fact they are one of the commonest flavourings in cookery. Just be careful you don't get the wrong laurel.   Y

KEYS SURVIVE   14 February 1985

One would imagine that with the snow and frost which was part of January the bunches of keys on the ash trees would have fallen away to be carried on the winds to the ground and a possible suitable site to allow them to germinate. Yet going into the second week of February they hold on grimly. Anyone anxious for a coppice of young ash trees can pull the keys off the lower branches and, sandwiched in a box of sand, they'll come up in anything from nine to 18 months.

A lump of fresh moss, if it is used to "bed" them, helps to bring on an early germination, but seeds put down this time of year will most likely need the best part of 18 months: the seedlings are sturdy enough and stand up well to an early transplanting into pots or a propagating bed.   H

MASSAGING PLANTS   20 January 1986

 When you first hear about the virtues of talking to your plants, you laugh. Then you realise that it is merely another way of saying that they need unremitting attention. But massaging plants is a reality, particularly in the greenhouse. The best, most green-fingered gardener this corner ever knew practises it all the time. He would brush the palms of his hands regularly over a tray of seedlings. Is it that this replaced the breezes they would have got outside and thus firmed up the roots? Try it when you have two trays of seedlings put down at the same time: brush one with your hands and leave the second untouched.

The same gardener would put his hand or hands around the bigger plants and gently smooth them from root to tip. Everything worked for him. Some may talk of electrical or other currents passing from hand to plant. Whatever it is, it is worth a try.   Y

MASSAGING PLANTS AGAIN   24 January 1986

The suggestion that young plants benefit from stroking or brushing with the hand, raised here a few days ago, draws a letter from Liam Ó Ceallaigh of Booterstown, Dublin. He remembers an article in *Reader's Digest* of some time ago, which touched on the theme. A major company was experimenting on plants, and the process involved transferring sprouting seedlings from one tray to another. It was found that the seedlings handled by one female developed more rapidly than the others. The company analysed samples of sweat from the fingers of all the handlers and it was found that the sweat of the successful transplanter differed in chemical content from the others. "I've forgotten what the particular substance was, but apparently it was what the doctor ordered for the seedlings," writes our correspondent.

What if the hands of the massager had been dry, as is so often the case when working in greenhouse soil? The original green-fingered gardener mentioned here the other day propounded no theory himself, but those who watched his success concluded that his handling or massaging of the plants was, in itself, a large part of his success.   Y

STRANGE FRUIT   11 February 1987

 Certain herbs and fruits, the old books tell us, have been applied to wounds that are not healing, in order to clear away pus and help knit the flesh. What of a fruit that mends *itself* when cut – a fruit that has long been parted from its tree. A correspondent says that the paw-paw or papaya has this quality in itself.

To explain: a paw-paw was cut open, lengthwise as you do with an avocado, but was found to be unripe. The two halves were put together again in the hope that the fruit would not spoil and might be ready to eat in a couple of days. So, days later it is picked up and, lo and behold, the skin has joined completely right around the cut. The wound has healed over. And, yes, it was edible when opened a second time. A slight touch of science fiction?   Y

GROWING YOUR OWN PINEAPPLES 13 February 1995

Fresh, exotic fruit all the year round is the norm these days, and not only in big cities. Cherries at Christmas from God-knows-where; grapes from half a dozen places, mangoes, paw-paws and some odd things you can't put a name on: "some of those, please". But there was a time when gardening books, while covering the usual range – the kitchen garden, the fruit garden, the flower garden – of long ago, used also to carry chapters on not only the greenhouse but also the hothouse. To keep a hothouse going you would need a staff, fuel for keeping the temperature up and unremitting care. Maybe some big houses can still do this; maybe even some of our own botanical and horticultural institutions. Leafing through the months of the year in an old book: *Every Man His Own Gardener*, you follow the growth of what are called pines month by month. For pines read pineapples. In January the pinery hothouse needs to be looked at carefully, for some of the pines begin to show fruit. The plants are in pots, buried to pot-level in tan bark. Take up the pots and see that the bark at the roots is warm enough; fork it over, maybe replace some, if it has disintegrated. The fires have to be made up every morning and evening. For watering, use soft water, the barrel near or in the hothouse to take off the chill. In February you may need fires all day, and not just morning and evening to keep the pipes warm. And watch your bark-bed for the same. March keep your heat going. Replenish your bark-bed; it may be compacting. The pines should now all have fruit showing well. By April you need to water them daily and keep a good moderate heat. Maybe more bark as it ferments down. Let them have fresh air on warm sunny days. June-July the pines are ripening. When they turn yellow (don't let them get overripe), cut them from the plants with about six inches of stalk. And, of course, with the green crown which, after being admired can be cut off the top and returned for planting, to produce fruit again in two years.

The book is dated 1809 and that marks the nineteenth edition. A nice touch that, *Every Man His Own Gardener.*   Y

IN NATURE'S WAY   6 February 1987

 Be like nature: scatter abundantly when you are planting. If you are putting down trees, don't listen to those who urge you to think of the right spacing and then to double the distance between them. If you plant close, you can always decide, years later, to trim the side branches and have some lovely, tall, stately boles, or you can dig up a tree here and there to let, say oaks, spread, and oaks do like to spread. Those select few who grow their trees from seed, know only too well that your acorn or your pine nut may well be hoked out by mice or marauding rooks before sprouting. Be like nature: be prodigal.

A reviewer of the first volume of a new edition of Gilbert White's journals, wrote recently in *The Sunday Times*: on 21 March he "sowed 12 seeds of Cedar of Libanus, a Crop of Larches, Weymouth-pines and Cluster-pines in two boxes standing in the morning sun in the field-garden and netted them. Planted Ivy round the little-house, and a bed of Raspberries at the north end of the House: Planted a fine Mulberry-tree, of my own raising from a layer, in the new opening in the new Garden." Not a bad day's work.   Y

MOON STORIES   14 February 2000

The moon has not ceased to be a thing of beauty, poetry and romance even since man first set foot on it all those years ago. Moonlight still transforms the night scene in town and country. And the planting of seeds is often influenced by the state of the moon, be it waxing or waning. The *Field Book of Country Queries* says plainly: "The simplest of several theories is: plant all crops maturing their produce above ground when the moon is waxing, preferably in the first quarter; plant all crops maturing below the ground, such as roots and potatoes, when the moon is waning, preferably in the third quarter . . ." Dr Rudolph Steiner, the anthroposophist, held that plants such as leafy greens and brassicas growing above the surface should be planted with the moon, Mercury and Venus in the ascendant. Then a following remark refers to the "rules" in inverted commas. There are beliefs which appear in various parts of the world which say how dangerous it is to fall asleep exposed to the rays of the moon. A current French magazine devotes many pages to the same heavenly body.

A farmer is quoted as saying that the phases of the moon are very important when it comes to felling trees. If you cut your firewood while the moon is waxing, he says, it will be difficult to dry: it will smoke, ooze and give you problems. So you should always cut it while the moon is waning. For wood that is to be worked, it is the opposite. You must cut it while the moon is waxing, so that it will last a long time. The tides of the seas, of course, depend on the pull of the moon, and there's not much you can do about that, though Laurence Grousset, a yachtsman of Brittany, warns of the speed with which water, on a change of tide, can rush through the many hidden rocky underwater passes and bring disaster to any who have failed to watch the tides, and thus the moon. And mycologists? The spokesman for the local society of Oléron, on the Atlantic coast, says that all connoisseurs of mushrooms watch the phases of the moon. The great time of growth begins three days before the new moon, more or less, and lasts for about a week. And he says he has never found anyone who can give him a satisfactory explanation of the phenomenon. A sea fisherman says that a full moon is bad for his type of surface fishing, even when it is hidden by cloud.   Y

TREES FOR STORMS   16 February 1988

Most people – real foresters and investors excluded – buy trees for their colour, grace, their shade, their fine bark. Or to block off an unsightly prospect. For shelter belts, too. Very few would think to buy a tree for its resistance to hurricane-force winds. If you did, you couldn't be sure of getting it right. The trademark of a hurricane-force wind, it is said, is that it snaps off a tree trunk like a broken pencil. Photographs of the effects of the October wind on trees in England showed many broken off just like that. In the Phoenix Park, Dublin, last week one ash, about a hundred years old to judge from the rings, and something like two-and-a-half feet in diameter, was broken off sharply at a height of ten feet or so.

In big storms, mature beech are vulnerable. They ride the winds gracefully, as a sailing ship at sea, but their roots are shallow. Many cypresses bit the dust last week, for not everyone thinks to have garden trees lightened, as the tree surgeons put it. Oaks, with plenty of space around them, are among the most resistant to wind, for even at three or four years, their tap root can be formidable. But no tree is entirely invulnerable.   Y

HEALTHY   21 February 1986

Gardeners live longer. Or at least they deserve to. For do they not relentlessly follow one of the most often repeated medical injunctions: to keep active? They bend and stretch; they are up and down on their hunkers all day every day; they breathe deep as they exert themselves; they sweat profusely and healthily; they are, more than most other people, out in God's fresh air. Then, those of them who grow their own vegetables are right in line with all the modern food gurus: raw, fresh and in most cases unchemicalised produce. An apple a day and all those lovely, healing herbs. And gardeners cultivate the quiet mind and the virtue of hope. They can plant an oak, knowing that it will be seen at its best only about the end of the next century.

All this has to be true. Or is it wishful thinking? For why, if it is so healthy, do most gardeners complain of creaks and cricks and knotty fingers? You can't have everything.   Y

"OH DAISY" WROTE THE REVEREND 17 February 1999

For those of us who welcomed the love-ly St Brigid's Day we experienced this year, there was always the reservation that it wouldn't all be so bland until summer finally reached us. There was the usual mention of a foot of snow early in May 1943, when wartime censorship forbade publication of the phenomenon. But how exceptional was it for these islands? Continuing yesterday's look at the work of a few diarists, consider the entry for Sunday 11 May 1872 of the Reverend Francis Kilvert in Wiltshire: "This is the bitterest bleakest May I ever saw and I have seen some bad ones. May is usually the worst and coldest month in the year, but this beats them all and out-Herods Herod. A black bitter wind violent and piercing drove from the East with showers of snow. The mountains of Clyro Hill and Cusop Hill were quite white with snow. The hawthorn bushes are white with May and snow at the same time." But there is consolation. Later that day he met Morrell, owner it seems of a nearby estate, whose keeper was carrying a beautiful salmon of nine-and-a-half pounds – the first of the year. Morrell invited the Reverend to dine "and we discussed part of the salmon which was delicious, a bottle of port, and some fine strawberries [from the hothouses of the estate], as well flavoured as if they had been ripened out of doors.

"Shrove Tuesday 13th February 1872. Dined at the Vicarage at 5.30 and 7 drove with the Venables and Crichton to the Rifle Volunteer Concert in the National Schoolroom at Hay. We had tickets for the first row, and in the third row I immediately espied Daisy and Charlotte. I had the good fortune to get a chat with Daisy before the seats were filled up and she was so nice and I was so happy . . . I had been hoping and thinking all day that I might meet her. But now the seats began to fill. Fanny Bevan her great and inseparable friend sat on one side of her and her father on the other. I sat in the row before them. Henry sang: 'Oh Daisy.' "

Yes, she gets one whole line to herself. Kilvert muses elsewhere as to why he keeps his journal (it makes three full printed volumes), and decides it's because life is such a curious and wonderful thing that even such a humble and uneventful life as his may amuse and interest some who come after him.   Y

TALKING ABOUT THE WEATHER   16 February 2000

"Why are you Irish people always talking about the weather?" asked a visitor from central Germany who had come over to improve his English. "Well, because it's there, because it is so unpredictable, so changeable." Whereas, in his own home surroundings, winter was definitely winter with snow, cold and ice; and summer warm and bright and dry . . . and soon. Yes, we do talk a lot about it, and often we get it wrong. Brendan McWilliams, in his *Weather Eye* of 9 February, put us grumblers in our places, when so many of us were saying that this February was extraordinary, we never remembered one like it, and wasn't March supposed to be the time for winds? For he opened up with: "A vigorous storm or two is the norm, not the exception, at this time of the year." And he gave us the reason: because the temperature contrast between the equator and the poles is greatest. And "the interaction between the very cold air in the north and the warmer air farther south provides the stimulus for the development of deep depressions which sweep across the Atlantic, and now and then wreak havoc on our Irish shores." He gives examples of previous Februarys which were very stormy. February 1990 was a very turbulent month from the first day and on a dozen subsequent days. Then in 1994, the 3rd had a storm with widespread damage. Perhaps the worst storm in Irish history, he says, was also in February but long ago, 20–27 1904. But the date of his article, 9 February, had, down the years, so often given storms.

Yes, indeed a lot about weather in our talk. But did we in the last week or two not have several days of brilliant sun? Cold but brilliant; and daffodils flowered before their time. But how many called out to their neighbour, "Lovely day, thank God"? 15 February used to be opening day for trout fishing in the eastern region, and a group of anglers remember often eating their sandwiches in the shelter of a disused shed while hailstones rattled down on the tin roof. And, come to think of it, there was the head of family who insisted that St Patrick's Day had to be celebrated with a picnic – always. And all of the brood had to come. Rain is the chief memory. Sheltering from it in hedges and behind walls; but food definitely better than the fare of sandwiches at the river. Why, now, do we, indeed, talk so much about the weather? Answer that.   Y

THE WINDS AT BANTRY   11 December 1996

 The discussion of wind-patterns is not the province of this corner of the newspaper, but before Christmas you will be hearing and reading a lot about it. For we are approaching the bicentenary of the attempted French invasion of Ireland at Bantry Bay. And, as everybody learns at school (you hope), after entering the Bay with 25 ships and 10,000 soldiers, on 23 December 1796, with Wolfe Tone, adjutant-general on board the *Indomptable*, a gale blew up and, in short, scattered the fleet, which a few days after "limped back to France".

The *Cosantóir* for November has an article by Captain Dan Harvey, curator of the Military Museum at Collins Barracks, Cork, which concludes that if the French had landed, such was the incompetence of the occupying army that "it is difficult to envisage how a rebellion could have failed". He packs a lot into one page, including the information that the French expeditionary army was numerically the largest French force that had left her shores since the Crusaders, exactly five and a quarter centuries before. Read it. He also gives several useful references.

All of you can fantasise now on this: if the French had succeeded, would they have stayed on as conquerors? Tone obviously thought not. But if they had, there is one thing you can be sure of. We would all now be French-speakers – as the first language. Great cultural imperialists, our friends the French.

Back to those winds. *History Ireland,* that most valuable quarterly, has an article: "Weather and Warfare, Bantry 1796 Revisited", which displays three maps with weather indications and the maps first remind us how close to Brest, from which the fleet departed, is Bantry and give us a fine perspective on the whole affair. The author, John Tyrrell, tells us that from "data contained in ships' logbooks, Tone's diary and from weather observations made at Armagh Observatory, Dublin, Manchester, Edinburgh and Rutland, weather maps have been reconstructed for each day between 1 December 1796 and 5 January 1797". Whew.

We think we suffer from annoyingly changeable weather conditions. John Tyrrell shows that December 1796 was characterised by a wide range "from almost summer-like calm, dry sunny weather to the most severe storms and intensely cool, snowy weather". Same here now, though not so much of the almost summer-like, etc.   Y

CRASHING WIND AND LASHING SEA   11 January 1996

Probably most people who saw the rerun of Robert Flaherty's *Man of Aran* on RTÉ on Monday night, were aware that, made in the early 1930s, it nevertheless, even then, depicted a lifestyle that had long vanished. The islanders, in fact, had been using paraffin for their lamps for 50 years already. But the dangers the boatmen faced were real enough, and Flaherty well knew it. He was later to say: "I should have been shot for what I asked these superb people to do for the film, for the enormous risks I exposed them to, and all for the sake of a keg of porter and £5 apiece." He gives one example. "There was one scene which took place so quietly in the finished film that most possibly it wasn't noticed. When the currach is racing and trying to get to land, suddenly a jagged tooth of rock is revealed by the momentarily sagging waters and the currach comes to within a foot of it. If it had struck that tooth of rock, the currach would have been ripped from bow to stern and the three men would have been drowned before our eyes."

For so many people, the smashing seas and the dangers involved were not to be doubted. And the coolness of the young boy, casting his fishing line down the face of a cliff which must be all of three hundred feet. Islanders still point out the very spot, not far from Dún Aengus. The film was premièred in London on 25 April 1934, but did not please all critics. Graham Greene, for example. He wrote: "Photography by itself cannot make poetic drama. By itself, it can only make arty cinema. *Man of Aran* was a glaring example of this: how affected and wearisome were those figures against the skyline, how meaningless that magnificent photography of storm after storm. *Man of Aran* did not even attempt to describe truthfully a way of life. The inhabitants had to be taught shark-hunting in order to supply Mr Flaherty with a dramatic sequence."

Another critic said it was "escapist in tendency". Sure. But it's still fascinating viewing in 1996. Quotes from *The Innocent Eye* by Arthur Calder-Marshall, 1963. Read, too, *Man of Aran* by Pat Mullen.   Y

PATRON OF BUTTERFLIES   25 November 1988

 People who leave money to pets and pets' homes are often mocked. Recently a woman in Norfolk gave her house and an attached acre of woodland (value £250,000) to the British Butterfly Conservation Society on the agreement that it would never sell the land and that she could occupy the house until she died. "Too much land is being taken over for building and not enough is being left for wildlife," she said. Is this eccentric or dotty? Not at all. An acre given over to wildlife, butterflies and everything else, is one small, but praiseworthy, effort to keep the ecological chain unbroken. Would it be daft if someone left in trust a few acres in which hares might not be shot or chased? Or the head waters of a stream in which salmon and trout spawned?   Y

WHAT YOU MAY NOT KNOW ABOUT HONEY
4 December 1989

Or maybe you do know what the bee does to make honey. A pamphlet issued from the south of France tells in detail of the goings-on in the hive: "The bee flies from

flower to flower, takes up the nectar through her pro-
boscis and fills her crop with it. [The word, nicely, is
jabot.] When she comes to her hive she regurgitates her
precious harvest onto the tongue of the first bee she
meets in the hive, which, in her turn, passes it on to one
of her sisters, who will continue the process . . . and so
on and the nectar becomes honey." Thus the transfor-
mation of nectar into, eventually, glucose and fructose.
"During all these absorbing processes, each bee incorporates into the nectar the secretions of its glands. These
substances, secreted by the young bees, are very important for the benefits they bring us. They are natural
antibiotics and fight the development of microbes and
bacteria or perform the office of catalyst, stimulating our
organs; and so the sugars are rapidly assimilated, from
which there is an immediate gain in energy." Such substances, the pamphlet says, are, of course absolutely
destroyed by heating or by long exposure to the sun. And
this for a punchline: "It is a shame to destroy in a few
moments that which our little pharmacists have spent so
long in preparing." That's what one beekeeper in southern France tells his customers.   Y

HONEY FOR A HANGOVER?   24 January 1998

 There are several ways to use honey, but
who has heard of it for curing a hang-
over? An account of a dramatic
employment in this connection is given by the famous
Vermont doctor Jarvis. It is in his *Folk Medicine*,
described as a book which "swept America" about four
decades ago. The good doctor tells how a man in his for-
ties had been drinking from 27 December to 10 January.
He was paralysed drunk, when seen. First he was given
six teaspoons of honey. And at intervals of 20 minutes
given the same dose again. In a bedside bottle there was
still one drink left. It was still there three hours later. The
dosage of honey went on, as above (Lor').

The book says that he was seen again next morning
at 8.30. The man had slept straight through the night,
something he hadn't done for 20 years (but he had
taken that last drink in the bottle). Believe it or not, the

previous day's routine of three more doses of six teaspoonfuls of honey. Then he was allowed a soft-boiled egg. More honey. For lunch: four teaspoons of honey, a glass of tomato juice and a piece of ground beef. For dessert: more honey.

Then, we are told, a friend brought him a pint of liquor. He pushed it away and said he didn't want it any more, and never took a drink again. The doctor tells us that folk medicine believes over-indulgence in alcohol to be evidence of potassium deficiency in the body. As honey is a good source of potassium, he says, the craving for alcohol is counteracted by taking honey regularly. He gives a list in which sherry, port and vermouth are described as "very acid"; beer, too; while whiskey is "weakly acid". He doesn't condemn the labourer for his beer after a hard day, nor begrudge the businessman his evening cocktail. There is endless food for thought in this off-beat volume. It was published this side of the Atlantic by W H Allen. *Folk Medicine* by D C Jarvis, MD.

Irish beekeepers may not make such claims, but they produce fine honey. The County Dublin Beekeepers' Association starts its 1998 beginners' course on 10 February, Litton Hall, Wesley House, Leeson Park, but you must book before 31 January. Phone 2888873.   Y

MID-MORNING WINE FOR THE GOVERNESS
16 January 1996

The benefit of a couple of glasses of red wine per day to stave off cardiac and other disorders is regularly canvassed in the press. Then we are told of the virtues of the Mediterranean diet as a whole. "More than a hundred years ago this gospel of the beneficent contentment of ordinary wine was the subject of a book by Dr Robert Druitt MRCPS: *Report on Cheap Wines, Their Quality and Wholesomeness with a Short Lecture to Ladies on Wine*, was published in London in 1865. The author dedicated his book to Gladstone, who, as Chancellor of the Exchequer, had tried to induce the British ordinary people to like ordinary wine. Dr Druitt even goes so far as to recommend a glass or two of claret (by which he means any reputable light clear red wine from France, Italy or Spain) for governesses and ladies who are compelled to earn their living. He suggests a glass or two at mid-morning as healthful, strengthening and enlivening." (It could certainly be enlivening, for a glass or two often means a glass or two or three or more.)

This quotation comes from a not obviously relevant footnote in a book by Moray McLaren, published just thirty years ago: *Corsics Boswell*. It is an account of a journey Boswell made to Corsica in 1765 to meet General Pasquale do Paoli, who, it is stated in the introduction, "was endeavouring to free his people from the tyrannical alien rule of the Republic of Genoa". Boswell's book was, according to McLaren, an eighteenth-century best-seller.

But, back to the wine and the governesses. McLaren comments: "How right! But one doubts if any mid-Victorian governesses would have had the moral courage to take his advice. Moreover, Dr Druitt, admirable though his intentions were, forgot that the kind of claret he speaks of, would have had to be 'fortified' before travelling to Britain. Perhaps some governesses in Europe took his advice, perhaps not. But Dr Robert Druitt's well-informed and delightful book is an encouragement to ordinary lovers of ordinary wine. It ought to be republished."   Y

QUIRKS OF ANIMAL AND INSECT LIFE
13 February 1999

 Three slightly off-beat or, if you like, quirky, items about animals and insect life, from the February/March edition of *The Countryman*. In a feature in which readers' natural history queries or observations are dealt with, a Mr Derek Ive writes from Spain to remark that while foxes have for long been foraging behind his house for what they can get ("alas that included our three bantams"), but mostly after moles and voles, this year after the meat course they have moved to the orchard and feasted on plums and apples, ripping bird netting off the plums, while apples are torn off, sometimes breaking young branches. Teethmarks are clear, and plum-stones are found in their droppings. The editor of this section, Brian Martin, replies that as well as mammal prey, British foxes take both wild and cultivated fruit and berries, also small birds, carrion, scavenged foods, insects, earthworms, beetles, crabs, etc.

Now wasps. Mrs Sheila Hayden of Sutton Coldfield was anxious when a wasp settled on her plate at lunch, "as I react badly to wasp stings. I quickly cut the insect in half with my knife, but the front half flew away and I assumed would promptly die." But two minutes later it was back, trying to land on her plate. She drove it off and it settled on the ground where she trod on it. She had heard of hens running around with their heads cut off, "but is this normal behaviour with a wasp?" Not so unusual, is the reply. The editor once saw a wasp cut a large moth in two and fly off with the abdomen, "leaving the head and thorax, with wings attached, fluttering in the grass for some minutes". As to decapitated hens, he writes that the spinal cord possesses considerable autonomy and can co-ordinate wing and leg movement for a short time after the brain is cut off.

Another wasp story. Mrs Joan Blewitt Cox from Devon writes that a wasp was being a nuisance in her room and started to make a hole in an apple. She drove it out about a dozen times, but it came back to dig into the same apple. Was it just one wasp or a series of them? So she dabbed a spot of Tippex-type white correction fluid on it while its head was in the hole it had made in the apple. Yes, the same insect came again and again. She shut the window and at dark the wasp gave up trying to get in. Next morning, the window opened, in came the Tippex wasp and made straight for the same hole in the same apple. "I could not help marvelling at its memory."   Y

YEATS'S HYPNOTISING OF HENS EXPLAINED
6 December 1996

You may remember an item here asking how Yeats hypnotised hens? It came from an account of Sundays spent by various friends of Katherine Tynan on her father's farm at Whitehall, Clondalkin. A bald statement requiring some development, you'd think: "Here", wrote John Cowell in his *Dublin's Famous People*, "on Sunday afternoons there would be a stream of callers with endless talk of poetry and Willie Yeats would hypnotise the hens."

Just that, no explanation. Now Dr Cowell writes to expand on, if not to explain, what it was all about. "I grew up in County Sligo where I often saw it done. And, very likely, that's where Yeats learned about it. You gently fold a hen's head beneath a wing, then hold the hen in both hands and rock it from side to side for a minute or two. Then just put it on the ground. It will remain in that position until you 'waken' it. Hindsight provides an idea: the cochlea [which Y finds in the dictionary as 'the spiral cavity of the inner ear'] of the human inner ear influences postural activity. It can be disturbed by swings, rough sea crossings and the like. Assuming the hen has an inner ear of some similar design, this may be the explanation. At any rate, it doesn't seem to do the hen the least harm."

How do we know that making a hen seasick, as it were, does it no harm? Today Yeats might have the cruelty people after him, if that's what he did. And when you see a hen with her head tucked under a wing – that is, if you ever see a live hen at all – what is she doing? Thanks, anyway, to Dr Cowell for his explanation of a parlour barnyard act of long ago. But is hypnotising the word? Ah, Sligo.

Interesting by the way, when the paucity of hens around the yard or seen rooting along the hedges was mentioned here not so long ago, how many people got in touch to say that they still kept them, free range, as we now say. From personal experience, their eggs taste as no eggs today taste. Even when they have to be crocked, according to season. Friendly, nice things, hens. Postscript. Notice in meat and poultry shop: FREE RANGE PHEASANTS.   Y

BANGING AWAY AT BIRDS 9 December 1989

 Around this time of year you often get protests against the hunting people. Do the protesters organise demos against big bird shoots? The big shoot concept is not practised here as widely as it is in Britain, where shooting people have become nervous because of the many abuses – such as birds being released from boxes which have been transported long distances to feed the cupidity and bloodlust of corporate asses. But still, even the quieter, more traditional English shooting gentleman manages to destroy quite a lot of life. Thus, a notable shooter, Sir Joseph Nickerson, has recently published a book and has received much publicity – sometimes of an oblique and quirky nature – as a result.

He gives his credentials. In 24 years he has shot 188,172 birds, or, per year, 7,841. Shooting for the pot is reasonable justification for the average sportsman who, we are told recently by a spokesman for the National Association of Regional Games Councils in this country, probably takes one game bird per week. But 7,841 over the few months of the game season would need a for-midable pot. Or course, most of the birds go on to the game market and, according to foodie correspondents, game is good for you.   Y

WELCOME BIRD 28 December 1985

Instead of a robin on the Christmas card, the forward looking might next year be thinking of promoting the lapwing as the Christmas bird. For, at this soft season, one of the delights is to watch a flock of a hundred and more tumble in their own distinctive way high in the clear air. The complete protection given to these birds by our Wildlife Act must be paying off. In one area of the country at least, there is no doubt that they are increasing. In the last week many flocks have been seen, but only once accompanied by their normal complement of golden plover. In England where plovers' eggs are a highly-regarded delicacy, the stringency of their own wildlife laws have been questioned. Some shooting and some culling of the eggs could be allowed, it has been argued. No such lobby is obvious here; to the non-specialist at least. Let them fly and tumble. We can eat hens' eggs.   Y

WINTER HEN-HARRIER   17 January 1987

Frost is hard enough on bird life but snow on top of frost makes life very difficult. Never mind that a foot or more of snow can release heat: the birds cannot scrabble in the sheltered places where the sun can ease the grip of the frost for a few hours.

It is a hard time for the hen-harrier as a bird of prey. The low tree-hopping flight at speed appears to be abandoned in frosty weather. Instead the hen-harrier slows down and uses staging posts far more often as he sits elegantly, swivelling the head to scan the landscape.

The fence posts of Achill, dividing the small fields, are a substitute for the lack of tree perches which the hen-harrier prefers: they have one obvious advantage for the biscuit-coloured bird in that he manages to blend with the post and the dead grasses in the field behind, so that unless you saw him land he could go unnoticed.   H

THE WOODCOCK STORY   19 January 1989

There are some wild tales that no one believes until he or she witnesses the truth of them. Thus, no one believes that the weasel really does dance up and down to hypnotise a victim until that remarkable performance is played out, before the doubting eye. (Yes, there are no weasels in Ireland, but we call our stoats weasels: see Fairley's *An Irish Beast Book*.) Another spectacle that scoffers have to see, is that of the woodcock carrying her young either between her legs as she flies or even piggyback. Has anyone ever produced a photograph of either phenomenon?

There seems little doubt; it does happen. Sir Ralph Payne-Gallwey, Bart, author of *The Fowler in Ireland,* and no old buffer where birds are concerned, says flatly that he had twice seen a woodcock carrying a young bird huddled up under the neck. And he quotes other sources as witnessing young birds being carried either clutched up and carried in the feet or partly supported by the feet and the bill. With all the nature programmes, especially on television, it would be remarkable if some of those patient camera folk have failed to get this one to film.   Y

LULLED TO SLEEP BY BIRDSONG   21 December 1998

If you find it hard to get to sleep, there are various tried remedies, but we won't go into them all. Some folks find that reading poetry helps, particularly poetry that is known to you. In one case, a man of some years can recall much of the poetry he learned by rote in school. "In Dyfed's richest valley, where herds of kine were browsing,/We made a mighty sally to furnish our carousing ..." – oh no, that's a war song. Not to be recommended. You want peaceful, romantic stuff.

In that case, you would be wise to turn, as another does, to CDs or tapes of birdsong. Can't fail. The best, to this man's mind, is a CD or compact disc of the singing of nightingales. This came as a gift from Switzerland and is hypnotic in its effect on him. It is of the nightingale ("thou wast not born for death, immortal bird") recorded in more than a dozen sites throughout Europe; mostly in France but also Finland, Romania, Greece. The background sounds are soporific, too – blackbirds, nightjars, woodpigeons, crickets, frogs, warblers, and in one case, faintly, the sound of a church bell. He says that now, when he occasionally puts it on when already in bed, he has gone to sleep before the first nightingale has ceased singing. There is another compact disc, also acquired in Switzerland *Le Reveil des Oiseaux* or "Birds Awakening" – the dawn chorus, if you like. It was recorded in a copse in the Alpine foothills and suffers from one disadvantage – like it or not, no matter what bird is singing, there always seems to be a damned cuckoo in the background all the time.

Not that the cuckoo isn't welcome, but not at the risk of spoiling another bird's song. But it is worth having this disc. The company is Sittelle, Rue des Jardins, F-38710, Mens, France. You can, of course, buy tapes of various kinds of birds, made closer to home. Some seabirds and shorebirds make delicate, tinkling sounds with waves breaking in the background. One bird brings back memories to Robert Louis Stevenson in the South Sea island where he was to die, far from his Scottish mountains: "Be it granted me to behold you again in dying/Hills of home: and to hear again the call;/Hear about the graves of the martyrs/the peewees crying,/And hear no more at all." Y

PS: The nightingale record is called "Rossignols" in French and in English "A Nocturne of Nightingales".

THRUSHES, GAMEBOOKS AND DOUGLAS HYDE
26 January 1999

Some people may have been shocked by the recent account here of the shooting of thrushes in France. And, by the way, the prescribed bag limit is, in one area, 15 thrushes per gun per day, in another, 20. The game shooting season ends shortly in these islands, but here is an account of fairly comprehensive slaughter in Scotland. We do not seem to see any more, in illustrated magazines, huge carpets of dead pheasants with the authors of their doom ranged, smiling over them. But shooting for the pot is one thing, while others make a ceremony out of gunmanship.

Anyway, the higher dottiness seems to be with the landed gentry, as told in a recent *Country Life*, the English magazine. Jamie Douglas-Home tells how his father, William, on their estate in Lanarkshire, some 30 miles south of Glasgow, in one day shot, purposely, one (and sometimes more than one) of every species of game. On 1 October 1931, William, aged 19, set out with one of his father's under-keepers to, as he puts it, get "Everything in the Game Book". By 10 am he had shot a teal and a woodcock, "usually the trickiest species to acquire". Soon he had a pheasant and three partridge, and in a piece of wetland a mallard and a snipe fell to him. A flock of golden plover flew overhead. He hid behind a wall while the keeper drove the flock expertly towards him. Five of them were in the bag. Now he was on moorland proper. Soon he had three grouse, two rabbits and two hares. He needed only one blackcock and pigeon to fill his list. He enjoyed his packed lunch and then set out "on the long trek home".

All blackcock haunts were empty. Finally, after a seven-mile walk he got "two old blackcock", in early evening. Rushing, now, not to be frustrated by "the humble pigeon", he did, in fact shoot one, and "everything in the Game Book" was logged. Even in recent years, he writes, the deed has been narrowly missed more than once. All good eating, though that's hardly the point. On then, or back then to 22 December 1876, when the young Douglas Hyde, nearly 17 years of age, recorded in his diary. "Snowy day . . . I went out shooting to the Currachs, Ballinphuill and the river. Shot a wild goose and a hare and six grey plovers, and a brace and a half of snipes, a partridge and three lapwings and a waterhen. Good fare for the rectory. The goose weighed about seven pounds." This from *The Young Douglas Hyde* by Dominic Daly.   Y

HOW MANY ACORNS IN A PIGEON?   6 January 1996

 It boils down to this. He wants to know how many acorns a pigeon can stuff into its crop. Big acorns, in this case, for the season produced the most magnificent specimens he had seen in more than thirty years. He has ruled out other predators. There were no badgers about in the area at the time. Squirrels hadn't been seen for decades. It has to be the birds, and pigeons were the prime suspects. And yet, two barrowloads of these acorns had lain at the foot of the tree for weeks, and only when the few days of very hard weather came in, did the pile diminish. One day they were still heaped high, forty-eight hours or so later, there was a thin enough covering of them on the ground. Then, overnight, or early in the morning, there wasn't one acorn to be seen.

Shooting folk will have heard or read about pigeons so heavily laden in the crop, that they could hardly rise from the ground. Indeed there was a query in an Old Field book of country questions about one shot pigeon which was found to have eighteen large acorns in its

crop. And some of them were germinating. The writer wants to know if they germinated in the bird's crop or were they already germinating when swallowed. The solemn answer was that germination even under the most favourable circumstances takes several days with acorns, although once the radicle or first rootlet breaks out, it develops quickly. Unlikely, then, that the germination took place within the crop. The pigeon clearly ate those acorns that were already sprouting. But of course, some further development might have taken place in the crop it was admitted. A bit prissy, that answer.

But back to the original question. A comparison might be made, and an estimate come to, when you read that story in White's *Selbourne*, where a woodpigeon shot at dusk was found to have its craw stuffed with "the most nice and tender tops of turnips", enough, when washed and cooked to provide "a delicate plate of greens" for shooter and wife.   Y

UNDER THE NUN'S PILLOW   15 January 1996

Sister Carmel Morris writes from Belfast about vanishing acorns, following the almost overnight disappearance of two barrowloads of the same, reported here on 6 January. "Several years ago I spent some time in Brecon, Wales, in a cabin (wood), situated in the hills overlooking the Beacons. I had a dish of acorns on a shelf in the living room, only room actually. I had picked them up somewhere. I noticed after a while that the acorns seemed to be diminishing! I was away for a few days and, when I got back, I noticed there were only 3 or 4 left. That night, to my horror, I found a few acorns under my pillow! I had stripped the bed before going away and knew it was clean and fresh. A fullscale inquiry revealed tell-tale droppings. The few remaining ones I threw out in the field around the cabin . . . they were gone within 24 hours. I wonder if some of our four-legged friends made love to your acorns? In my case the culprit was a mole, [surely not? Y] rat or vole. There were no squirrels around at the time. The time of year was end of March, beginning April. It was very cold at the time and a lot of hard frost. I did not mind sharing the acorns with my friends, but I did find it hard to find them in my bed. However, I hope they were enjoyed and helped them make the spring."

A footnote says "I am a Little Sister of the Assumption and was on sabbatical in Wales and enjoyed the beauty of that country." In Sister Carmel's case, wouldn't the layer-up of treasure be a mouse, perhaps. Used to domesticity. In the case of the two disappearing barrow-loads of (very big) acorns, while some four-legs may have had their share, the bulk of the crop went, almost certainly, to the pigeons. Anyway, this year's superabundant crop helped out some wild creatures at a time of bitter cold and frost. Thanks Sister Carmel.   Y

BREAST OF SEAGULL, STEWED   30 December 1998

At Christmas there was turkey, of course; there was goose, and some people went for pheasant. Not ruling out chickens and ducks. And for some time the game season has been on and snipe, mallard, woodcock fall to the guns. Naturalists of the last century were given to eating the oddest creatures – for purely scientific reasons, of course. But seagulls no; though puffins have been on the menu with many around these islands and in Iceland. Anyway, our roving friend Arthur Reynolds came across a new one some years ago: plain, ordinary seagull. He was spending a few days in Skagen, which he describes as a 400-vessel fishing port in north Denmark. He was noting differences of procedure – thus, he observed, the fishermen pack their plaice white side up in boxes, so that, he says any sunshine would not warm the fish so much. In Britain, he tells us, and Ireland, it is always white side downwards.

Anyway, he got a surprise when, on the third day there, he saw a seagull and suddenly realised that it was the first one he had seen during all his daily wanderings in the port, noticing vessel features. Irish ports always have hundreds, "because, unlike in Denmark, fish and fish scraps are left lying around". That evening he remarked to a friend that he'd seen a seagull for the first time. The friends inquired if it was fat. "Why ask?" Arthur responded. Answer: "Don't you know that in Denmark we eat them? We simmer the breasts in milk, sometimes with a little spice. Lovely." Arthur himself wasn't too surprised that seagulls provide food, for as a schoolboy, he used to collect seagulls' eggs in season on Ireland's Eye and sell them to a Dublin exporter who sent them to London restaurants. He earned more, he says, at this part-time trade than did his teachers.

Back to the seagull. Is this widespread, using them for home cooking? A Norwegian friend was asked; he hadn't heard of it. Logically there is nothing against it: eat puffins, eat seagulls. Last comment. On a later visit our friend asked a citizen how it was that their town was so civilised, with no evidence of crime or vandalism. "That shows you haven't been here for long. In this very bar a man had his overcoat stolen three weeks ago. I read it in the newspapers."   Y

BIRDS WITH A BELLYFUL   16 January 1998

A friend sends for Christmas a lovely print from one of her drawings, of a dozen or so cormorants on a rock in the sea, flapping their wings or, wings outspread while digesting their dinner; some, maybe just asleep. The focus of this inspiration is just off Groomsport, County Down. A peaceful scene. Now, a couple of weeks later a gruesome photo spreads into two pages of the *BBC Wildlife* magazine. It shows a dead cormorant, shot by "a marksman employed by an angler", and spread over the corpse are 13 perch, the alleged contents of the bird's stomach, about four inches long, apparently skinless, i.e. in process of digestion at the kill, and pinkly repulsive.

These birds are hearty feeders. Around the picture the pros and cons of seriously culling them is argued. Against the proposition is a representative of the RSPB (is that Royal Society for the Protection or Preservation of Birds?).

His argument is condensed into four sentences set out over the article. One: people *like* birds and want to see them given appropriate protection. Two: the law allows for limited, local cormorant control to protect human interests from serious damage. Three: a cull could threaten cormorants' conservation status but is unlikely to improve fish stocks. Four: our wetlands and rivers can support healthy populations of both fish and their natural predators.

To all of this, the response must be, "as long as you are not a fish farmer".

The anti-cormorant view is given by a fisheries management consultant. When the birds stay on inland waters for months, he says, the effect can be dramatic. There are enough predator/prey relationships; cormorants add to this. Many fisheries managements, he claims, have been forced into culling the birds illegally. The process of getting a licence to shoot the birds is so long and often turned down anyway, that managers just shoot.

Cabot tells us that we have about 5,000 pairs, well scattered. Some of the young take themselves away to France, Spain and Portugal in the winter! The cormorant is the one with the white patch on chin and cheeks, also a white patch on the thigh in breeding times. Very like it is the shag – smaller, no white patch, thinner beak, 8,000 pairs. Has anyone ever eaten a cormorant or a shag?   Y

BIRDSONG UNDER SHELLFIRE   27 January 1999

 Recently a report on the effect on birds of modern motorway traffic, especially in Britain and Holland, was commented on here. One aspect was a possible change in birdsong, also the effect on breeding. As a postscript this corner raised the question of how birds fared at the front lines in the First World War in France; also how they survived the incessant bombing from the air around such cities as Berlin in the Second World War. Now John B Doherty from Ballyraise, Letterkenny, writes enclosing a print-off from a chapter in *The Square Box* by Saki, or H H Munro. The essay is "Birds on the Western Front". Saki was known for piquant, ironical short stories above all.

According to him, in spite of the huge impact of war on the front, "there seems to be very little corresponding disturbance in the bird life of the same district". The rats and mice that swarmed into the trenches were followed by barn owls. As for nesting accommodation, the barn

owls found whole streets and clusters of ruined houses. And, typically Saki, "as these birds breed in winter as well as summer, there should be a goodly output of war owlets to cope with the swarming generations of war mice". (His natural history may not be as good as his prose.) The rook, normally gun-shy, is not at the front, but "I have seen him sedately busy among the refuse heaps of a battered village, with shells bursting at no great distance and the impatient-sounding rattle of machine-guns going on around him. All this has made his nerves steadier than before." He notes that crows and magpies are nesting "well within this shell swept area".

The skylark, amazingly, has stuck to the meadows and croplands, "now seamed and bisected with trenches and honeycombed with shell-holes". And, on a misty morning, would suddenly dash skyward "and pour forth a song of jubilation". To which Saki, the ironist, had to add that it "sounded horribly forced and insincere". And once, he writes, he had to throw himself down among all those shell-holes and whatnot, to find himself nearly on top of a brood of young larks, two of which had been hit by something but the rest were normal nestlings. He came across a "wee hen-chaffinch" which he suspected had a nest in apple trees nearby. All the deafening explosions had not scared local partridges away, and they were raising their broods. Saki was killed in France in November 1916.   Y

BIRDS KNOW   3 February 2000

St Brigid's Day is past (did you see many of her crosses around, or any?) and we're surely coming into mating and nesting time for the birds. And those children who notice such things will be asking: "Daddy, why do blackbirds always build the same sort of nests and blue tits and other birds make quite different homes for themselves? And, Daddy, why do they continue every year to follow their own kind of home? Blackbirds never build like tits . . ." and so on. You can put them off by referring to instinct, something automatically placed in their brains from time immemorial, and maybe quieten them. You can't tell them that the parent birds teach the young how to build, for the young are usually pushed off as soon as they can make their own way. So some birds go on making cup-shaped nests and others domed nests, and yet others scrape a hole in the ground and take their chances. And it's probably the sheer ingenuity of the threading and cementing with mud of the grasses that makes such a mockery of us humans talking derisively of bird-brained people, said a friend.

And the sharpness of bird perception was the subject of a letter written many years ago and incorporated in a volume called *Harvesting The Field*, referring to the English magazine. A man wrote to say that he was sure birds could tell in advance when a tree was going into decay and thus was dangerous. Two large elm trees, he wrote, had had nests in their tops for at least 10 years. Then the birds ceased to build in them. Five years later these trees made no fresh foliage and showed dead twigs at the top. When cut down they were found to be rotten and dangerous. Another elm which had plenty of foliage never had birds' nests, although birds built in surrounding trees. "This particular tree was blown down last month and was found to be completely rotted through at the base." Another elm, this correspondent writes, has had no nests in it for about 10 years, although earlier they did build in it. "Last week I decided to examine this tree and cut the top portion. It was rotten from the centre to within three inches of the bark and yet has thick foliage and shows no sign of decay from the outside." Perhaps, he writes, the birds can recognise a smell of death in trees.

And another correspondent on the same topic concludes: "My experience of birds has taught me that they have far more practical common sense than most people believe."   Y

A BULLFINCH AND ANGELS   8 February 2000

 A friend phones about that question of uniformity within bird species of patterns of nest-building, to say that his own answer had been to dig out an essay by John Ruskin – that sage of the 19th century who wrote about art, architecture, travel, natural phenomena, education, ethics and religion; more too in volume after volume. And in one of his collected works is an essay on nest-building. Ruskin tells of going to see an ornithologist whose collection of birds was said to be unrivalled in Europe. Mr Gould showed Ruskin a nest of a common English bird "which was altogether amazing and delightful to me. It was a bullfinch's nest, which had been set in the fork of a sapling tree, where it needed an extended foundation. And the bird had built this first storey of her nest with withered stalks of clematis blossom, and with nothing else. These twigs it had interwoven lightly, leaving the branched heads all at the outside, producing an intricate Gothic boss of extreme grace and quaintness, apparently arranged both with triumphant pleasure in the art of basket-making and with definite purpose of obtaining ornamental form."

Having led you on, he then wags a finger: "I fear there is no occasion to tell you that the bird had no purpose of the kind. I say that I *fear* this, because I would much rather have to undeceive you in attributing too much intellect to the lower animals, than too little." The bullfinch, he went on, has just enough emotion, science and art as are necessary for its happiness. The clematis twigs were lighter and tougher than others, and the beauty of the result was much more dependent on the blossoms than the bird, writes Ruskin. Then, the big leap: "Does it never occur to you, then, that to some of the best and wisest artists among ourselves, it may not always be possible to explain what pretty things they are making and that, perhaps, the very perfection of their art is in their knowing so little about it? Whether it has occurred to you or not, I assure you that it is so ... And, assuredly, they have nothing like the delight in their own work which it gives to other people."

We have strayed far from the original questions put here a few days ago, but let us end for today on Ruskin's final line of thought: "Why should not our nests be as interesting things to angels, as bullfinches' nests are to us?" (*Selections from the Writings of John Ruskin, Second Series 1860–1888*, George Allen.)   Y

PHEASANTS KNOW

14 February 1987

Yes, the pheasants *do* know that the shooting season is over. On a County Meath side road verging on a famous shoot, no less than five cock pheasants strolled along, taking leisurely refuge in the ditch when blasted at close quarters by the horn. And yes, they do become fairly domesticated if you put corn out for them. One correspondent boasts that a pheasant (hen) which roosts in the trees near her house, spends most of the day rooting around with her bantam brood, and nobody takes any notice. It is said that an English newspaper has had an item about pheasants and bantams cross-breeding. Would there be any virtue in breeding pheasants in a farmyard for the table or laying? How many generations of scientific breeding would it take, without fancy hormones, to get pheasants to lay for 200 days or more per year? And why would you do it? Well, if the present fad for tiny quails' eggs can take on, why not those of pheasants' which are between bantam and hen size?   Y

"QUOTH THE RAVEN . . ."

15 February 1999

 The raven in Edgar Allen Poe's poem of that name, which goes on repeating to his uneasy if not distraught host the one word "nevermore" may not be alone as the one talker of his species. Ravens not only mimic other birds, train-whistles and the jingle of bells, but Douglas Chadwick in a recent *National Geographic* magazine declares that, like parrots, they will learn to imitate our speech. He even tells us that some people have told him of being startled when a raven alighted nearby and spoke to them in human phrases. To which he comments, "Hmmm". The raven, *Corvus corax*, is distinguished from other crows by its size: wing-span of four feet, by its wedge-shaped tail in flight; and it may weigh up to four pounds. David Cabot figures we have about 3,500 nesting pairs in Ireland. They build in cliffs or abandoned quarries, sometimes in trees. A couple from the midlands often see of an evening, while they are out gardening, a pair flying northwards before dusk. The ravens will divert to pass directly overhead and give a friendly croak, a sort of casual "howya".

The man in the *National Geographic* tells us how cute they are at untying knots, undoing zips and even opening Velcro fastenings. Always use straps in raven country, he advises. They live for decades and must go on learning. Diverse diet: worms, insects, grains, berries, nuts, which they break open on stones, like thrushes with snails. They thieve from other hunters. And there is always carrion. They may drop clods on nesting birds such as kittiwakes to scare off the sitters and steal the eggs. Smart. They have been known to kill new-born sheep and seals, usually by pecking out the eyes. A biologist of Vermont University tests their acuteness by putting a snake or frog (at various times) into one end of a pipe. The young ravens watch, then run round to wait at the other end. A raven has been seen eating groceries out of a brown paper sack on the back of a speeding truck.

Chadwick says he owes his life to a raven. He was driving up a mountain road when "the sudden passage of a shouting raven left me unsettled enough that I slowed down and pulled towards the shoulder a bit. A moment later a logging truck came roaring into view on the wrong side of the curve ahead. Had I not already moved aside, the hurtling truck would probably have killed me. Though I realise this only proves that big talkative birds naturally compel our attention, I still owe a raven my life."   Y

KINGFISHER: BLUE OR GREEN?   16 February 1998

Quite a few people in this country will tell you they have never seen a kingfisher. They are not that scarce; estimated breeding pairs are from 1,300 to 2,100, and these are, according to Cabot, scattered thinly throughout the island. The same authority says they are to be found on freshwater canals, sluggish rivers, streams and lakes. Anglers of the more relaxed sort, who find as much pleasure in observing all around them as they do in landing a trout – at least they excuse themselves with the explanation – will confirm that on the smaller rivers of the middle of Ireland, there is hardly a stretch where you won't sooner or later see that exciting flash of brilliance.

There is some difference of opinion on the exact colours of this small jewel. Upper parts are a greenish-blue, underparts a chestnut. The throat is white and there is a white patch on the neck or cheek. It is a bit bigger than the robin. A book published in 1997 explains a colour dilemma that one family argued long about. Appalled, looking out the main window they saw twitching on the grass two small objects, green and flashing. On inspection they found two kingfishers. One died quickly, one, taken to the vet, died the next day.

They had, possibly fleeing from some predator, come around the bend of the river and mistaken the glass sliding doors as an extension of the water. But kingfishers are blue on top, aren't they? Now Charlie Hamilton James in his book *Kingfishers* (published by Colin Baxter) explains: "Their bright feather colours are not due to true pigment, for true blue pigment does not actually exist in birds. Rather, the astonishing colours of the upper parts of the kingfisher are the result of a complex structure in the layers of the feathers, which filters out certain colours of light, reflecting back only blue. This is known as the 'Tyndal effect' and as a result of it the kingfisher can appear to turn from bright blue to the rich emerald green with only a slight change in the angle at which the light falls on it."

If you live on or near a river and kingfishers patrol it, you might be able to hammer a post in midstream. They will appreciate it, and often land on it, either for rest or to dive for fish from it. An oak tree, which grew laterally instead of vertically on a river bank, made a fine platform from which to dive for minnows.

(The book, so brilliantly illustrated, cost £5.40 from Fred Hanna in Nassau Street, Dublin.)   Y

THE SEASON   14 January 1989

"From age to age the rural pastimes grew,
Necessity first urged, then pleasures new
From wants supplied arose, and none more pure
Than from the deep the finny tribe to lure."

Which means that the season is due to open in a few short weeks: the real season, the trout fishing season. And those are the opening lines of Mr Thomas Ettingsall's ode to the art. He goes on:

"The high, the low, the simple, and the wise,
Make it a study how a trout to rise.
The pale mechanic hails his holiday,
And to the gurgling streamlet speeds his way;
There, in the lonely vale, to praise his God,
And seek contentment from his pliant rod."

After the lyricism comes advice on which flies to employ; the advice still good after a hundred and fifty years and more. And why wouldn't it be good advice, for Mr Ettingsall was proprietor of a sporting tackle shop in Wood Quay, Dublin.   Y

PASSION ON THE RIVER BANK   2 January 1989

"Could never be an angler. Haven't the patience," say those who don't know anything. There is no question of patience being involved. Anglers are passionate people. The angler has a capacity for excitement beyond the average. Even in youth, it appears, these characteristics appear. So runs the findings of "a study of the massive database on teenage behaviour held by the university's Schools Health Education Unit in Exeter". Teenagers who go fishing, according to this, are twice as likely to smoke as their non-fishing counterparts, and they go to discos and most have a drink at least once a week. The head of the unit said, according to *The Times* of London, that the survey started with the assumption that fishing provided an opportunity to withdraw from the hurly-burly and quietly recharge batteries. Not a bit

234

of it. The converse is more likely. And you can't argue with databases can you?

The older generation is emphatic, too. There is a suggestion that gravel is going to be extracted from the famous English trout river, the Test, that and all sorts of wicked engines will despoil the scene. A knight writes to *The Daily Telegraph*. The river, he says, must not be used for any purpose other than fly-fishing "for which God created it". There's certainty for you.   Y

JEALOUSY IN SPORT   27 January 1986

The trout season opens in certain areas on 15 February. Earnest anglers are tying new wet flies, though the more usual practice is to soldier on year after year with a particular cast that has proved successful. The fly may be ragged, the barb in need of sharpening, but as the whole operation is such a matter of luck in the early part of the year, that hardly matters. One angler who fishes only in the first couple of months boasts that he has not even dismounted his rod nor taken off last year's cast. There it stands, ready for at least a ritual throw in three weeks' time.

There are certain constants in this game. One is that when you meet a fellow aspirant on the bank and he shows you a good fish he has taken, you'll never know just where it came from. "Down there, round the corner", or something of the sort will be the answer. Not that they are mean, anglers; just jealous. For example, in reviewing a book on fishing experiences a recent reviewer had this to say: "The trout the author catches are for the most part *gratifyingly* small."   Y

LAST OF GIANT PIKE, PLEASE   28 January 1999

This might be the last of the Giant Pike stories, as it offers a possible – just possible – solution to tales of 10-foot monsters seen lurking in dark waters but never landed. It comes from Jim Leonard, formerly of Meath, now living in Tramore. His letter, incidentally, is a marvel of penmanship, beautifully laid out and every single letter perfect. Anyway, there was plenty of water about in

Meath: lake and river, but the Dee was a prime goal for its many large pools. "Rivers were considered dangerous (which of course they are) but young bloods did not see it that way. Our trips were secret, but we had been warned that the Dee was populated by giant pike which could break an arm or a leg with a single bite. A sharp look-out was kept, but was never rewarded by a sighting or punished by a biting."

Now he comes to the real news. Some years later he did see a big one, in the flesh, in Carrick-on-Shannon. It was in a pub belonging then (maybe half-a-century ago) to a notable citizen named Ging Duignan. Ging's father, who was a well-known fisherman, landed a real whopper of a pike, which was put on show in the pub. It was strung up to the ceiling in the bar area. The ceiling was low there, probably about 8ft 6ins or so. In position the fish's nose was tight to the ceiling, while its tail was touching the floor. "Surprisingly, the weight was only twenty-nine and a half pounds. It was suggested that it must have suffered from some parasite, such as tapeworm, which kept it from putting on weight." And our friend adds: "And a creature of that length, viewed through the magnifying medium of water, could easily be regarded as 15 to 20 feet long." (Especially, he might have added, if you happened to be in the water with it, swimming or snorkelling or whatever.) He ends: "Of such sightings, I suppose, legendary monsters are born."

He saw the fish himself and admits that if the ceiling wasn't exactly eight foot and a half, it must have been nearly so. He is quite sure that nose and tail touched, respectively, the ceiling and the floor. No, he doesn't think the bar owner had the fish preserved in any way. It would have been a great curiosity for the pub and the town if he had. Our friend supposes it was got rid of when it began to smell. It's a fine story. Was a photograph taken? Did the local newspaper carry a story about this monster? Anyway, here it is in print and Jim Leonard of Tivoli Terrace, Tramore, County Waterford, remembers it well.   Y

SALMON LEAP   6 January 1987

There was a bit of a hubbub the other day about the first salmon of the year in the Liffey actually being a salmon of last year. In other words it was caught on the way down-stream, after a year spent spawning. From the legendary Salmon of Knowledge – and even before that, no doubt – this fish has been bound up with our life and culture. Its fate is a bit doubtful today. But a traveller around our island in the year 1764, one Mr J Bush, writes in his *Hibernia Curiosa* that there was hardly a river here "but what is ornamented, more or less, in its course, with beautiful cascades, water-falls or salmon leaps as they are usually called, from the infinite number of salmon that, at the season of the year for spawning, are seen leaping up the falls, many of them to the height of 15 or 20 feet".

One of the most beautiful was at Leixlip. The author was in awe before the leap of the salmon. Some people argued that in the leap they would start from the bottom of the river, i.e. 30 or 40 feet. Not so, he says, for he noted salmon bobbing up to the surface to measure the distance to the upper level before taking off. "The manner of giving themselves this surprising leap, is by bending their tails almost to their heads; and by the strong reaction of their tails against the water it is that they spring so much above it."   Y

CORPSES ON THE RIVER BANK   30 January 1999

We've been lucky in Ireland – well, certainly in the eastern part – not to have been overrun by mink escaped from farms where they were being cultivated for their skins. For a while there was real worry that they were going to devastate our rivers, trout, salmon and what-not, but it seems that they have been absorbed in many parts and are even failing to reproduce in any great number. Certainly in one tributary of the Boyne, three separate observers are agreed that hardly one seems to have survived, or if they are around, the damage they are capable of doing is minimal. One hadn't seen a mink for over a year, and he is almost daily on the river; another, a keen fisherman and river-watcher, says it is about two years since he came across one, and the third has had no evidence since he shot one five years ago across the river from his house. Maybe the news from elsewhere is less encouraging or maybe they have just blended into the general background. Aren't we lucky that we are not reading in our newspapers of the depredations of wolves and bears, as the French are. Or rampaging wild boar. Or even beavers with their tree-felling to make their dams, as might yet happen in Britain.

Would mink be responsible for hauling salmon out of the river, spent male salmon, on their way down river after the spawning act; that is, dying salmon? For Gerry Farrell has found something like eight of them near where he lives on the river (the Borora properly called, though often referred to as the Moynalty). Probably, he thinks, the work of otters, which another observer says, he came across for years. The otter usually takes a good hunk out of the fish when he gets it up on to the bank and then leaves the corpse to be disposed of by the usual other carnivores and carrion-eaters – rats, foxes, crows. Plenty of salmon must have come up the river this year, Gerry reckons, because it was for so long in flood.

Yes, he says, as if in answer to a query here, there should be a good number of fry out or coming out from now to April. They are not without their enemies. Gerry says the heron has a good eye for these youngsters. He has watched one of them standing among a host of such fry in the shallows and picking them off one by one. You wouldn't mind, so much, he said, seeing the heron take a one-pound fish, but think of so many potential one-pound or more fish gone before they had lived to grow. Nature red in tooth and beak.   Y

SEAHORSES COMING OUR WAY   8 December 1998

 The seahorse or hippocampus looks like some mythical creature – head not unlike that of a horse, but the rest of it a scaly, crustacean body ending in a hugely curved tail. The whole is not more than three inches long. It rides upright. Mostly found in the waters of the Far East, though also in the Mediterranean and once in a blue moon in these waters. We'll come to that. The German newspaper *Die Zeit* carried a long article, "Ballet on the Seabed", which tells of research and help to villagers in a village on the sea-coast of the Philippines in helping preserve this creature, by Amanda Vincent, assistant professor of environment biology at McGill University in Montreal, Canada. This village was put to such straits as patrolling its shore with guns because of poachers, for harvesting the seahorse gave them half their income. By marking out fixed territories and in general a sort of fish-farming, the tide seems to be turning.

What an odd creature. After mating, a delightful ballet-dance it is said, the female squirts her eggs into a pouch in the male, who then impregnates them and keeps them with him until the little ones are ready to go forth. She visits him daily. But apart from their value as decorations for watch-chains or earrings, the trade in their use for medical or quack reasons is enormous. The article says that at least 20 million dried seahorses per year are sold. Live in aquariums, too. China imports around 45 tons for medical purposes. Most of these come from India, Vietnam, Indonesia and the Philippines. Pliny the Elder recommended ground seahorse mixed with soda and pigfat as a cure for baldness, and *The Gentleman's Magazine* of England in 1753 recommended extract of seahorse to women to increase their production of milk. In China, Japan and Korea, ground or otherwise, it is recommended as a tonic, also for sore throat, asthma, infertility, kidney and liver disorders.

Where and when does the seahorse appear here in Ireland? Rarely. On 18 August 1989 a *Hippocampus ramulosus Leach* (that's the full name) was found in Lough Hyne, the marine nature reserve in County Cork. There had been only seven recordings previously around Ireland, the nearest being 1956. Mark Holmes of the Natural History Museum in Dublin, most helpful as always, thinks in future we may have more due to global warming and perhaps changing of ocean currents. Go see this one in the museum. His daughter caught it. Space runs out. We'll be back on the subject.   Y

LOBSTER LORE   14 December 2000

Ever wonder, asks Arthur Reynolds, old-time colleague and former member of Bord Iascaigh Mhara, why, in the season of festive and luxurious eating, one rarely sees lobster in the shops? From time to time the Dublin supermarkets offer cooked frozen Canadian lobster tails, which are just above the minimum legal size, but their flavour has mostly been left behind on the other side of the Atlantic.

He goes on: The reason is that the lobster is very sensitive to disturbance by wave motion, as its nerve system is linked to its shell. So, not wanting to be bumped or jostled, they move into deeper water or hide away in deeper rock holes well away from lobster pots. They also dislike fresh water, and will die quickly if left in it.

Not that really big lobsters are ever caught in pots or traps, since they cannot enter the funnel hole. Big ones get taken in trawls or tangle nets. And speaking of large ones, off the Cornish coast there is one of over 50 lb that is regularly visited by divers but is not disturbed. In Ireland it is illegal for a diver to take any lobster.

While if big lobsters are relatively safe to crawl about in their watery environment, tiny lobsters are prey for many fish. For that reason BIM, in conjunction with a local co-op and rural development board, runs a hatchery at Carne, County Wexford, which has released 25,000 juveniles this year and will step this up to 50,000 a year for the next three.

But, unlike prawns, they are slow growers, so that when you are eating even the smallest legal size lobster, note that every minute's chewing has taken a year to grow. That is, five to seven years.

On a certain part of the east coast a retired fisherman used to go out in his rowing boat to haul his few pots and often as not he was "under the weather" when doing so. Then younger colleagues got the idea of boiling a lobster to put in one of his pots. They said that if he went out "under the influence" he certainly came back sober. A good story, Arthur. Thanks.   Y

LOVELY FISH AND NASTY ICE FLOES   2 February 1999

Greenland, described in a recent magazine article as being an ice mass 14 times the size of Britain and a home to only 55,000 people, is one of the latest places to appear in the holiday lists. In this case, specifically for anglers. And John Bailey, writing in the English *Field*, tells us – hard to grasp – that the ice sheet covering the country contains 3 million cubic kilometres (repeat, kilometres), "which is the vast majority of freshwater contained in the entire universe". The short summer is, apparently, brilliant – flowers, mushrooms, mosses. You may see whales, and other large sea creatures, and on land musk oxen, ermine, lemming, arctic foxes, reindeer and others. But angling – for arctic char – is the main theme.

Now, quite a few years ago a local supermarket in Dublin displayed largish steaks of what from a distance looked like salmon, but which were marked as arctic char. A lighter pink than salmon, a more delicate flavour, perhaps; quite an experience. Then no more. It is known that char, here since the ice age at the bottom of lakes, are now being farmed in Ireland. But these supermarket fish came from northern waters.

The writer in the *Field* says of those he fished in the rivers of Greenland: "They are large, long, streamlined fish, burstingly strong from a diet of shrimp, krill and immature cod . . . These fish come from the world's most unpolluted seas and somehow you can taste it in every mouthful." Virtually all rivers are netted by the Innuit people who nevertheless allow "sport fishermen", if they behave – i.e. put back all fish not needed for the evening supper. Not until late August will you need a torch at night. That's summer on Greenland. Winter conditions for visitors (in this case a film crew) we read of in the memoirs of that formidable woman Leni Riefenstahl, who is chiefly known for her film *Triumph of the Will* which records the Nuremberg Nazi Party rally with intricate and massive formations of Blackshirts, Brownshirts and the Labour Services, etc., a triumph of presentation. She also did a film on the Berlin 1936 Olympics. Both Hitler and Goebbels, according to her memoirs, pursued her, but in vain.

Anyway, for five months on Greenland, a film unit in 1932, a long time before the fishing brochures, after pleasant summer weather, ran into autumn and winter conditions and were projected off ice floes when they broke up. Some nearly drowned, others froze or got fevers. Wild dogs broke into their tents and ate leather boots and even Leni's sealskin trousers "my beautiful film costume". At the age of 88 she published a book of underwater photographs taken while diving in the Red Sea and elsewhere. What next?   Y

LIVE BAIT   2 February 1987

The cold east wind is not one which winter pike anglers welcome because fish won't bite in an east wind. Frosty weather is the kind of weather which pike anglers like: there is generally a good take by hungry pike in the thaw. A mackerel or herring bait on ledger tackle is a favourite in the absence of live bait.

Small perch used to make a favourite live bait but in recent years there is a public opinion building up against the use of live bait – even live minnows. At this time of year the herring is a fish readily available in the fish shops so it is convenient.

So far, apart from the frosty period we had with the snow, the pike anglers have had a lean year of it but February is the favoured month as the big fish come in on flooded grasses on most of the midland lakes to spawn. The big henfish, of 20 lb or more, are getting scarce and anglers are encouraged to return them if they have spawned: the smaller jack pike of four pounds, who attend the spawning hens, are good sport on a light spinning rod and are good to eat as well.   H

THE MICE ARE AMONG US   18 December 1984

One of the steadiest sellers in the hardware business throughout the year – with the exception of high summer – is the ordinary, spring-activated mousetrap. So said a Dublin city merchant. And in Duke Brothers in Kells – a vast storehouse of everything from a bath-stopper to a furlong of chicken wire, to tools of every shape and size, not to mention cardboard boxes of screws, nails, switches, fittings of every metal you can think of, and in short everything you need for farm or home – in that same house of wonders they will tell you it is not unusual for customers to buy the traps in half dozens. Mice we will always have with us. You see a mouse, you have mice. And if there are fistlings behind the cupboards with paper, you have many mice, the little ones so dainty that it is indeed a shame to execute them. They tire of the same bait. Cheese dries out. Melted chocolate say the experts. The author of that famous dictum, "if a man write a better book, preach a better sermon, or make a better mousetrap than his neighbour, though he build his house in the woods, the world will make a beaten path to his door", was wise indeed. (Ralph Waldo Emerson, very likely, according to the *Oxford Dictionary of Quotations*.) But the world is still beating a path to the sellers of the ordinary, tuppenny (as it used to be) trap.   Y

RABBIT IN THE DIET   10 December 1988

Well, rabbit is a fair substitute for chicken, isn't it? It's mostly farmed stuff. The French, as always, are well up on such matters. For, they say, with a rabbit 80 per cent of the live weight is edible flesh as against the chicken's 65 per cent. Rabbit is high in protein and has more calories than chicken. It is not fatty and is suitable, according to this pleading, for all diets and all ages. And the creature is easily raised, even by the amateur. *Le Chasseur Français*, invaluable sporting magazine, lists some of the main breeds. There have been as many as 44 in that country alone, and then, of course, cross-breeding.

There is the Flanders Giant, a monster, with the male reaching seven to eight kilos and the female eight to nine. One metre long in some cases. A snag: the flesh is sometimes a bit coarse compared to others. There is the tawny Burgundy rabbit, half the size of the monster, finer flesh and a skin that sells well. Then, too, the silvery Champagne rabbit was much prized in Poland, it is said, in the last century for it's fur. Now it's purely for eating.

243

Two more main breeds are the Californian and the New Zealand white, both smaller than the above. Both white. Maybe everyone already knows all this?   Y

HUNTING INSTINCT   31 December 1988

 Do many people have an inborn desire to hunt and kill? Wilfrid Thesiger, author of *The Life of my Choice*, thinks so. Right enough, big game hunting should now be condemned, but 50 years ago when he was active in Africa, things were different, he tells us. There was no threat of extinction to any but a few species. He shot often to feed himself and his retainers. And he shot lions which were killing people and cattle when the local tribesmen asked him to. They had only spears. "The memorable occasions were when I hunted dangerous game or tried to secure a really fine head of a rare or elusive animal."

Asked why he did not just photograph them, he would answer: "For me, the sound of the bullet striking home in a clean kill, with the animal dropping where it stood, was the climax of the hunt, all the more rewarding if it followed upon days and even weeks of testing and arduous hunting or a really difficult stalk. With photography, and the uncertainty of whether the picture would be a success, there would be no such climax."   Y

ONE MAN AND HIS GUN   13 January 1988

Shooting rabbits wouldn't occur to you at first as one of the most difficult of gun sports. But, according to Richard Jefferies, the great writer on natural history, "rabbits, although of 'low degree' in comparison with the pheasant, really form an important item in the list of the [game]keeper's charges. Shooting generally commences with picking out the young rabbits about the middle or towards the end of the hay harvest . . . It requires experience and skill to select the young rabbit just fit for the table from the old bucks, the does which may yet bring forth another litter, and those little bunnies that do not exceed the size of rats." (*The Gamekeeper at Home*, 1878.) He writes that it is difficult to judge at 30 yards when only the ears appear over the long grass. But while one pair of ears may look very like another, the developed ear is less pointed than the other.

This book came to mind on reading another engaging piece in *Country Life* by Richard Plantaganet, who says he has always seen himself as a rough shooter, and details what comes to his gun within his own few acres and beyond. As to rabbits: "In one corner of my garden I grow vegetables which I share with several thousand rabbits. They eat my sprouts and I eat them in return, which seems a reasonable exchange to me." Hare and pheasant come into the garden, but he rarely shoots hare (decent man); a cock pheasant striding through the cabbages is fair game.

He has also shot "particularly stupid mallards", the stupidity lying in the fact that they have flown in to visit our man's tame ducks and stayed, rather than making off to safety. More falls to his gun. For pigeons roost in the trees around a ruined hay barn and come down to forage any spilled corn the chickens miss. "Occasionally they invite their wild cousins in for a beano, and I can top up the deep freeze."

He says that, over a year, he must walk hundreds of miles with a gun. He sees himself as "a rough shooter . . . a practical, unpretentious breed, spiritual descendants of the old journeymen gunners, skilled artisans who go out into the fields seeking our suppers rather than waiting for them to be handed to us on a plate".

Query: does anyone agree that rabbits today, perhaps as a result of the myxo war, are much smaller than before? Certainly in one patch of Meath this is noticeable.   Y

UNPOPULAR ANIMALS   21 December 1989

Shooting a fox, instead of hunting it to death on horseback, may still be regarded as a dreadful solecism in parts of England, but in Antrim and other northern counties, there is a real concern at the depredations of this animal. D C Kinney writes on outdoor affairs for the Belfast *News Letter* and, week after week, he has been deploring the lack of control of what he sees as only a pest. And they may number 20,000 in the whole of the Six Counties. There is no shortage of evidence. One man lost 143 red-legged partridges in a night. The fox dug under wire which was sunk six inches. He ate 10, mauled the others and left one hen.

The price of the pelts used to make it profitable for organised parties to go out at night with searchlights for the kill. Now there is no money in the game. One man alone shot 67 in a winter. Shortage of staff makes control difficult, but the authorities need support from the farmers and gun clubs. They recommend snaring and it only takes a few minutes to learn. At one time there were two men employed to control foxes in County Antrim, the *News Letter* writes. Apparently such services are needed again.   Y

RUNNING WITH THE HOUNDS   28 January 1988

After Kingsmill Moore's story about the rabbit chasing the stoat, the following extract from a recent book lands on the desk. "Some people cannot understand this hunting instinct; they say all sport is 'cruel'. But their ideas are wrong-headed. When I tell you that only this year I saw a fox leave cover with hounds on his brush and – lo! – running in the middle of the pack, also after the fox, was another fox! Surely that gives food for thought? I have seen a fox toiling after the pack which has 'gone away' after his brother. He seemed puzzled and disappointed when they left him behind."

It takes all sorts in the human and the animal world. This extract is from *Fisherman's Folly* by B B, recently published by The Boydell Press.   Y

UNEATABLE? THE FOX?   14 January 1999

 Has anyone ever eaten a fox? When the subject of fox-hunting comes up, someone is certain to quote Oscar Wilde's summing up of it as "the unspeakable in pursuit of the uneatable". Do we know for certain that someone has experienced and judged the flesh inedible or uninteresting or horrible? After all, there are parts of the world where dogs are eaten. Anyway, edible or not, foxes are fascinating creatures, and city-dwellers are seeing more and more of them. The other day a woman walking her dog along a suburban avenue wondered why the Dalmatian made a lurch towards the gate of every house they passed. Finally, as a small side-avenue came in sight, a fox boldly stepped out of one drive, with satchel-toting schoolgoers all around, with cars almost bumper to bumper alongside, and skipped down towards a field which bordered the Dodder.

On thinking over this, a man was reminded that, although he has spent good periods of his life in Meath, even living for long periods there and fishing devotedly for days on end, he has seen more foxes in Dublin in his life than in the greenery of Meath. And if city-dwellers hear a piercing, heart-rending squeal just about now, it is likely a fox, for this is the mating season. To come back to the "uneatable" aspect. Is it because of his diet of worms and beetles and other creepy-crawly things; and hedgehogs, according to one authority? And slugs and snails? But do not free-range hens and ducks eat the latter? And God knows what the battery hens are fed. And do we not know that a Young Irelander, in 1848, fleeing the country, was fed badger ham in Kerry? The badger diet would not be so widely different from that of the fox: well, give and take a bit of carrion here and there.

A remarkable aspect of the fox is an apparent inbred gift for family planning or, if you like, contraception. And if you try to wipe them out, they have the capacity to reproduce, to level up again. James Fairley, whose *An Irish Beast Book* is wonderfully informed about foxes, remarks that in Northern Ireland 290,000 bounties were paid out between two and three decades "with no noticeable benefit". He dissected 1,000 fox carcasses. His chapter on the fox in this book is a masterpiece. All this is not a plea for us to eat fox; just wondering why we don't.   Y

TARGET: BADGER   8 November 1999

The badger hasn't got much going for it. It is big and shambling; it can, David Cabot reckons, attain 27 kilos, and that's some weight. It's not easy and comfortable. It lives underground, and issues at night. Nor is it handsome to look at, though you could make a case for the young with the little black stripey face. It is not an animal of which much is known, except among the experts. Many know it only as a corpse on the roads. The only cosy badger, probably, is a "gruff but lovable father figure" as the London *Times* put it the other day, from Kenneth Grahame's *The Wind in the Willows*: "We are an enduring lot," said Badger. "And we may move out for a time, but we wait and are patient . . . and so it will ever be." And the badger, for some superstitious reason, arouses passions. How else explain a story in the same newspaper of a slaughter of badgers on the grounds of Lord Rayleigh in Essex, where a sett, as their underground habitations are known, was blocked up, all 15 entrances, and cyanide was pumped in, thus killing all within. Is this a fear of the unknown? It has nothing to do with bovine TB. There is none in the area, and no campaign against the badger is necessary on that score. One of the oldest-inhabited setts in this country used to be in Woburn estate near Millisle, County Down, the seat of Denis Pack Beresford. Naturalists used to come to see the badgers whose sett was on the edge of a small stream. Woburn is now an institution of some sort.

An Broc, the newsletter of Badgerwatch Ireland for Autumn 1999, notes that the organisation sent a submission to the standing committee of the Berne Convention questioning the legality of the culling of badgers that is going on, and requesting that a file be opened on their complaint. Nuala Ahern, Green MEP, had already lodged a complaint. They contend that the Irish government is in contravention of European Wildlife and Natural Habitats in several articles of the Convention. The newsletter complains that the government, in the matter of bovine TB should closely monitor various aspects of the cattle industry, including restrictions on the interherd movement and correct treatment of slurry. Well, we'll see in due course. Recent revelations of what our cattle – herbivores – have been fed, must at least raise some doubts.   Y

BADGERS AS GRAVE-ROBBERS   4 December 1996

Have rare wild animals been conserved, protected, cosseted, sanctified, almost to the point where they are rare no longer and are even endangering others? This is a question raised about Britain in an article in the London *Times* by one of their country writers, Paul Heiney. There are mutterings, he writes, that something will have to be done. In last Saturday's paper he quotes from a letter by Mrs Buddy Trahair from near Salisbury, who included "a lurid set of photographs of decapitated hens, mutilated cockerels and general carnage". It was a badger that did it, writes Heiney. You wonder if it was seen at the killing or left undisputed paw marks. For, more usually, this kind of slaughter is carried out by a fox or, perhaps, a mink.

But Mrs Trahair tells Heiney that the badgers in her area do not stop at hens. Fields, hedges and gardens have been dug up, with dire effects on trees, plants and road safety. Hard to credit. But there is more. One badger raided the churchyard and dislodged human remains, which the widow had to re-bury. But then the badger returned and dug them up again. Presumably this badger, alone or with help, was trying to establish a new sett, rather than going after human remains.

The people in a farm in the same area had so many setts that they marked them on the map with red spots. The ministry did admit it looked like an outbreak of measles. But there was nothing it could do. (Surely this cannot be so. Does the British Wildlife Act or series of Acts not allow culling or remedial measures by designated officials in certain cases. Such as, for example, the shooting of cormorants fishing off the mouth of a salmon river at the time when smolts are going out to sea?) This badger outbreak, remember, is from one area only. And, incidentally, thinking of our own country and the charges against badgers on the TB question, it is perhaps on the cards that someone will try to pass off BSE as being spread by the same. No, we're not as daft as that.

From badgers to otters. Heiney's article tells us that crofters on North Uist are reported to be calling for the culling of otters because – wait for this one – flocks of poultry were wiped out, "endangering already meagre earnings". Could it be mink again?

His worry is that "as we have been sold conservation as a fashion accessory without which no late 21st-century life is complete, badgers and the rest of them will wake up to find that they have joined the hula-hoop, the slow-cooker and the prawn cocktail on a heap of discarded fads. They are too important for that. But so are young hens about to come into lay." Y

BADGERS AND SQUIRRELS   23 December 1998

Reports from badger-watchers in south Dublin tell that winter has set in and this means for the badgers, not hibernation, but a reluctance to travel any distance in search of food. A couple of months ago, or less, the sound of the first handful of monkey-nuts and bread landing at the edge of the shrubbery would have one white-striped head edging out of the shadows, often followed immediately by a second. By the time the provider had got back indoors he could look out the window and see three, four or five hovering over the grass. For the past few weeks, hardly any showings. In fact, in the morning there are a couple of magpies or pigeons or both pecking away at last night's offering. Badgers don't hibernate, we are told, but in mid-winter they stay nearer to their setts. They don't need so much food to sustain them, having stored fat in the summer and autumn. You miss them, the badger-man said, but they'll be back.

Grey squirrels up in Meath, according to another correspondent, are now less visible at the bird feeders. But still there, he thinks. Or maybe the odd gunshots at the weekend have wiped them out or scared them off. Squirrels do not hibernate. These are all grey squirrels: no reds have been seen in the townland for decades.

And the badger controversy goes on in Britain, though we haven't heard so much here recently. A writer in the English bi-monthly *The Countryman*, under the heading "Country Diary", tells us that, in common with his neighbours, he got a letter from the ministry to say that a scientific study to investigate the link between TB in cattle and badgers had been given the go-ahead by the government. "It now intends to put the policy on a scientific footing, which has not happened in the past." There will be 30 recommended areas, each of about 100 square kilometres. In some no badgers will be culled, in others all will be killed, sorry culled. And the writer adds that the pre-election document of the Labour Party, signed by Mr Blair, stated that no badgers would be killed. (So many claims and counter-claims.)

The writer in *The Countryman,* Humphrey Phelps, has it thus: "The only direct evidence for transmission was obtained in the 1970s when healthy calves were housed experimentally with infected badgers, which strikes me as rather a put-up job." He adds: "It seems a case of 'We've tried slaughtering badgers to stop TB; it wasn't a success, so we'll do it again.'" Are we still not clear which infects which first?   Y

HEALTHY HARE DIET   10 February 1988

 With the grass growing so voluptuous-ly, you congratulate yourself that the hares now won't need to chew on the bark of your young tender trees. You look closely to make sure that you haven't missed something. And, sure enough, while the bark of the slender little trunks is virgin, nearly all the buds at the tip of the side shoots have been nipped off as cleanly as a sharp pair of secateurs would do it. A hare all right. The diet-conscious observer points out that hares, too, need fibre, roughage, just like humans. Particularly, it may be said, coming in to the mating season. They need all their strength to sustain them in the Mad March Hare days when, in a spirit of innocence, some human observers claim that they are boxing. Bonking, in fact.   Y

BATS   28 February 1986

You will have read in this newspaper yesterday an informative piece about the fact that it is National Bat Year in Britain. One of the more quirky sidelines to it all is that a houseplant fertiliser made of bat droppings is being sold in England – and the price is 50 pence for just under two ounces. Just what bat manure has over cow or horse or any other manure is not explained, but it makes a good bit of publicity and adds to the gaiety of life.

There are shibboleths about the value of various sorts of natural manures. There has long been the idea that hen manure is too "hot" to be used. In fact, the mix of hen manure and peat which you get from using deep litter as fertiliser can, from experience, be excellent for vegetables and soft fruit anyway. If you find a few bats hanging up by the heels in a barn or ruin or hollow tree, do scrape up some droppings for your stephanotis or the herbs in your window box. Dr Robert Stebbings, a noted bat expert, it is said, claims that the droppings are amongst the richest of natural fertilisers.   Y

NORMAN DOGS   15 November 1988

 To keep you warm in bed there are hot jars, electric blankets – and dogs. You know those sarcophagi of Norman knights and their ladies, he resplendent in armour and with sword, she in all her coiffure, and both with a dog under their feet. They are small dogs, but maybe that was a matter of scale for the sculptor. And what do you bet that the Normans – and the mere Irish of the day – took kindly to having a dog in the bed to keep them warm? Ecclesiastes, the Preacher, tells us that "a living dog is better than a dead lion". Maybe he didn't quite mean that a warm dog under your feet was better than a smelly lion skin over you, but you can take that meaning out of it; a living dog is at least the equivalent of a duvet – provided he's big enough. Or she.   Y

HORSE SKULLS UNDER THE FLOOR   4 December 2000

Why would anyone want to bury a horse's head or skull under the floor of his or her house? Or more than one? Often quite a serious number? This is one of the questions arising from a splendid book issued by the Institute of Irish Studies at Queen's University, Belfast, with authors from many sources and not only Ireland.

From Corrib to Cultra, a series of essays on folk-life, is in honour of Alan Gailey, who has retired as the second head of that great institution, the Ulster Folk and Transportation Museum at Cultra, County Down.

It is a museum, of course, with a difference – most of it open-air, with, for example, a rural schoolhouse taken down and reassembled *in toto* there in County Down. The cover picture is a handsome white-painted house, cobbled yard and handpump, all neat and tidy just as it was when it left Drumnahunshin, County Armagh.

An article by Eurwyn William gives acknowledgement to the work of Seán Ó Súilleabháin, which linked the practice of burying horse skulls in churches with a view to improving their acoustics, to the same practice in many houses which were found to have been used for dancing and music-making.

But, according to the article, this was a secondary motive – rationalising a basic, primary notion of foundation sacrifice designed to keep the house safe from evil.

The author quotes Scandinavian reasoning that the skulls were buried under threshing floors to improve the echo and let the sound of solid threshing be heard by neighbours. Well, Alan Gailey added Northern Ireland examples to the lists.

A great number of such houses are from Wales. When a house in Wales was rebuilt in 1870, 40 horses' heads were taken from under the floor of what originally had been a hotel. A case for acoustic reasons?

All very mundane, but the writer of the article has his doubts, and quotes a woman under whose house five skulls came to light, that while she didn't believe in some of the superstitious theories about the real reason for these skulls "you never know what can happen, so we decided to rebury the skulls".

And who would fault her?

From Corrib to Cultra, £9.50 stg. Much more worth looking at, including an article on Francis Joseph Bigger: Donegal bothógs for summer transhumance, and other subjects. Why Corrib? Well, Gailey had a connection with that lake. Makes a good title too. Y